SOUVENIRS

OF

SOME CONTINENTS

SOUVENIRS

OF

SOME CONTINENTS

BY

ARCHIBALD FORBES, LL.D.

The Naval & Military Press Ltd

in association with

The National Army Museum, London

Published jointly by

The Naval & Military Press Ltd
Unit 10 Ridgewood Industrial Park,
Uckfield, East Sussex,
TN22 5QE England

Tel: +44 (0) 1825 749494
Fax: +44 (0) 1825 765701

www.naval-military-press.com
www.military-genealogy.com
www.militarymaproom.com

and

The National Army Museum, London
www.national-army-museum.ac.uk

In reprinting in facsimile from the original, any imperfections are inevitably reproduced and the quality may fall short of modern type and cartographic standards.

OF the papers which make up this extremely discursive book, some have already been printed in periodicals ; others appear now for the first time.

June 1885.

CONTENTS.

	PAGE
SKOBELEFF	1
HOW I BECAME A WAR CORRESPONDENT	47
THE EMPEROR AND HIS MARSHAL	71
SOCIAL AUSTRALIA	96
MACGAHAN, THE AMERICAN WAR CORRESPONDENT	120
WHERE WAS VILLIERS?	141
WOLSELEY: A CHARACTER SKETCH	156
THE AMERICAN GENTLEMAN WITH THE MOIST EYE	183
INTERVIEWED BY AN EMPEROR	199
SOME SOCIETY ASPECTS OF AMERICA	225
DOUGHTOWN SCRIP	270
A POET WAIF	290
CHRISTMASTIDE IN THE KHYBER PASS	306

SKOBELEFF.

IT was in the early summer of '77. A month had passed since I had seen that *avant-courier* of active hostilities, Schahofskoy's advance-guard Cossack, ride his shambling pony up the main street of Galatz, and pushing on through the swamp-land beyond, annex the bridge of Babosch at the point of that long lance of his. Ever since that afternoon the main tide of the Russian march on the Danube had been steadily flowing onward over the dusty Moldavian plains from the willows that line the banks of the sullen and sluggish Pruth. Jassy, where the dark-eyed gipsies love to make their headquarters, had become all save in name a Russian city, its cafés crammed with white-coated champagne-loving Russian officers, its squares and streets thronged with flat-faced, small-eyed, pug-nosed Russian linesmen, stalwart of frame, strong of odour, placid of demeanour, even when the vodki was in their noddles—which was very often. Already shells had whistled across the great river of Separation, from Braila, from Oltenitza, from Giurgevo. Already the fated Lufti Djelil, sitting there on the calm river water, trim, taut, and jaunty, behind the tall alders in the bend of the Old Danube between Matchin and Braila, had with an appalling suddenness blackened the air with the smoke of her explosion, and strewn the bosom of the river with shattered fragments of crew and ship. Dubassoff, the daring lieutenant who had so dashingly steered the Russian steam launch to the destruction of the Turkish gunboat, was the hero of the hour, and he was flaunting his brand-new Cross of St. George among the feather-headed revellers of the *cafés chantants* in the gay Roumanian metropolis. Czar Alexander had taken the war-path, and for the nonce had his quarters in Ploesti, eighty miles behind Bucharest, where Ignatieff and Nelidoff transacted bellicose diplomacy under the fragrant lime-trees in the garden of the Boyard's mansion, while the unvenerable Gortschakoff, when he was not dallying senilely in the boudoir of Mademoiselle Sara in the Hotel Boulevard, or hobbling with tottering jauntiness among the fair pedestrians of the *Allée Vert*, was concerning himself with chartreuse and affairs in the chancellerie of the Russian legation in the Podo Mogosoi of Bucharest. And that capital—the Paris of the East—was throbbing in a delirium of wild pleasure, accentuated by the clank of martial accoutrements, the clatter of the sword scabbards on the parquet floors of the restaurants, and the steady tramp of the cohorts which poured through her seething streets. Bucharest was a ballroom wherein Mars, Venus, and Bacchus were dancing the cancan in a frantic orgie. Princes, grand-dukes, countesses without their counts, *ci devant* operatic ladies, whose troupe had dispersed itself in favour of more probable engagements that did not strain the voice, diplomats, aides-de-camp, Polish Jews, maquereaux, and war correspondents belonging to every European nation, jostled one another politely in the broad staircase of the Hotel Broft.

In the garden-restaurant of that phenomenally expensive hostelry gay guardsmen from the Russian headquarter staff—youngsters as reckless as they were blue-blooded—were piling up the dead soldiers of the puissant "Mumm" regiment; scornfully glancing, as they drank, on the adjacent group of swarthy, slender, classical-featured officers of the Roumanian Guard, who had not yet lifted the cloud from their military reputation in the fierce fighting and terrible carnage around the great Gravitza Redoubt. At a little table in the shady corner, under the drooping willow tree, there sat poor MacGahan, the "Cossack war-correspondent," the hero of that wonderful lonely ride through the great desert of Central Asia that had earned for him, by the unanimous voice of the Russian army, the title of "Molodyetz" or "brave-fellow," quietly gossiping with another war-correspondent, myself, who had only a few days previously made his personal acquaintance, and who was interested and fascinated by this new colleague of mine in the service of the Daily News.

MacGahan was a brilliant talker when his topic interested him, and now his fine face was aglow, and there was a sparkle in the fine brown eyes—into which, alas, I shall never look more. For MacGahan's theme was a certain heroic young Russian general named Skobeleff, an old Khivan comrade of his, a man of whom until then I had barely heard. But MacGahan knew Skobeleff to the backbone, and thus early was predicting in his confident, emphatic fashion, that as he had been the hero of the Khivan campaign, so Skobeleff would prove himself the hero of that far more stupendous struggle whose shadow was now luridly slanting athwart the broad current of the Danube. Skobeleff was a colonel and barely thirty years old when MacGahan had been his comrade in Central Asia. Kaufmann had reached the environs of Khiva, and was training his cannon on its ramparts and preparing for an assault in form, when suddenly on the fortress wall above the closed gate which Kaufmann was threatening, there stood displayed against the sky-line the tall figure of Colonel Skobeleff. With a handful of Cossacks that heroic madcap had quietly ridden round to the rear gate of Khiva, carried it after a flicker of resistance, taken the town by surprise, and was now beckoning to Kaufmann to limber up his batteries and countermand the detachments told off for the assault of the place that had been already won. Of another exploit performed by Skobeleff, MacGahan told me as we chatted. Of the five Russian columns which had set out on the desert march from different points with the common object of reaching Khiva, only four had made good their destination. Markosoff's column had not yet arrived when the time approached for Kaufmann to evacuate Khiva. It could not be left to its fate,—it was necessary to ascertain whether, thwarted by adverse conditions, it had turned back; or whether it was struggling on through the hordes of Turkomans who infested the region through which lay its line of route. For this hazardous enterprise Skobeleff volunteered. He took his life in his hand with a light heart. With three friendly Turkomans, himself disguised as a Turkoman, he rode away into the desert on his perilous task of exploration. Ten days passed, and he returned not; he was given up for lost; and Kaufmann, unable to tarry longer, reluctantly made his preparations for departure. The day before Kaufmann's evacuation of Khiva, Skobeleff reappeared there—alone, on foot, half dead. He had lost his companions and his horses; he had run the gauntlet of the marauding Turkomans time after time; but he had accomplished the task he had undertaken. He had struck the point at which Markosoff had for want of water been forced to turn back, and so had attained the solution of the problem of that commander's whereabouts.

After Khiva, continued MacGahan, Skobeleff's career had been singularly brilliant. Kaufmann had given him, now a major-general—the youngest in the Russian army—the command of a force intended to operate against the Khanate of Khokand. That country, with a population of some two millions he had conquered and annexed, after a three months' campaign so fiercely pressed that when the vanquished Khan surrendered, his first words to Skobeleff were, "Before we begin to talk, let me sleep, for I have not had a night's rest nor a sound sleep for more than a month." Of the new acquisition to Russian territory in Central Asia, renamed Ferghana, Skobeleff had been appointed governor. In the course of his two years' administration there, the enemies whom a young, energetic, and thorough man is always sure to make, had accused him to the emperor of malpractices. He was charged with ruthless cruelties, and of having stolen a few millions of roubles more or less. From needful severities Skobeleff was not the kind of man to be backward; but wanton cruelty was abhorrent to his nature. He was not the sort of man to be dishonest. Of money he was splendidly careless; and when I knew him he was always poor. In the early days in Bucharest, when as yet his father had not opened his purse to him, he had to take credit for his hotel bills; and he was indebted to his father for his equipment as a lieutenant-general, which would scarcely have been the case had he stolen in his Central Asian Government. But his enemies prevailed against him; he was superseded, and with contumely, if not disgrace. With witnesses and vouchers to disprove the charges against him, he had hurried to St. Petersburg, to find that the enemy had already departed to join the army at Kischeneff. Tarrying in the capital until the official auditors had gone through his accounts, and had cleared him of the accusation of peculation, he had then hurried after the emperor and begged for an audience. But this was denied him. Skobeleff's enemies had poisoned the ear of the Czar. But Skobeleff was recognised, nevertheless, as too good a man to be altogether left out in the cold when hard fighting was in the air. To his father, General Skobeleff senior, had been assigned the command of a division of irregular cavalry made up of Cossack regiments from the Caucasus, charged with the duty of covering the main advance and overrunning the lower region of Moldavia adjacent to the Danube. Skobeleff the younger was temporarily appointed Chief of Staff to his father, with a sort of informal open commission to risk his life pretty much where he pleased, and a tacit understanding that he should be at liberty to show the way in any hazardous adventure that he might contrive or hear of. In a word, he was a chartered free lance.

As MacGahan gossiped with me over the flagon of Pilsener, I chanced to notice two men enter the garden-restaurant in which we sat. The two were arm in arm. One was dressed in the ugly plain blue uniform of a private of dragoons—a small, slight, swarthy man, whose face seemed not unfamiliar to me. His companion, tall, stately, and blond, was dressed in spotless white, and wore the insignia of a general officer. The curious spectacle—we were not in France—of a private and a general arm in arm struck me; and I called MacGahan's attention to it. He sprang to his feet at a bound, with the exclamation, "Why, it's the very man—it is Skobeleff himself!" and running, or rather limping across the garden—for he was lame—greeted his friend, or rather his two friends. Let me first dispose of the dragoon-private in the shabby uniform. He was Prince Tserteleff. He had been secretary to Ignatieff when that diplomat was Russian ambassador at Constantinople, and had accompanied his chief later on that wily Muscovite's mission to London to hoodwink Lord Salisbury, in the course of which visit I had met him casually more than once. Now, finding his diplomatic avocation gone, panting for action yet knowing nothing of war, he had taken service as a private in a dragoon regiment; and Skobeleff had found him bivouacing in a swamp on the Danube side, and had annexed him as his orderly. Such enthusiasm for active service was no rarity among the Russian nobility. At a later stage of the campaign a private dragoon was detailed to me to escort my waggon to a general's headquarter near Simnitza. Riding with this man I found he talked English like a native, and was familiarly versed in London society. He turned out to be one of the Princes Dolgorouki, and had been attaché in the Russian embassy to the Court of St. James. His brother was a general and the governor of a province; his sister was the morganatic wife of the Czar, to whom, therefore, the private soldier on duty as escort to my baggage-waggon bore the relationship of left-handed brother-in-law. Again, in Bulgaria, I remember a venerable man riding as lieutenant in Staal von Holstein's cavalry division. This mature subaltern was seventy-three years of age, one of the emperor's chamberlains, and having the relative rank of a full general; the bearer, too, of an historic name, for it was his father, Count Rostopchin, to whom the sad but grand task of burning Moscow was confided, when Napoleon's legions were thronging into the venerable capital. The old man, nominal general though he was, had no military knowledge, and was glad to content himself with a lieutenancy in the Achtirski Hussars, with whom he had ridden every yard of the way since the regiment had crossed the Pruth. But to return for a moment to Prince Tserteleff. It was he who afterwards discovered the hill-track through the Hankoi Pass, by which Gourko penetrated beyond the Balkans in his summer raid; later he helped Ignatieff to draw up the treaty of San Stephano. A life of excitement overturned his mind; he became hopelessly insane, and not long ago he died in a private madhouse. He had given to Russia more than his life.

I looked at Skobeleff with all my eyes as he stood there on the garden path, the cynosure of every gaze ; his fine face glowing with pleasure as he returned the greeting of his old friend. I thought then, as I have never ceased to think, that I never looked on a finer man. Six feet high, straight as a pine, the head carried high with a gallant debonair fearlessness, square across the broad shoulders, deep in the chest, slender of waist, clean of flank, the muscular, graceful, supple figure set off to perfection by the white frockcoat with the decorations and the gold lace on it, Skobeleff, with his frank high-bearing, looked a genial king of men. Presently he came and sat with us, and I was introduced to him. As we talked I looked into his face, partly because I was curious, partly because he fascinated me so that I could not help myself, and indeed did not care to try. Except MacGahan himself, I never knew a man so winning. No wonder that soldiers, friends, and women loved him! It was impossible to know him, to have him smile on you with that sweet grave smile of his, and not to love him. As I write I see before me—ah, that I shall never see them again in life!—the broad lofty forehead shaded with the chestnut curls; the clear, frank, manly blue eyes that met yours so staunchly; the long, straight, decisive nose,—the kind of nose Napoleon said he looked for among his officers when he wanted to find a general; the beautiful mouth, with its wonderful mobility of expression; the well-turned compact chin, with the deep dimple in its centre. At this time he wore only whiskers and moustache—

later in the campaign a silky chestnut beard flowed over his broad chest. I could not fancy this man a foreigner who sat by me talking, in purest idiomatic English, of common English friends; he looked to me like an English country gentleman of the best type—such a man as Miss Braddon has depicted in Lady Audley's husband. It seemed to me that this young man—he was then scant thirty-five—had been everywhere, seen everything, done everything, and read everything. He was familiar with episodes of my own professional career; he had carried a flying reconnaissance from Khokand over the Pamir Steppe, round Lake Victoria, and right into the flanks of the Hindoo Koosh; he quoted Balzac, Herbert Spencer, Hamley's Operations of War, and The School for Scandal; he had no belief in the first favourite for the approaching Derby; he thought Madame Chaumont very *chic*, and considered our household cavalry rather underhorsed; he imparted the information that the upper fords of the Oxus were dangerous because of quicksands; and gave it as his opinion after deliberate consideration, that you could get as good a *suprême de volaille* at the Café Royal in Regent Street as either at Bignon's or the Café Anglais. We dined together—Skobeleff prescribed the menu and won little Müller's heart by his discrimination; and after dinner we went—he, MacGahan, and I—into the empty music-room, where Skobeleff, to his own pianoforte accompaniment, sang songs in French, German, Russian, Kirghis, Italian, English, and wound up with "Auld Lang Syne" in unimpeachable vernacular. Between whiles we talked in a desultory, fitful sort of way, Skobeleff always leading the conversation with an imperceptible masterfulness; and I took to bed—it was a very late bed—the impression that he was out of sight the most muscular and independent thinker of any Russian I had met; and, although I have never been accused of magnifying geese into swans, that I had for once found a Muscovite, or rather, indeed, a cosmopolitan admirable Crichton. But thus far I had not seen manifested Skobeleff's most striking attribute. I had yet to see him fight. That experience was soon afforded me.

He had but an evening's leave from his father's dreary headquarters down at Guirgevo in the Danube, opposite the Turkish fortress of Rustchuk. Next morning I accompanied him to Guirgevo, at his invitation—thus early had we taken to each other, at least I can speak for myself—and in his society had a few days of about the riskiest fun that the most adventurous man could covet. Skobeleff's amusement for the time was laying torpedoes in the bed of the Danube to close in the Turkish flotilla over the way at Rustchuk. He had, it seemed to me, a positive delight in drawing the enemy's fire, and went back to his quarters happy if he had teased the Turks into expending half a dozen shells in blazing at his little cockleshell of a steam launch. But it was rarely that we saw quarters. Sometimes we slept in the launch among the bulrushes; other nights we would bivouac on the bank by the fire of a Russian picket, whose soup we were glad to share. As we lay there in the calm balmy nights under the beautiful stars ere yet the ruthless summer heat had set in, Skobeleff would beguile me from sleep by the varied charm of his conversation. I believe that the man opened his soul to me. He burned with ambition to distinguish himself; he had a superb confidence in himself that he would do so; yet he did not expect to survive the campaign. He was sore under the unmerited stigma that had attached to him; what he craved beyond all other aspirations was the opportunity to distinguish himself conspicuously under the very eyes of the Czar himself, and then he would die with a light heart. He was no Nihilist, and yet in his independence, in his scornful recognition of so much that was rotten in the Russian State, in his contempt for high-placed duffers and dotards, there was a leaning in the direction of what was virtually Nihilism. He had an unreserved confidence in the military virtues of the Russian soldiers, if only they had fair play and were well led; he over and over again quoted Napoleon's jibing compliment that it did not suffice to kill the Russian soldier—he was such an obstinate dog that you had to take the trouble to knock him down after he was killed. In the days I speak of he was keen for a Russian invasion of British India, and laughed at my representations of the virtual impracticability of that enterprise; after his Turkoman campaign he was fain to own that he underrated the difficulties of it. Dissolute man as he was—it must be confessed that in the intervals of campaigning he drank as deep as any man of the cup of dissipation—he had yet a strong although vague religious sense, though he was as much a fatalist as any Turk. He disliked the Germans root and branch, thought them prigs and pedants in a civilian sense, and although he recognised their military virtues, held that their reputation for those had been won comparatively cheaply, because of the inefficiency and degeneracy of the enemies whom they had worsted. England and Russia together, it was Skobeleff's expressed belief, could "whip creation," if only the two nationalities were loyally and thoroughly banded together. But then he himself exemplified the difficulty of any such union ; he confessed as it seemed to me with an undertone of angry respect that he hated England ; yet paradoxically he loved individual Anglo-Saxons better than any folk in all the world. His whole heart went out to MacGahan, for instance. From the premature grave of that beloved friend and tried comrade he turned away with an irrepressible burst of loud sobbing, nor for weeks after did he recover his accustomed serenity. Alike in Bucharest on campaign, and in Constantinople he constantly, as a matter of social preference, sought the company of Anglo-Saxons ; and he was an assured, although perforce of circumstances a somewhat irregular member of the little English coterie in the Roumanian capital in the earlier days of the campaign, ere yet the crossing of the Danube had been achieved.

Presently, in anticipation of that event, came the general move of the Russian army corps down to the vicinity of the great river, and with the army naturally went the war correspondents. The secret of whereabouts the crossing was to be tried in earnest, the Russians were singularly successful in keeping up to the very eve of the attempt. Then indeed, by the merest chance of good fortune, what sporting men used to call "the office" was confided to me, and it was my luck to be the only representative of journalism present at its inception. For days before the sudden coup, we correspondents were straggling around the convexity of the bend between Simnitza and Turnu Magarelle, in a fog of the blindest bewilderment. Every Russian was courteous; and every Russian was irritatingly noncommittal. Not even to MacGahan, far less to me a much later friend, would Skobeleff emit one significant word. The night but one before the actual crossing I chanced to find Skobeleff in the town of Alexandria behind Turnu Magarelle. I hoped as I saw him that here at last surely was a gleam of light on the path that was so dark to me. But he was resolute in refusing me even a hint. "Haven't the faintest idea!" was his answer when I asked him where I should head for; and he bolted from the embarrassment of my question to assist a lady out of her *calèche* with a sedulous leisurely grace that was characteristic, in the midst of a whirl of bustle and excitement as he was. Thirty hours later I was down among the willows on the Danube shore in front of the bluff of Simnitza, just as Dragomiroff's first pontoon was launched amid the strained silence into the swirling water. Through the sullen gloom of the night I could discern a man in a white coat jump into the pontoon, and there came the low impressive command, in a voice I knew well, for the nearest soldiers—the voice called them "brothers" in the pleasant familiar Russian officer fashion—to get aboard. "All right, little father," was the response; and so set out the first boat on its voyage across the great river toward the Turkish bank. Skobeleff was the first man to spring ashore on that bank, and when I reached it an hour later he, Dragomiroff, and Yolchine the brigadier, were standing up in the gray dawn under the straggling fire from the Turks above, while boatload after boat-load of reinforcements were coming across the river through the shell-fire that tore the water into ribbons, and were being landed to lie down among the slime under the bank, and wait till the party should be strong enough for effective action. When that time came—and already ere it came the slime was the moister because of the blood that had soaked into it—it was the chief in the white coat, it was Skobeleff, who gave the command, and that command was characteristic of the man. This time the voice rang out loud and clear—the need for quietude had passed by. From flank to flank it echoed, "Get up, brothers, and follow me!" All through that hot morning Skobeleff was being followed for the simple reason that he was always leading. After I had recrossed to the Roumanian bank, I could see through my glass the white coat heading the dashes of the sombre-clad Russian skirmishers, as they pressed higher and higher through the straggling trees that dot the steep slopes up to where, outside the high-perched town of Sistova, the steadfast Turkish gunners were plying their shell-fire on the Russian masses crowded on the flat shore below Simnitza, and in the loaded pontoons that were toiling across the current. In the summer season the Russian troops march and camp in white clothing, or rather clothing that once was white; but they always put on their uniform coats of dark cloth to fight in. They "dress" for the fray as the duellists used to do; and there is another reason. The Russian ambulance service is not very alert, and there is a chance, even with the alertest ambulance service, that wounded men may lie all night before being removed. The cloth coats are warmer than the white canvas blouses for men in this plight. One of Skobeleff's singularities—and he had many—was that he always, no matter what the weather, made it a point to go into action in a white coat. His explanation was racy of his nature. "It is that my fellows can see where I am, and know whither to follow."

The day after the passage of the river had been forced the emperor crossed the Danube, to visit and congratulate the troops who had performed the exploit. In front of the long massive line drawn up on the crest of the slope east of Sistova stood three men awaiting the coming of the Great White Czar—General Dragomiroff, who was the commander of the division that had crossed first; Yolchine, the chief of the brigade of that division which had been first over and had borne the brunt of the fighting and the loss; and Skobeleff, who had shown the way to all and sundry. The emperor embraced Dragomiroff in the Russian fashion, and gave him the Cross of St. George; he shook hands cordially with cheery little Yolchine, and gave him too a St. George to add to others which this blithe fighting man had been picking up since he was a boy, all over the Caucasus and Central Asia. Then he came to Skobeleff, and men watched the little scene intently; for it was as notorious that Skobeleff was in disfavour, as that on the previous morning he had behaved in a manner that might have wiped out any save the most inveterate disfavour. For a moment Alexander hesitated as the two tall, proud, soldierly men confronted each other; you could trace on his features the short struggle between prejudice and appreciation. It was over in a moment—and the wrong way for Skobeleff. The Czar frowned, turned short on his heel, and strode resolutely away, without a word or a gesture of notice. A man of strong prejudices, he had still the poison in his mind of the calumnies that had blackened to him the character of Skobeleff. Skobeleff, for his part, bowed, flushed scarlet, then turned pale, and set his teeth hard. It was a flagrant insult, in the very face of the army, and a gross injustice; but Skobeleff took it in a proud silence that seemed to me very grand. Nor did I ever after hear him allude to the slur. It was not long ere he could afford to be magnanimous. This despite was done him on the 28th of June. On the 3d of September Skobeleff, after having heaped exploit on exploit, led the successful assault on the Turkish position in Loftcha, and drove his adversaries out of that strong place, not less by the splendid daring he so conspicuously displayed than by the skilfulness of the tactics he had devised. On the following night at his own dinner-table in the Imperial marquee at the Gorni Studen headquarter, the Emperor stood up and bade his guests to pledge him in the toast of "Skobeleff, the hero of Loftcha!" It is not given to many men to earn a revenge so full and so grand as that.

On the afternoon of the crossing of the Danube I had to ride back some distance to arrange the transmission to the telegraph wire of my despatch describing it. On the road to Alexandria I met General Skobeleff senior, at the head of his Cossack division marching down on Simnitza. I stopped the old gentleman, and told him of the prowess of his gallant son. He was moved to tears, solemnly descended from his saddle, approached me, threw both arms round my neck, and kissed me on both cheeks effusively and with loud sobs. The good old general always wore a huge diamond ring on the thumb of his right hand, and I remember how this ring scratched the back of my neck while its owner was hugging me with a fervour and emotion that I respected indeed, but with some of the demonstrativeness of which I might have readily dispensed. After Skobeleff senior had blown his nose on my moustache, he remounted and set off for Simnitza at a canter, eager to see and congratulate his son. There had been some coolness between them—for the old gentleman was close-fisted, and the son, although not *alieni appetens*, was *sui profusus* when humour and opportunity prompted, and he had a cheerful habit of regarding his own and the paternal purse as identical, a view which Skobeleff senior did not unreservedly share. Besides, both now and later, the latter had a comical jealousy of his son's military reputation and rapid promotion, and was drolly savage when before Plevna he was actually under that young chief's command ; and he was especially mad in a half serious way, when Michael threatened in jest to put him under arrest unless he forked out the money to pay for the irreverent youth's outfit on promotion to lieutenant-general. But the father, nevertheless, had a genuine pride in the son, and I have noticed the shaggy veteran sit silent for long watching with a kind of self-complacent contentment, the rapid play of the young man's handsome features, as he poured forth talk on some subject that exceptionally interested him. As soon as Skobeleff senior reached Simnitza, Skobeleff junior zealously urged him that he should swim his whole division of Cossacks across the Danube. The old man refused. He might think of such a thing, he said, if there were an emergency, and there were no other means of crossing; but for the moment there was no urgency, and to-morrow the bridge would be ready ; and what, pray, was the use of a bridge if not to cross by ? The son was very angry at the paternal resistance to his quixotic proposal. His contention was that Cossacks were fit to go anywhere and do anything, and that they should snatch at this opportunity of vindicating the possession of such attributes, quite irrespective of common sense. So he set out to swim the Danube—about a mile and a half wide with a four-knot current, with one special henchman, a wild Kirghis lad whom he had found a child in his dead mother's lap after a Turkestan skirmish and had adopted, a quaint profane imp in purple and white dimity, who never left his master in the thickest of the fight, and was perpetually getting flesh wounds at which he laughed—and with his personal escort of three Cossack orderlies. Skobeleff swam his first charger, a noble Turkoman chestnut which he had brought from Central Asia, and which was afterwards killed under him in the July Plevna fight. He and the Kirghis got safely across. Three men of the escort were found two days later on an island about three miles below; and were buried there. It was generally considered that the result proved that in this affair the father showed more sound sense than the son. But then the father had made his career.

After this for a time I parted company from Skobeleff. I went east with the army of the Lom, expecting that it would have the earliest fighting. But although we were no longer together I heard of Skobeleff from time to time. Thus early he had become the most talked-of man in the Russian army; later Lord Beaconsfield perhaps shared with him that pre-eminence. There came to us the news that he had been the first man over the Schipka Pass, crossing it with a mere adventurous handful the day after Prince Mirski's more strongly supported attempt had been balked by the Turks with heavy loss. Then we heard of dashing forepost enterprises of his on the Selvi-Loftcha line; and I for one had the most fervent wish he would come east among us, and galvanise us out of the torpidity that seemed to have enwrapped us for an indefinite period. Hearing casually of the project that Schahofskoy and Krüdener should make a combined attempt to dislodge Osman Pasha from the position which he had so masterfully and inconveniently taken up at Plevna, I left the army of the Lom to its stupor, and crossed Bulgaria in the direction of Plevna, bent on seeing whatever there might be to see. On the 29th of July we were in bivouac at Poradim with Schahofskoy's force, waiting for the word to assail Plevna—a word that was uttered on the following night, and that carried in its echo the death-mandate to many a gallant man. After sundown there came galloping in on us a man in a mighty hurry—a man whose advent was like a gust of wind. It was that stormy-patrol Skobeleff, who had got permission from the Grand Duke Nicholas to take command of a brigade of Caucasian Cossacks that had belonged to his father's original division, and that had been watching Loftcha, a town to the southward of Plevna, which Osman had sent a force to occupy ; and of a stray couple of battalions of infantry which had been supporting that brigade. His instructions from headquarters were rather vague, as indeed the Russian headquarter's orders mostly were ; he was to do what he might, to cover with this little force the region and roads between Loftcha and Plevna, so as to hinder supports being sent from the former to the latter place ; and in the event of Osman being expelled from Plevna, to impede his retreat on Loftcha if he should seem inclined to head that way. If he saw an opening to do anything else that promised to be useful, there was no prohibition against his striking in ; and Skobeleff was the sort of man to make an opening of this kind for himself in the event of one not presenting itself in the ordinary course of nature. He had come round by Poradim on his way from Tirnova to join this little command that had been given him, in order to report himself to Schahofskoy, and to ask that commander as his superior officer, whether he had any instructions to give him, or any suggestions in the way of co-operation to make. Schahofskoy was a gruff bear and hated Skobeleff because of his enterprising nature; and he was, besides, in a worse humour even than usual, because his reluctance to make an attack which he foresaw would result in failure, had been overruled by peremptory orders from the headquarters of the Grand Duke Nicholas. So Schahofskoy would have nothing to say to Skobeleff, and did not even ask him to supper. Skobeleff accepted the rebuff with characteristic cheerfulness. "I'll have all the more freedom to do a stroke of independent business on my own account," he blithely observed to me, as he gulped down the last drop that was in my flask—I hadn't eaten myself that day, and had no food to offer him—and with a shake of the hand he galloped away out into the darkness of the summer night, with his faithful Kirghis behind him.

The morrow was a terrible day—a day at the recollection of which, after all this lapse of time, one's blood turns with a spasm of horror. Schahofskoy's men could not get into Plevna on our side, the south, any more than could Krüdener's on the north side. After carrying the first Turkish redoubt, they were brought to a dead stand by dint of the tempest of hostile fire that struck them; and not being the kind of men to go back, they stood there gazing into the face of death, poor gallant fellows, till 8000 of them littered with their corpses the long gently-sloping natural glacis whose face the Turkish rifle-fire swept with such workmanlike steadiness. Ever between the blue-coated column of them standing up there out in the open, and those spires and minarets yonder, on which sparkled the rays of the low afternoon sun, there heaved upward into the calm blue sky the white bulwark of smoke from the deftly-plied rifles of Osman Pasha's staunch Moslems. But all of a sudden there was carved a rift in that white fleecy bulwark, and there came to us on the faint wind the noise of a bicker of musketry-fire, away in the rear of it, about the mouth of a gully which debouched on the little plain on which stands the town of Plevna, far away to the left of the Radisovo height which was Schahofskoy's initial position. What could this mean? It was clearly in the nature of a diversion, only who or what could be carrying it on? None of Schahofskoy's force had been despatched for such a purpose; that was all too plain. That force was all down below in front of us, dying there with stolid inactive fortitude. Yet the devilry went on right in the Turkish rear, till the turmoil of the din seemed actually inside Plevna itself! Then smoke began to rise from a house that had been fired right on the edge of the town under the near shadow of one of the minarets. Gradually the firing fell back again toward the mouth of the gully. The assailants, whoever they were, had been thwarted and forced to retire. And who, think you, were those assailants that seemed to us with Schahofskoy, as if they had dropped from the clouds? Skobeleff and his petty force of two infantry battalions, or rather, indeed, but a part of it. Yes, he had thrust down the Loftcha-Plevna road, past the spot where later stood the Krishine redoubt in the vain effort to hold which he shed blood so profusely in September, and had made an audacious dash right for the town of Plevna itself—right at the very core of the Turkish position. I do not speak on Skobeleff's own authority, for I never talked over this day in detail with him; but it was reported with seeming authenticity in the Russian army that on the evening of this disastrous day he was actually inside the town of Plevna for ten minutes, and had expected to make good his position had it been possible for support from Schahofskoy to co-operate with him. Frank Greene, the American military attaché, says in his history of the war that Skobeleff got no nearer than the heights 300 yards southwest of the town; and Dr. Charles Ryan of Melbourne, who was the only Englishman then with Osman, assured me that although there was among the Turks a momentary scare that he would penetrate into the town, he never actually did so. But it is certain that he did work yet more purposeful. Recognising the danger that impended over Schahofskoy's left flank which circumstances threw into the air, he dashed resolutely at the immensely superior Turkish force which, but for his bold stroke, would

have had freedom to enfilade Schahofskoy. He
kept up the unequal fight all the afternoon, and well
into the night; although he lost nearly half his
little force he was able to remove his wounded,—
more than Schahofskoy could do,—and he finally
made good his retreat deliberately and in order.
What he had done for Schahofskoy was this. He
had so utilised his few hundreds as to cover the
shattered debris of that general's division from a
flanking attack that would have annihilated it,
and enable its remnants to rally into something like
cohesion at Poradim on the following morning. It
is quite unnecessary to add that Schahofskoy never
acknowledged the obligation, or gave him so much
as a word of thanks.

Immediately after this catastrophe Skobeleff was
directed to turn his attention to Loftcha. Offensive
action was hardly a word in the mouths of the
Russians just then; they had all their work cut out
for them to hold their own. Skobeleff's prescribed
duty was to mask, with an absurdly scanty force,
the Turkish division holding Loftcha so as to prevent
it from molesting the Russian flank and line of communications during the period of shock, disarray, and
prostration resulting from the disaster before Plevna.
He fulfilled this task by keeping up a series of reconnaissances in force, in which his great trouble was
to restrain his men from turning the feints into real
attacks. The bulk of his little force still consisted
of Caucasian Cossacks. Those "Kubanski" men,

as they were called, are nearly all Mahommedans, and the Russians were at first rather anxious how they would turn out when asked to confront in battle their co-religionists. The Kubanskis did not care a cent about the Mahommedanism of the Turks; it sufficed to know that they were enemies whom they were to have the inexpressible luxury of killing. The Don Cossack, with his pug nose and tow hair, is a fraud as a fighting man. He has a genius for plundering and makes a capital scout, but he has an instinctive disrelish for anything like close fighting. He infinitely prefers running away. But those Caucasian Cossacks are men of quite another stamp. They gave the Russians an infinity of trouble before their mountains were conquered; now they serve Russia with a whole soul and are the hardest, staunchest, and most ruthless of fighting men. They shoot well, and do excellent work as mounted infantry. They will charge knee to knee as regular cavalry, and odds make no odds to them. In temperament, as soldiers, they resemble the Goorkhas more than any other soldiers who serve under the British flag. Like them they kill and spare not; they have no comprehension of the meaning of giving quarter to an enemy, who they consider deserves extermination to say nothing of rather free-handed mutilation in the course of the operation. Skobeleff had a great liking for the cheery, enduring, ruthless Kubanskis, and never wanted to command better troops. They served him right well both at Plevna, and now before

Loftcha ; but he had to risk his life very lavishly to hinder them from forcing the fighting. MacGahan thus relates an incident of those Loftcha days :—

"The fire was still raging along the Turkish entrenchments, and the Russians (the Kubanski Cossacks skirmishing) were still pushing forward. Skobeleff mounting another horse, a chestnut this time, again galloped forward. He reached the foot of the hill shouting and gesticulating, while his trumpeter kept sounding the retreat apparently with effect, for the skirmishers began to withdraw. Then I saw him go down, man and horse together, and I said to myself, 'He has got it this time!' He had had two horses killed under him at Plevna. If it be the horse only, it is the fourth within ten days. It is impossible for him to go on in this way long without being killed. He is fairly under the Turkish entrenchments, and within easy range of the Turkish fire which is growing stronger and stronger. The roar is continuous and rolls up and down the hollow like one continuous crash of thunder, only broken by the heavier booming of the artillery. The bullets must be falling about him there like hail. It will be a miracle if Skobeleff comes out of it alive. Here a cloud of dust and smoke gathered for a few moments, and when the wind swept it away I saw Skobeleff again on another horse, coming up the road at a trot, cool and fresh as ever. He had not received a scratch, and the reconnaissance was over."

Skobeleff later, in the beginning of September,

took Loftcha by storm. It was the first regular systematic enterprise that had been entrusted to him since the war began. Prince Imeritinski was in nominal command, it is true, but Skobeleff was his chief of staff, and Imeritinski left to him the arrangement and execution of all the details. Skobeleff, the evening before the successful assault, promulgated elaborate instructions to the officers, with some words of sound soldierly advice to the men. This "Scheme of Attack" has become a standard in the war schools of all continental Europe, as a model of tactical conception of lucid clearness, of careful provision for any and every contingency. I am content to stand by it alone in my contention that Skobeleff is to be reckoned, not as some reckon him, a mere dashing fighting man, but as one of the great generals of modern times. Soldiers can appreciate injunctions such as those as I am about to quote, although few commanders since Napoleon have given themselves the trouble to realise that it is worth while to recognise the private man as a creature to whom God Almighty has given some modicum of comprehension. "Do not forget the necessity of supporting your comrades at any sacrifice. Do not waste your cartridges. Remember that the nature of the country renders it very difficult to supply ammunition. I mention once more to the infantry the necessity of order and silence in fighting. Do not cry 'hurrah' till you are close to the enemy, and are preparing to charge him with the bayonet. I call the attention of all the soldiers to the fact that in an intrepid attack the losses are a minimum, and that a retreat, especially a retreat in disorder, results in great losses and in shame." Were ever words so few more pregnant with compressed yet forcible meaning? These few sentences are worthy to be hung up in every barrack-room in the world; they comprise the whole duty of the soldier in the hour of battle.

Having planned, Skobeleff executed. By virtue of his detailed instructions every man knew his place and his work, without reference to him. As for Skobeleff, the place he naturally chose for himself was at the head of the assault; his task was to take Loftcha, and to this end it seemed to him he could thus best contribute. And so it was that on that day as ever, the soldiers, looking out to their front, saw that broad back in the white coat showing them the way. Skobeleff in the assault was never the chief to use the word "go;" no, he bade his men "come." And no man who saw how the Russian soldiers followed Skobeleff can with truth aver that he ever made his appeal to them in vain.

The exploit of Loftcha brought for Skobeleff restoration to Imperial favour (for which, since it had been unjustly withdrawn from him, he had rather a contempt), and it brought him what he prized more —promotion to the rank of lieutenant-general and the command of the famous 16th Division (it was he who made it famous), which he subsequently led to the shores of the Sea of Marmora, and would fain

have led indeed into the heart of Constantinople. He
and I made a hurried rush back to Bucharest for a
few days ; he to order the outfit commensurate to
his new position, I to make sure of my telegraphic
arrangements for transmitting the intelligence of the
impending struggle, which promised to be more
momentous than any fighting that the campaign had
yet developed. We were barely back into Bulgaria
and he had just actively assumed his command, when,
in the foggy day-dawn of the 7th September, there
began the third attempt on the part of the Russians
to make themselves masters of Osman Pasha's
positions around Plevna. To gain what was thought
sufficient strength for this undertaking, steadily as
its difficulties had been increasing because of the
Moslem general's assiduous and judicious spadework,
the Russian invasion had stood still, paralysed by
Osman's bull-dog attitude there on their right flank,
until the stream of reinforcement pouring in from
Russia had filled up the war-depleted battalions, and
added regiment after regiment, brigade upon brigade,
to the "Order of Battle." Ninety thousand men
now stood around Plevna, waiting for the signal to
assault. Skobeleff had the extreme left flank, on
ground wherewith he gained some familiarity in his
dash on Plevna when co-operating with Schahofskoy
in the end of July. But that ground had taken on
a new and more formidable face since then. Osman
had been using the spade to great purpose during
the five weeks' interval. On ground whereon, on

the 30th July Skobeleff had manœuvred unimpeded, there cumbered the earth now the formidable Krishine series of redoubts, constructed and fortified with all the skill of Osman's engineers and artillerists. That undulating region where in peace time the maize-fields are so luxuriant, now serrated with trench and piled high with parapets, was once and again to be drenched with Russian blood before the day should come when Osman, as he was carried away wounded into a captivity more honourable than many triumphs should look his last around the scene in which he had fought so long and stout a fight.

A preliminary bombardment was to prepare the way for the Russian assault. Twenty great siege cannon and 250 field guns, from the morning of 7th September until the afternoon of the 11th, rained an iron hail-storm on Osman's positions. The 11th, Czar Alexander's name-day, was chosen for the assault. What happened elsewhere on that lurid afternoon in the rifts of the bewildering haze need not here be recounted; I concern myself only with Skobeleff's glorious although unsuccessful part in the stupendous tragedy that was being enacted. He had made his preparations with timely skill. He had pushed seventy guns forward to the very verge of safety, and prepared with their fire his grand attack, for which he had in hand four regiments of the line, and four battalions of riflemen. Still keeping up his crushing artillery fire he formed under its cover two regiments in the little hollow at the foot of the low hill in which stood the Turkish redoubt that was his objective, together with two battalions of his sharpshooters. The distance was not more than 1200 yards up to the scarp of the Turkish work. His arrangements complete, he himself took up a position whence he could watch events, and ordered the stormers to fall on. The assaulting column moved forward, rifles on shoulders, with music playing and banners flying, and soon had all but disappeared in the fog and mist. The outline of the column was barely visible, a dark mass in the obscurity. With his finger, so to speak, on every throb of the pulse of the battle, Skobeleff discerned that his first line was wavering and hesitating under the stress of the Turkish rifle-fire. On the instant he hurled forward a fresh regiment to invigorate it, and watched attentively the effect This added force carried the mass farther forward with its momentum and its dash, but the Turkish redoubt flamed and smoked, and poured forth such a torrent of bullets that the Russian line was again staggered. Skobeleff stood up unharmed in this shower of balls as if he bore a charmed life. All his escort were killed or wounded, and the Kirghis lad sat there mopping the blood from a bullet wound in the shoulder. As he watched the line sway and heave in its hesitation, he flung forward to its support his fourth and last regiment. Again this new and fresh wave carried farther forward with its momentum the earlier waves, whose force had been all but spent, until the now ragged and disordered line all but reached the lip of the glacis. But there it swithered. On the panting soldiers poured steadily that deadly shower of Turkish bullets, men were falling in hundreds, and the issue swayed to and fro in the balance. It was a time when the hearts of the onlookers stood still, and the current of blood seemed to cease to flow in the veins. There was not a moment to be lost, if failure was not to be the issue of the attack.

Skobeleff had now in reserve but two battalions of riflemen, but they were picked men, the best soldiers in his command. He closed his glass, he swung himself into the saddle, his sword flashed from the scabbard, his voice rang out loud, clear, and calm, as he galloped out to the front of the deployed riflemen, and bade his "brothers" to follow him. As he rode on he gathered up and rallied the stragglers; he reached the wavering, fluctuating mass swaying there in the hell-fire, and sent thrilling and tingling through it the sublime inspiration of his own high courage. He caught up, as it were, the whole mass, and carried it bodily forward with a rush and a cheer. The whole redoubt was a pandemonium of flame and smoke from out of which rose screams, shouts, cries of agony and defiance, along with the deep-mouthed bellowing of the cannon, and the steady, awful, ruthless crash of the deadly rifle-fire. Skobeleff's sword was cut in two in the middle, as he waved it above his head. Then, a moment later, just as he was gathering his horse together for the leap across the ditch, horse and man rolled together on the ground ; the horse shot and done with, the man alive and unharmed. Skobeleff sprang nimbly to his feet with a shout ; the men he led responded ; then, with a sharp, savage yell the whole mass of men streamed after the white-coated leader across the ditch, up the face, over the parapet, and swept down into the redoubt like a whirlwind. There ensued a few fierce moments of desperate hand to hand fighting ; then numbers and the bayonet had done their work, and a hoarse shout told that Skobeleff had captured the Krishine redoubt, and that at last one of the most important defences of Plevna was in the hands of the Russians.

But at what a sacrifice ! In that short rush of a few hundred yards 3000 men had gone down— one-fourth of Skobeleff's whole force ; and the slope, the glacis, the ditch, and the scarp were strewn thick with the fallen. He was not responsible for the assault ; he was ordered to take the redoubt, and he was the man to obey orders when they enjoined fighting. Then he tried to hold what he had won, but at a dreadful disadvantage, for the adjacent redoubts commanded it, and poured into it a continuous shell-fire. He prayed even pathetically for reinforcements, urging with stern yet piteous vehemence that if only they were sent him he would guarantee to serve the other redoubts as he had done this one, and so gain Plevna. There was little doubt that he could have made good his words. But unspeakable ignorance, carelessness, and folly refused him the reinforcements for which he entreated. Still he clung fiercely to what he had won, loath to relinquish the vantage ground such as it was. By the afternoon of the 12th, 3000 more of his men had gone down. He had lost 50 per cent of his command. At length, late in the afternoon, the Turks took the offensive in overwhelming numbers, and drove Skobeleff's shattered remnant out of the work so long and so obstinately held. Such indomitable spirit had he been able to inspire that, after thirty-six hours of continuous fighting, some men had not then enough of it, and actually 200 men under Major Gortaloff would not quit the place, but fought it out in a desperate hand to hand struggle until the last man of them was cut down. As Skobeleff came out from the long devilry at the head of his dauntless remnant, MacGahan met him, and I know nothing in the language more luridly vivid than his pen picture of Skobeleff in this unique crisis: "He was in a fearful state of excitement and fury. His uniform was covered with blood, mud, and filth; his sword broken; his Cross of St. George twisted round on his shoulder; his face black with powder and smoke; his eyes haggard and bloodshot, and his voice quite gone. I never saw such a picture of battle as he presented. I saw him again in his tent at night. He was then quite calm and collected. He said, 'I have done my best; I could do no more. My detachment is half destroyed; my regiments do not exist; I have no officers left; they sent me no reinforcements; I have lost three guns.' 'Why did they refuse you reinforcements?' I asked; 'who was to blame?' 'I blame nobody,' answered Skobeleff, 'it was the will of God!'"

The Russians had got their stomachful of assaults upon Plevna. Todleben came down, with his project of slow scientific starvation, and the deliberate siege began. Skobeleff had the brunt of the hard fighting that had to be encountered in the course of drawing tighter the cordon of environment, and lived perpetually in the trenches under the Turkish fire, sleeping on a stretcher. In one of the almost daily encounters he received a severe flesh wound in the back, which he did not allow to exile him even temporarily from his duty, but which I believe left its effects on his constitution. This was his only wound throughout a campaign in which he exposed himself with a recklessness which no remonstrances could abate, and which seemed to indicate that he was courting death. Now that he had a definite and permanent command, he had organised a staff, the personnel of which was of quite another stamp from the usual staff *entourage*. Skobeleff, although himself a dandy who went into action scented like a popinjay, did not believe in "fancy" soldiers for his subordinates. He had got about him a rugged motley crowd of staunch fighting men of whose martialism he had had experience in his Asiatic warfare. The young men were of the *enfan perdu* class who having come to grief in the Guards accept a warlike exile beyond the Caucasus. With them were grizzled linesmen wholly destitute of any accomplishment save the accomplishment of fierce and resolute fighting. Skobeleff did not affect scientific staff officers, but he would have about him men who without swagger or bravado, but simply as a matter of course, would fling themselves at his bidding into any enterprise however desperate. On the man who hesitated or even who argued he would turn his back with contemptuous abruptness. His chief of staff, Kurupatkin, was a silent, dogged, bloodthirsty fellow, with bull-dog instincts of savagery and tenacity. Skobeleff harboured semi-civilised Circassian officers, not because he had any fondness for their society or any belief in their capacity as staff officers, but simply because the Circassian was a fighting man in whose dash and constancy he could implicitly trust. What science was needed to shape the exertions of this gang of desperadoes, Skobeleff could furnish himself; but in truth the work they were engaged in was of a nature in which scientific warfare was rather at a discount. The great scientist of the Russian army in Bulgaria was Levitsky, the under-chief of the Grand Duke Nicholas' headquarter staff; and Levitsky's "science" it was that contributed more than anything else to the successive reverses sustained by the Russian arms in the earlier period of the campaign. Levitsky was too scientific to be practical. He failed to comprehend that successful war does not consist in obstinate endeavours to carry out a theoretical plan with a theoretical army, but in the ready and dexterous adaptation of existing means to required ends.

At length, came the closing scene of the great Plevna drama, when the wounded Osman at the head of his sortie, ended the long gallant struggle by his surrender. Skobeleff was among the group of generals who cheered the valiant Moslem as he came out. The Grand Duke Nicholas presented them to him one after the other. As Skobeleff was introduced the two men stared hard at each other, with a gaze of mutual curiosity and respect that was surely natural. Then there came on Osman's dark face a grave smile, and his hand went out and was grasped in Skobeleff's. The pair recognised each " a foeman worthy of his steel ; " they bowed, parted, and never met again. At the fall of Plevna, Todleben raised his voice in favour of quiescence in winter quarters ; and all the generals joined him save only Gourko and Skobeleff, who vehemently urged on the Grand Duke Nicholas that the Balkans should be crossed at once, in the dead of winter though it was. Nicholas was not much of a commander-in-chief ; but he was a man of action, and he took the advice that had a ring of energy in it. Gourko went over the mountains toward Sofia, while Skobeleff, with his own division and some detachments, struck across the Balkans by a precipitous hill-track to the right of and near the Schipka Pass. On the inhospitable summit of the latter had long been camped stout old Radetski, confronted from below by Vessil Pasha in the lines in front of the village of Schipka, at the head of some 40,000 Turks. The Russian advance against that Turkish chief was a combined movement, Radetski in the centre standing fast, while Mirski on his left, Skobeleff on his right should descend and turn the Turkish position, Radetski himself co-operating in the offensive scheme by striking at the Turkish centre when Mirski and Skobeleff were hurling themselves on its flanks.

It was a strange time for a combined movement of considerable delicacy, for success in which were essential synchronous punctuality and accurate prearrangement. The snow lay ten feet on the rugged Balkans, and whole companies were engulfed in the fathomless drifts. The artillery had to be abandoned in the snow; what fighting would have to be done, and it was bound to be severe, must be done solely with the rifle bullets and the bayonets, and this against prepared positions heavily armed with cannon. The 8th of January was the day named for the combined attack. But the combination had been thwarted by the difficulties of weather and mountain, and by the stubborn resistance of the Turks. Mirski was fighting up to the hilt all that day, and by nightfall was all but spent. Radetski sent him word to brace himself for the following day; he would himself strike in with a diversion, and Skobeleff by that time would surely have got within operating distance. On the morning of the 9th, then, Mirski and Radetski renewed the struggle with resolution, but under desperate difficulties. A tempest of wind was raging that filled the air with blinding snow, and made a dense bitter fog of particles of frozen mist. No man could see ten yards before him. After hard fighting and terrible losses Mirski and Radetski had to own to the impossible. As they hung there in suspense, unable to advance farther, there came to them the strange glad tidings that the whole Turkish army had surrendered to Skobeleff. Yes, that wonderful man had added another laurel to his chaplet. He had wallowed on through yard-deep snowdrifts, set his face hard against the blinding snowstorm; and having at last got down into the valley, it was in the very nick of time that with colours flying and bands playing he fell, or rather rolled, on Vessil's flank. After a desperate struggle he carried the Shenova redoubts, and in the short pause after the bayonet work came to Skobeleff the officer sent by Vessil Pasha, to tender the surrender of the whole Turkish forces, consisting of 36,000 men with ninety-three guns.

Skobeleff, leaving Radetski to pick up the pieces, hurried on down the Tundja valley with his face set straight for Adrianople. He got there by forced marches—once he marched fifty miles in forty hours—almost before its Turkish inhabitants had heard of the Schipka catastrophe; and leaving a Russian governor in the capital of Roumelia, he pushed on at the top of his speed to reach the lines of Tcheckmedjee that cover the peninsula on the Bosphorus point of which stands Constantinople. He was in front of them, and ready and eager to assault them, when the armistice was signed on the evening of 31st January. The march from before Plevna to the shore of the Sea of Marmora Skobeleff's men had made absolutely without baggage, and without any provision train whatsoever. They drove their meat on the hoof, their biscuits they carried in their haversacks. Their boots were worn out like their greatcoats, and they tramped along in mocassins made of the canvas that had been their tents. They were in high spirits, high health, and ready for any service, no matter how arduous. No service that could come to them could well be more arduous than the service out of which they had already come victorious.

In the long weary interval between the Treaty of San Stephano and the final accomplishment of peace by the Treaty of Berlin, the Russian soldiers, lying inactive on the low unhealthy ground between the Black Sea and the Sea of Marmora, died like flies of typhoid fevers and camp pestilences. But Skobeleff's division remained healthy. He alone of the Russian leaders was a practical sanitarian. He kept his camps clean; he made his men wash themselves—a sore torture for the Russian soldier; he gave them exercise; he saw to the baking of bread for them, and bought them vegetables out of his own pocket; he lived among them, encouraged them by the exuberant vitality of his own presence, and staved off nostalgia by maintaining a steady series of amusements. He became very popular in Constantinople during his short visits to the Turkish capital, and was free of the British coterie there, with whom he liked to associate, partly for good fellowship, partly for the sake of amicably hostile controversy. He professed to hanker after its members as prisoners of war. If he had got his way, the Russians would certainly have occupied Constantinople—and then? Of the five leading card holders in that game of bluff which came so near being played out in grim earnest, three, the Czar, Lord Beaconsfield, and Skobeleff are dead; the Grand Duke Nicholas is "living in retirement," and as for Ignatieff, he is temporarily at all events an extinct volcano.

Of Skobeleff's subsequent career I have only the same perfunctory knowledge that any man may have who cares to read and to listen. His Turkoman campaign was toilsome, thankless work, and I know that he pitied the poor wretches whom he had the commission to exterminate. He had little happiness in the last few years of his life. His father died suddenly when he was in Asia, and the cruel assassination of his mother, whom he fondly loved, was a blow which I fancy he never recovered. He had no married life, although he was married before I knew him. His marriage was one of the strangest episodes in his strange career. He had wooed and won a lady of, if I remember correctly, the Gagarine family; they were married with the approbation of all concerned, and there were all the anticipations of a life of wedded happiness. A fortnight after the marriage the lady left him, went back to her friends and never lived with him again. I happen to know through relatives of hers that the explanation of her conduct given by her to her own family, was regarded by them as affording the fullest justification of the action she had taken ; nor did Skobeleff inferentially combat this conclusion by making any attempts to re-establish conjugal relations. He was not ancestrally of noble family ; his grandfather began life as a private soldier, but his sister since the war has married one of the Leuchtenbergs, cousins of the present emperor.

After the Russo-Turkish war I saw Skobeleff but once again, and that only for an hour during his visit to Paris in '81. He seemed to me greatly changed. The old buoyancy had faded out of him ; he was grave, and even sometimes sombre. His face had lost its glow of health, and the brightness of the eye had dimmed. But his intellect possessed all its pristine strength, and in a sense of responsibility as in scope of apprehension, he had perceptibly matured. As we talked of MacGahan his eyes filled with tears, and he said, with a break in his voice, that "he had loved that man like a brother." The true story of his woful and awfully sudden death has never been written, nor can it be written. He did not commit suicide, at all events with intent ; he was not assassinated ; he did not die of heart disease. He sacrificed his life to a paroxysm of what was perhaps his chief weakness—sensuality. And in his death Russia sustained a loss, in any war in which she may engage, which I estimate is equal to the deprivation of an army corps. My heart swells now at the sad thought of Michael Skobeleff's frank eyes clouded in death, of his gallant, manly spirit gone from among us.

HOW I BECAME A WAR CORRESPONDENT.

BEFORE passing to the subject of this paper I must premise that it was originally written under the irresistible force of an editorial injunction. I would not have it thought that I am other than proud of the profession in which I have spent the best years of my life; but, on the other hand, I was anxious to guard against the imputation of seeking to thrust under public notice personal details in relation to my own career. It was so received that my solicitude on this score is dispelled; and so I do not scruple to reprint it.

I became a war correspondent because I had previously been a cavalry soldier, and it was a war correspondent who made me become a cavalry soldier. My earliest bias towards the profession of arms came to me from listening to a lecture on the Crimean war, which William Howard Russell delivered in the Music Hall of Edinburgh in the winter of '57. I had read his war letters piecemeal, but his lecture forced me to buy his book, and the description of the cavalry work at Balaclava I read in its pages kindled in me a great ardour for the mounted arm. This remained but a theory until follies and extravagance abruptly terminated my university career, when it had a practical outcome in my accepting "the Queen's shilling" from a fine old recruiting sergeant belonging to the Royal Dragoons. It was not long before I realised that cavalry regiments do not hurl themselves in wild career against hostile ranks with so great frequency as to impart to the pastime any character of monotony. I was disillusioned, yet the glamour did not wholly fade—no, nor is it dead yet, although I have no hope ever again to hear the trumpets sound the "charge," and see the war horse pawing in the valley. I suppose I had a natural affinity for soldiering; anyhow I took to its drudgery with as much zeal as if I had never learned to conjugate Greek irregular verbs or make bad Latin verses. Five and twenty years ago there were few gentlemen in the ranks even of our cavalry regiments, and of the few who were fewer still had their heart in their work. When the little remittance came to me from home, most of it went in standing beer to old troopers, who, as they drank, could talk with spirit and force of the old "active service" days—how "Joey Yorke" still bade his men close in knee to knee and ride straight, after the bullet had smashed his knee; how "Duck Wilson," the sergeant-major, had ridden down the Russian colonel, and given him "point one" before he had time to go to ground; how young "Jack Noakes," whom I met the other day a retired major in New Zealand, having had his horse shot under him, serenely killed a Russian cavalry man and so remounted himself. The oldsters drank my beer, and I suppose laughed at me as they wiped their moustaches on their shirt sleeves ; but, although I had no thought save for the present pleasure of listening to their tales, told as they were in the quaint forcible idiom of the barrack room, it was I who was the gainer. I was saturating myself with practical soldierhood, while the grizzled veterans were swilling my beer. Then when the troop-horses were bedded down for the night, and my comrades sallied out "into the town" to keep tryst with maid-servants, or to swell the chorus in some beer-house taproom, there were for me, till the watch-setting trumpet sounded, three happy hours in the regimental library over the pages of Napier, or in tougher wrestle with the war problems of Jomini.

Then there dawned in me the desire to write something descriptive of the manner of life we soldiers were living. I remember as if it were but yesterday, under what conditions I wrote my first article. It was at a table in the barrack room, amidst din and turmoil. Fellows were singing as they pipe-clayed belts or burnished sword scabbards. I was interrupted by the necessity to clear the table away to make room for a fight. The first page of my manuscript was smeared with chrome yellow that dropped from the stripes of a pair of overalls hanging overhead. When I returned to England after the Russo-Turkish war, some partial friends who were so good as to admire some exertions of mine in that campaign, did me the honour to entertain me at a banquet in Willis' Rooms. It was a coincidence passing strange that, as I rose with a heart overfull for eloquence, even were that gift at my command, to strive to stammer a few words in acknowledgment of the magnificent eulogium which George Sala had allowed himself to pronounce, my eye should have fallen on two men sitting by each other, Frederick Greenwood and Justin M'Carthy, of whom the former, in his capacity as editor of the *Cornhill Magazine* had accepted the first contribution I ever dared send to a periodical, the latter had made a "Starlight Reading" of the first paper I submitted to a daily journal. I have often wondered whether Mr. Greenwood regarded the chrome yellow drops as a species of voucher for the authenticity of the barrack room origin of the article he accepted with words of encouragement that I can never cease gratefully to remember.

But ill-health cut short my soldiering days, and I had to lay down the sword for the pen. The pen has kept me and mine ever since, yet indirectly the sword has furnished the greater share of our rations. In the early days I lived a good deal on military sketches contributed to the "Starlight" column of the paper which Mr. M'Carthy then conducted. Later I staked my small fortunes on a now long-forgotten journal which tried to prosper under the title of the *London Scotsman*. This paper was my own in every sense. I was the proprietor and the sole contributor. Week after week it saw the light —my work from the first leader to the compiled " Births, deaths, and marriages " immediately preceding the advertisements, some of which, too, I had gathered in. Sketches, short stories, reviews, reports, each and all, such as they were, came from my pen. I wrote a novel in its pages to fill up space—a military novel, of course ; a tale of the Indian Mutiny. I had not participated in the Mutiny campaign, nor had I ever been to India ; but that was a matter of detail. Some readers may yet remember a stalwart medalled soldier, wearing too the Victoria Cross, who did duty as a private constable outside Moses and Sons' ready-made clothes shop in Oxford Street. This was " Hollowell of the deadly rifle," one of the nine heroes of " Dhoolie Square." Hollowell is long dead, and Moses no longer exposes his cheap goods in the windows of the commanding corner over against Mudie's. Hollowell had been a soldier of the gallant Ross-shire Buffs, who played so valiant a part in Havelock's advance on Cawnpore and first relief of Lucknow. One day I fell into talk with him, and found him a man with a singular memory for picturesque details, such as give local colour and verisimilitude to descriptions. Every week I leased two hours of Hollowell's time and talk, at a tariff of five shillings the interview ; and as regularly incorporated what he told me into the week's instalment of my novel in the *London Scotsman*. I regarded it as in a sense a compliment when long afterwards the present Sir Henry Havelock, as the result of a perusal of the story in book form, expressed to me his firm conviction that I must be a deserter from the Ross-shire Buffs, since no man who had not actually made the campaign in that regiment could have given the story the local colour which he was pleased to ascribe to it.

Anyhow it was the descriptions of battles in this poor hand-to-mouth story which has long sunk into deserved oblivion, that earned for me my first commission as a war correspondent. In those days the late Mr. James Grant was the editor of the *Morning Advertiser*. I have heard men laugh at Mr. Grant, but it would ill become me to have aught but kindly memories of one who was to me a good friend. He had come from our neighbourhood, where in early life some of my people had been able to show him some favour, and this he remembered on my behalf. I never was on the staff of his journal, but he gave me a good deal of casual work, some of which was scarcely in my way, although I made a struggle to compass it without flagrant failure. The most trying commissions he gave me were to write notices of minor musical affairs, such as concerts. Now of music I know absolutely nothing—nature had given me no ear, and I never was able to whistle a tune in my life. I fancy Mr. Grant knew little more about music than did his "critic," nor probably were his readers very censorious ; so I was able to wriggle along somehow, earning my half-guineas until an unfortunate misconception on my part put an end to my work in the musical department of the *Advertiser*. I was sent to a music establishment in Bond Street to write about a gentleman who performed on a new instrument which he called a " pedal-pianoforte." He played not less with his feet than with his hands, and his physical exertions were at once arduous and grotesque. It seemed to me that it was of his dexterous agility of which he desired to make exhibition, and I wrote of him more in the character of an acrobat than of a musician, without the faintest idea that I was not doing him the fullest justice. My praises of his phenomenal activity were duly printed, and, judging by the tone of his remonstrance, Nature had not bountifully endowed him with the emotion of gratitude. So strenuous were his expressions that they caused an arrestment of my musical commissions.

On that day of July, '70, on which France declared war against Germany, Mr. Grant sent for me, and startled me with the abrupt question whether I should care to go abroad for the *Advertiser* as its war correspondent, having been moved to ask this question, he said, because of the battle pieces he had read in my story in the *London Scotsman*. Far off, as a child might sigh for the moon, this work had been the dream of my life, ever since I had come to realise that I could write matter that men would print, and that other men would read. It had been never more than a dream. I had a diffident half-belief that some work I had put out of hand was not perceptibly worse than work I saw in the dignity of large type in important journals. But I was so absolutely out of the running. In the journalistic swim of the day I had neither part nor lot. Of editors and managers of the daily papers I knew not even the names. And lo! the thing had come to me, unasked; the moon had dropped into my arms! I never realised that there were two sides to the question—that the *Advertiser* was scarcely a journal whose correspondence was likely to attract the notice of a wide circle of general readers; that my own little paper must suffer during my absence; that I might be flinging away a substance, such as it was, for a vague shadow; and that because of the hostages I had given to fortune it behoved me not to be rash. No, I grasped Grant's hand in a rapture of gratitude; I stipulated for no remuneration save that he should pay a modest specified subsidy for the maintenance of those I was leaving behind; I took £10 for outfit, and £20 in my pocket as campaigning expenditure; bought a knapsack and a note-book, and started by the mail train (second class) the same night. A friend had taken charge for me of the *London Scotsman*.

Luck, in a way, was on the side of the enthusiastic novice. Mr. Grant seemed to have little more conversance with the theatre of war than that it would be somewhere in continental Europe, and he left it to me to make choice whether I would see what was to be seen with the Germans or with the French. Since leaving the army, I had made some study of the military organisations of the great European powers; I had read Colonel Stoffel's warning letters; and I felt the conviction that even if the French were in condition to essay their old accustomed *rôle* of the first offensive, German method, system, and copiousness of available resource would ultimately bring victory to the Teutonic banners. How purposeful were the German military people, how smoothly and efficiently worked Moltke's vast machine, was demonstrated so powerfully in Henry Hozier's *Seven Weeks' War*, that I wondered even then, as I have wondered in a growing ratio ever since, how so many clear-headed Britons should have been so implicit believers in the French supremacy. I, for my part, needed no moment for consideration before I decided to choose the German side of the great cockpit, and with little less deliberation I selected the point for which to make, with intent to see the earliest fighting. I left behind me when I quitted England the address of "Poste Restante, Saarbrück." In regard to the all-important question of "legitimation," the German term for permission to accompany armies in the field, I was in utter and happy ignorance. My assumption was that I could get along somehow; and so, while the great ones of the profession in whose ranks I was the humblest of raw recruits were haunting the Berlin bureaux in quest of their credentials, I was already looking at the fighting. I was very lucky. I saw everything up to Gravelotte in virtue of an informal scrap of permission General von Goeben had given me as I passed through Coblentz on my way to the front. It was not until the day after Gravelotte, when the German hearts were mellowed by victory, that I got the "Great Headquarter Pass," signed by Podbielski, the quartermaster-general of King Wilhelm's staff, which was so potent a voucher wherever exhibited. Nor for this puissant document had I to beg and intrigue and use influence. I had no influence to use. I simply called, the evening after Gravelotte, at the bureau in Gorze of the general staff. There I found a friendly sergeant, to whom I explained what I desired to have, and with whom I left the credentials I carried from my newspaper, and the scrap Von Goeben had given me. I was bidden to return in an hour. I did so, and the friendly sergeant handed me the Podbielski legitimation, with the stamp and seal on it of the Royal Headquarter, and the injunction to all and sundry to regard me as a fully accredited correspondent. The sergeant did my business for me; in connection with this affair I saw nobody save that genial spectacled non-commissioned officer.

We—I had found a staunch comrade in poor young Jacob de Liefde, who was representing the

Glasgow Herald—had a strangely adventurous time of it between the frontier and the vicinity of Paris. Save for the occasional hire of a vehicle, we covered the ground on foot, knapsacks on backs. We were independent of quarters, for we bivouaced with the lightest hearts, and we carried our rations and did our cooking gipsy-fashion, under the lee of a sheltering hedge. We could scarcely be called war correspondents; rather we were journalistic tramps writing letters to our newspapers, which we posted in any field-post waggon we chanced on, with a vague hope that somehow or other they would reach their destination some day. We had no money for couriers back to the base with our despatches, no resources that would justify resort to telegraphic communication, no affiliation to any headquarter through which our letters could be expedited. In the fullest sense of the term we were "unattached." It was an adventurous, racy, picturesque life; but it was not war correspondence in the more modern sense of that term. Later, it came with me to be a grievance—a matter of chagrin—that I should see anything notable, the account of which English newspaper readers should not have before them within three days at latest. The feeling grew up in me, so centred did I become in my work, that I would rather not see such an occurrence at all than see it and not be able to justify my existence in relation to it by getting the description of it home *ventre à terre*. But this unquiet sense of responsibility had not got its grip on me, while as yet I promenaded Lorraine for the *Morning Advertiser*, with knapsack on back and a very small handful of napoleons in my pocket. It was not my affair that I had neither horses nor couriers. I have often thought since, had all the appliances been then at my command such as in later campaigns I originated, elaborated, and strained many a time to their utmost tension, how I might have made the world ring in those early, eager, feverish days of the first act of the Franco-German tragedy! For we two reckless adventurous pedestrians seemed somehow to drift into the very heart of everything that was most sensational of those sensational days. I believe we were the last in the Saarbrück Exercir Platz on the day of the "baptism of fire," before the red-trousered skirmishers swarmed on to its level expanse. We were in Saarbrück during the three days of the French occupation. Sometimes, in the advance, we were outside the German ground altogether, and drifting about in villages where no Uhlan had yet been. We drove through Chalons after the Germans had cleared out of it for the turning movement towards Sedan, and were gravely warned by the burghers against taking a road on which we were likely to meet the troopers from which they had been happily, although only temporarily, delivered. We were inside Sedan before its surrender was consummated. We saw Napoleon meet Bismarck on the Donchery Road, and witnessed the subsequent interview between the two. We were with Von Tümpling's advance patrols all the way from Rheims to before Paris, and my first meeting with the diplomatist who is now Sir Edward Malet occurred almost within the fire-zone of the cannon of Fort Nogent, when the French escort who brought him out from the beautiful capital over which beleaguerment impended, handed him over to a stolid corporal of Silesian Uhlans, whose file was patrolling the road between Torcy and Claye. But, alas, it might have been in another world that all this good fortune of opportuneness had befallen me, for all that it made for any prestige to me in the character of a war correspondent. There had been one chance, indeed, to emerge from the rut of obscurity, but of that chance loyalty and honour forbade me to take avail. After Sedan I met Sutherland Edwards, who was acting for the *Times* as William Russell's colleague. I had told Edwards something of the singular luck in being in the heart of the throes of momentous events which had come to us in the adventurous haphazard life we were leading; and he had spoken of our conversation to Russell who, always full of single-hearted zeal for the interests of the great journal whose pages his genius has so often irradiated, made me the offer to recruit me into the cohort of which he was the captain. It was with a pang the poignancy of which wrung me sorely, that I was forced gratefully to tell him that not even for such promotion could I desert the colours under which I had taken service, futile in the way of making a name for myself as I had come to realise that service to be.

It was on the same day we had met Malet at the fireposts that there somehow came to me a letter which Mr. Grant had written to me. The casual field-post waggons had not carried my correspondence either with speed or certainty. Probably he had expected greater things than the means he had accorded to his representative had enabled that representative to accomplish. I had written with a copiousness and alacrity such as I have never since excelled, but letters had miscarried, and others had tarried cruelly long by the way. Anyhow, his letter was a recall, the specific reason assigned being that since the Prussian troops had now advanced on Paris, and a siege of that capital being imminent, his correspondent inside Paris would now suffice to keep him informed of the progress of events. The German environment, as might have been foreseen, did not long delay to cut off from him the channel of supply on which the worthy editor professed to rely. It was a curious irony of fortune that, when I penetrated into Paris immediately after the capitulation, one of the first Englishmen I found there, eating horseflesh and scanty bread that was half sand, was the correspondent whose existence formed the pretext for my supersession, eager to gather from me some scraps of intelligence concerning that outer world from which he had been so long isolated.

Mortified by the tone of Mr. Grant's letter my heart sank. The moon that had fallen into my arms I had found mere dust and ashes. My essay in the profession after which my soul had longed was an ignoble failure. The iron of disappointment and shame ate into my soul as I ruefully owned that I had tried to soar too high; and that my proper sphere was petty paper-staining for the *London Scotsman* and such-like kindred grovelling.

I would not linger in the arena of my discomfiture. I happened to make the acquaintance of a German King's Messenger, who the same night was leaving Meaux with despatches for the German embassy in London. He was to travel with all speed, and he kindly accepted me as his companion. The journey was through Rheims, Sedan, Bouillon, and so to the railway at Libramont. On the third day from that afternoon when in the dim heat-haze I saw afar off the glitter of the gilded dome of the Luxembourg, I stood forlorn and disconsolate in Fleet Street. Barely six weeks had elapsed since I had trodden that pavement buoyant with high hope, in a quiet delirium of joy that I had at length got my career; and now that pavement was again under the feet of a man overwhelmed with shame, crushed by the sombre consciousness of having proved unequal to the career which fortune, conscious of his inaptitude, had mocked him with, humiliated now in the inverse ratio of his former confidence in his own powers. One drop was yet wanting to the bitter cup. It seemed my duty to offer Mr. Grant a final letter on the military situation I had so recently turned my back on. That letter he coldly and curtly declined. I was thought so unworthily of that a letter from my pen was summarily declined, notwithstanding that it would have been gratuitous, and would have contained details of the most utmost moment, for which, as a matter of fact, the world was anxiously waiting!

I think this cut me deeper than any previous stroke of malign fate. But as I walked and smoked there befell me a recoil from utter prostration. My war correspondent delusion was dead; but was that collapse to reduce me to drivelling idiocy? Had I not left still, then, some faculty of perception? Did I not stand here, in these somewhat dilapidated boots, the sole man in all this vast expectant London outside the German embassy, to whom belonged the knowledge of the dispositions of the German troops engaged in weaving round Paris that environment of blood and iron? I was a failure, but all the same, before I went back into the mill-horse round of drudgery, was not this knowledge marketable? Then why not try to find the market for it, and go back to the grind with at least a few guineas in the pocket?

I took my resolution. I went into a shop, bought a blank visiting card, wrote on it my name with the legend underneath—" Left German front before Paris three days ago, possessed of exclusive information as to dispositions for beleaguerment." Then I put out my pipe, tramped down Tudor Street, struck across for Printing House Square, entered the *Times* office, and asked to see the editor. The door-keeper smiled —it was not yet noon; and informed me that the editor was not to be seen. In reply to my question whether there was any one acting for him whom I could see, he offered to take my card and bring back a reply. He was gone a few minutes, and the reply he brought back was to the effect that if I cared to write anything on the subject indicated in the memorandum on my card the proper course was to forward the article in the ordinary way, when the editor would have an opportunity of judging of its eligibility.

I left the *Times* office divided between two opinions. Was that journal omniscient, and so in a position to be indifferent to any information offered it, no matter how valuable on the face of things that information was; or was its wooden, stolid, grandiose manner so rigid in the phlegmatic routine of it that a relaxation was a matter of simple physical impossibility? I could not solve this problem; but this I was ruefully firm upon, that the off-chance of having a paper accepted on the given condition was not worth the trouble of writing it. Perhaps I was wrong in coming to this conclusion, but my soreness made shipwreck of my temper. I shook the dust of the *Times* office from off my feet, and wandered out again into Fleet Street. One more opportunity I resolved to give Fortune, if she had a mind not wholly to flout me. There were three other daily papers—the *Daily News*, the *Telegraph*, and the *Standard*. I would not importune each of these in succession, but to one of the three I should make an application for the acceptance of this information of mine; if that application were unsuccessful I should resign myself and go and put together the births, deaths, and marriages for the wearyful *London Scotsman*.

But which of the three papers was I to try? They were all strange alike to me, except that once the *Daily News* had paid me ninepence for a paragraph nine lines long—a fact which scarcely constituted a claim to introduce myself to its further notice. As I stood in front of the tobacconist's shop at the corner of Fleet Street which Ludgate Circus has swept away, I fell on the device of deciding by the toss of a copper to which of the three penny papers I should address myself. The *Daily News* won the toss, if this be the right phrase to use. To Bouverie Street I accordingly hied myself. It occurred to me on the way that I had heard the name of Robinson somehow, in connection with the management of that paper. It was a vague impression, thus little was I conversant with daily journalism; but it grew on me so that when I reached the office I asked for "Mr. Robinson." Had I been told there was no such person I think I should have gone away.

A memo, with my name, and the same legend as I had sent in to the *Times*, went up to Mr. Robinson, and presently I followed the memo. I said my say very succinctly, and probably a trifle cavalierly, for I had not great store of temper left. A quiet-mannered man with a high forehead looked steadily at me through his spectacles as I spoke, and then said, "Yes, that sounds very interesting and valuable. Will you oblige me by writing three columns on the subject, and will you consider five guineas a column adequate remuneration? If so, please let the copy be sent in as rapidly as possible." They were kind and considerate words, that at once restored me to my sense of manhood, and yet went some way towards unmanning me, so strained by humiliations was my nervous system. I expressed my content, and it was arranged that a boy should be sent round hourly for copy to the chambers which I occupied in the adjacent Tudor Street.

In those days I had the gift, of which mental and physical strain have deprived me, of writing like a whirlwind, and I always found that the faster I wrote the better I wrote. As I painted, the picture breadthened on the canvas. I caught the details with alert ardour; I had that glow and sense of power that come to a man with the consciousness that he is doing good work. In three hours' time, or thereabouts—it had not seemed ten minutes to me—I had written my allotted three columns, but the canvas allowed me would not hold half my picture. I did not like to spoil it by cramping it up. But then again, I was chary of exceeding the bounds assigned to me, lest it should seem I was greedy after more than the stipulated guineas. I determined I would go round and see this considerate Mr. Robinson, tell him how the case stood, and offer, rather than spoil my picture, to finish it in a fourth gratuitous column if he would have the charity to spare me the space.

Mr. Robinson had gone. Was, then, the editor there? The editor was absent holiday-making, but I could see the acting editor. The acting editor was reading a proof. I thought him a trifle gruff for the moment, but long since I have grown to know how little of gruffness there is in the sweet and genial nature of Edward Pigott. I explained my dilemma to him—briefly, because he gave me the idea of being impatient.

"Is this your stuff?" he trenchantly asked, laying his finger on the slip of proof before him.

I glanced at it and said it was my stuff.

"Well, then," said he, "we'll take as much of this kind of stuff as you care to write!" And this remark terminated the interview. Laconic as was his utterance, it went straight to my heart; I did not care that he should be a syllable more diffuse. I went to my chambers and reeled off three more columns with a lighter heart than I had known since before Mr. Grant's letter came to me at Meaux. This done I returned to the office to read the proofs.

Pigott was there, and not so busy as he had been in the afternoon. He expressed a wish for further contributions, and that these might be talked over at leisure, he gave me an invitation to breakfast with him next morning. I walked on air up to South Bank, for I had read my six columns, and not only did I think them good work, but I realised that they meant thirty guineas—far and away the best day's work I had ever done.

It was arranged between Pigott and me that my next contribution should concern itself with the narrative of what I knew about that lurid episode of the battle of Sedan that occurred in the village of Bazeilles. Other topics had been adumbrated, and I rejoiced to think that I had found a crutch to supplement the somewhat feeble and precarious staff of the *London Scotsman*. I looked in at the office to bespeak the same arrangement in regard to sending round for copy as had been in force the previous day. I was shown up to Mr. Robinson.

"You've come for your cheque, I suppose," said he, as it seemed to me a little shortly.

"No," I explained. "I have arranged with the acting editor to furnish some further contributions, and by his directions I have called to ask you to have a boy call round for copy in the same way as yesterday."

"I think not," said Robinson, with what struck me as an intentionally aggravating drawl. "I don't think we will trouble you to write these contributions you speak of. I will explain the matter to Mr. Pigott."

I don't quite know what I did say; I know I lost my temper vehemently, and I believe I used strong language. I think I said something about having believed in editorial omnipotence, and my inability to understand this business of one man blowing hot and another blowing cold. Anyhow, I was not going to stand being made a fool of in this offhand easy style; and I'd take good care I didn't darken the doors of the *Daily News* any more. And with that, the *perfervidum ingenium* of my northern nationality being all ablaze, I removed myself abruptly from the presence, and swore my way downstairs into the street.

"Here, come back!" Robinson had shouted after me. "I want to speak to you!"

I fear that if he had acted on the strict letter of the brief retort I threw over my shoulder he would have had no occasion to give any subsequent orders to his coal merchant.

I was striding up Bouverie Street, fiercely fuming behind my beard, when I felt a hand on my shoulder, and simultaneously I heard a voice—"Don't be a fool! I was going to say that I want you to start for Metz to-night!"

I turned and stared at Robinson—for it was he who had spoken—in the blankest amazement. Then he had meant no insult after all, but something, indeed, of quite a contrary tenor. And here was the real chance come at last, then, with all the prestige of a great paper—whose war correspondence was already the talk of the town—at the back of the offer; all the scope for making a name, if indeed the power to do anything in this direction did abide within me. It was a wonderful chance; but again, what a risk! With my recent experiences should I dare to take that risk? The struggle of conflicting emotions made me dizzy.

I will not weary the reader with the recital of the arguments that seemed to forbid me to accept Mr. Robinson's offer. It is possible that had I declined it I might have been a happier man to-day, for I have been a widower now for some thirteen years. I might have been a haler man than I am to-day at forty-five, my nerve gone, and my physical energy but a memory. Yet the recompense! To have lived ten lives in as many short years; to have held once and again in the hollow of the hand the exclusive power to thrill the nations; to have looked into the very heart of the turning-points of empires and of dynasties! What joy equal to the thrilling sense of personal force, as obstacle after obstacle fell behind conquered when one galloped from the battle-field, fraught with tidings which peoples awaited hungeringly or tremblingly! If the *gaudia certaminis* have an enthralling fascination for the soldier, scarcely less does the war correspondent share in the fierce rapture of the fray: and there may be for him joys and triumphs such as cannot light up the career of a soldier.

I requested Robinson to give me the day to decide, and to make arrangements should the decision accord with his wishes. At 7 P.M. I kept tryst at the rendezvous he had named, equipped for the journey. He gave me his good wishes and a roll of notes. I left England by the mail steamer the same evening, and in two more days had my share of the straw in a Prussian "field watch" on the east side of Metz. It was then that in reality my career as a war correspondent began.

THE EMPEROR AND HIS MARSHAL.

PERHAPS in all history there is no episode so barren of touches of nature as was the Second Empire. From first to last it was a mere scaffolding of meretricious artificiality. There was the sham Cæsar, a flaccid person with a knack of uttering obscurities conveying a vague flavour of ominousness at which the nations pricked their sensitive ears. The inner life of the empire was a strange mixture of rottenness and gimcrackery. What a court! The atmosphere of Compiègne had a confused aroma of bastardy, the demi-monde, the bourse, bogus nobility, journalism in the degradation of prostitution, militaryism half bravo, half *galant;* of intrigue, of dissoluteness, of insincerity, of ghastly hollowness. It is among the most humiliating problems of modern times how long this nasty gaudy caricature of Empire was able to impose on the world. It is a poor consolation for the world's long self-delusion that when the windbag was once resolutely pricked, it should have collapsed with such headlong swiftness. The humiliating memory cannot out of that eighteen-year-long imposition.

Almost in vain does one range through the record of the Empire in quest of but a glimmer of naturalness. There is a boy in the story, it is true, and surely, hopes the inquirer, some trait of nature is to be recognised in connection with him. But no; he was a buckram boy from his swaddling clothes, poor little toy and tool of sham Imperialism, down to the "baptism of fire." No trace is discernible of him as a boy in the fashion of other boys; he is ever found a mere padded clothes-horse, or rather clothes-pony. Now attired in the cumbrous uniform of the Compiègne hunt, with a *couteau de chasse* and a huge hunting horn hung about the poor melancholy little chap; now bedight in military garb, with a puny bit of a sword dangling about his shins, and his gloved hand raised in the frequent formal salute. The boy of the Second Empire is perhaps the most melancholy figure in its story, because we are fain to expect some human nature of boyhood, and the boyhood of this unfortunate child was as unreal as was the fantasy of which it was a victim.

It is an old story now, you will say, this Second Empire; and why recall the half sombre, half ludicrous memory? I do not know that I have a valid excuse. Not many have had such stimulus of personal interest in the successive catastrophes of the late Napoleons as that which the chances of my profession have brought to me. I have seen Napoleon III. at the pinnacle of his hollow splendour. From the German picket line on the 2d August 1870 I heard the distant cheering on the Spicherenberg that greeted him and the lad whom he had brought from Metz to receive that day his "baptism of fire." Again I saw him on the morning after Sedan, as the broken man—broken in power, in prestige, in health, in spirits—sat with Bismarck on the grass plot in front of the weaver's cottage on the Donchery Road. Next morning I witnessed his departure into his Wilhelmshöhe captivity. I have seen him doddering about Brighton and strolling under the beech trees that encircle Chislehurst Common. And for the last time of all I saw that stolid careworn face, as it lay on the raised pillow of the bier in the broad corridor of Camden Place; and when the face was no more visible I witnessed the coffin laid down in the little chapel among the Chislehurst elm trees. I knew the boy of the Empire when the shackles of the Empire had fallen from his limbs, and he was no longer a buckram creature, but a lively natural lad. My acquaintance endured into his manhood. When the twilight was falling on the rolling veldt of Zululand, and his day's work in the staff tent was done, he liked, as it seemed to me, to gossip with one who knew the other side of the picture about the early days of the Franco-German war—a war that had wrought at once his ruin and his emancipation. And finally, poor gallant lad! I saw dimly through tears the very last of him, as he lay there dead on the blood-stained sward by the Ityotyosi River, with a calm proud smile on his face, and his body pierced by countless assegai stabs. Men have called his death ignoble. Petty as was the quarrel, wretched as was the desertion that wrought his fate, I call him, rather, happy in the opportunity of his death. Had he lived, what of artificiality, what of hollow unreality might there not have been in store for him! As it was, he had moved in the world a live ghost. Better than this, surely, to be a dead hero :—to end the Napoleonic serio-comedy with his young face gallantly to his assailants, and his life-blood drawn by the cold steel!

Poor Prince Louis' life was fragrant with naturalness from the time that the fall of the Empire emancipated it; but before then it was among the most artificial of the Imperial phenomena. Nevertheless it mingles itself almost accidentally in the sole episode of the story of the Empire in which I have been able to detect anything of natural beauty and tenderness. Perhaps it is because I am an old soldier that there has come to me the recognition of a certain pathos in it. I do not know whether others will discern aught of this in the little narrative I am going to try to relate. It ought to be told on what authority rests the relation. I piece the story together from three sources: Marshal Bazaine's recent book detailing his own connection with the war of 1870-71, some conversations with the Marshal, and others in the earlier days of the Zululand campaign with Prince Louis Napoleon.

I do not know how the palace of St. Cloud looks now, but when I saw it last it was a ghastly fire-blackened wreck. A German picket of infantry men were quartered in the roofless salon, where they had built themselves a shelter of a kind of scorched tapestries and singed carpet scraps. A troop of Uhlan recruits were practising the *manège* on the little bend bordered by the stream—a spot that had been the empress' flower-garden. Six months earlier who, in the wildest speculation of fancy, could have imagined the possibility of such a fate as this for the beautiful château? There was the gaunt framework of a bow-window whose outlook was up the Seine in the direction of Paris; this was the chief window, I was told, of the room that had been virtually the private bureau—the "study" as we should perhaps call it—of the Emperor Napoleon. At that window he sat late on the afternoon of 16th July 1870. It was a fair scene that lay before him. Out on the lawn close under his eye was the toy railroad-track that had been one of the rare playthings of his boy. But it was hardly a time for admiring scenery or thinking about toys. The dreamy-eyed man with his head on his chest had more serious food for reflection. War had been virtually declared. The Germans were mobilising like clockwork; the French were trying to mobilise, and finding that the attempt produced chaos. Ollivier had proclaimed his lightness of heart in accepting the arbitrement of war. It was in the council chamber next door where Le Bœuf had proclaimed the army ready to the last button on the last soldier's gaiter. But the gloomy, brooding man shared none of Ollivier's levity; and he knew too well how hollow had been Le Bœuf's swagger. Ever a puppet, whose wires men with stouter will pulled, he was never a stupid man. His intelligence was so keen as to impair his happiness; had he been a duller man he would have had a much better time of his spell of Empire. He saw himself poised between the all but certainty of a revolution and the all but desperate chances of a war. In the one direction there was no hope; in the other he could not but realise there was only a forlorn hope. For he had read those ruthlessly lucid letters of Stoffel, detailing the German preparedness; he had seen that loyal officer's finger of warning held sternly and nakedly aloft. He knew that the sham Empire had deteriorated the once puissant French army into nearly as great a sham as itself.

Who were his servants? His lip must have curled as he thought of his ministry. And his generals? In MacMahon, a valiant chief and a fair tactician, he might put some faith, begotten of experience. Le Bœuf, his chief of staff,—for, heaven help him, he himself was to be his own commander-in-chief,—he knew well had come in by the back stair behind a petticoat. The others were mostly grown in the imperial hothouse, forced products of the *sabreur-bon-vivant* family of military botany.

He knew of some tried and clean officers, but then they were not Imperialists, and such was the precariousness of his position he could trust only Imperialists. "Ah, Bazaine!" Well, in him was one Imperialist at least, true and honest; whose allegiance had not been won and kept by invitations to Compiègne. Perhaps he was not a profound military genius; but he did not regard *déjeuner* as absolutely indispensable; he had an un-French capacity for taking pains; he knew the theatre of war; he was a favourite with the troops (it had come to that with the French army that this was a consideration); and he was coming this very afternoon to pay his visit of farewell before going away east to take the command to which he had been nominated the same morning. This was he whom the page was ushering in.

Not a very grand soldier, in the physical sense, this man, who in forty years of steady purposeful duty had raised himself from out the very ranks to the position of Marshal of France. He was short, somewhat fat, long in the body, short and bulgy about the legs, and with a puffy, rather pasty face. But there were physical features that were to be marked favourably, He had a good, straight, manly eye; his mouth had a habit of setting itself firmly; his voice, rather hoarse in its lower notes, had a clear-sounding ring when raised, as it many a time and oft had been raised to bid men follow him in the charge. He could be silent, and he could sit still—two rare virtues in the Imperialist soldiery.

He was an Imperialist because he was a soldier and worshipped *le petit Caporal*. He had owed not a great deal to the Empire; he had made his mark as a soldier before it began. Worthy soldiering in the Crimea had brought him his division; if the Mexican business could have been made a success by force of arms that success Bazaine would have achieved, and the bâton was but his due. He had been always a "duty soldier," to use the expressive phrase of our own army; never a carpet knight of the salons. The Emperor had for him that sort of regard which an unpractical and loose person has for a man who is trustworthy—somewhat rugged, not over-congenial, but staunch; some such regard as that in which young Charles held stout old Marshal Lesley. Bazaine, for his part, had a faithful, honest love for his emperor. I assume that he knew that emperor's faults; but he had a very tender spot in him for kind words, and Napoleon knew at least how to speak to men who served him well. It is to be said of him that no man has spoken ill of him who was much under his personal influence. Either it came natural to him, or he had learnt to speak as became a monarch. To sum Bazaine up, his good soldierhood and the regard his sovereign held him in for it, had earned him the jealousy of the soldier-fribbles of the Empire; a feeling nowise modified by the circumstance that he had been a "ranker," and had not come into the army through the fashionable gateway of the schools.

The interview was doubtless cordial enough, but there could have been little comfort in it for the emperor. Bazaine had lately held a district command on the north-eastern frontier, where the army was concentrating, and which a German offensive would menace. He could tell, and no doubt did plainly tell, of the state of universal unpreparedness, the inefficiency of Metz for resistance, the emptiness of the local magazines, the studied neglect of the requisitions he had made while in the Nancy command. He would do his best, of that his master might be sure; but "beware the offensive!" was his reiterated caution. Bazaine had gathered some knowledge of the German military system; he knew that the French army had degenerated to no system at all. The defensive might be possible with energy and good fortune, but the offensive could have no other significance than ruin. And so the simple soldier-man took his *congé* and went to pack his campaigning trunk.

He had been nominated to the command of an army corps, with a sort of supervision over two more, the three lying in the neighbourhood of Metz. But after he went out from his audience the emperor took a second thought. "This man," he said to himself, "had some purposefulness at least;" he would give him further charge. So he ordered Le Bœuf to intimate to him that he would have the interim disposition of all the seven corps which formed the Army of the Rhine, until the emperor himself, in his capacity of commander-in-chief, should take the field. Within twenty-four hours Bazaine was on his journey to the frontier.

What chaos he found there need not be described, because for one thing it would be indescribable. No money, food already scarce, ammunition defective, fortresses inadequately supplied—are not those things written in the histories of the period? Bazaine could not get the chiefs of army corps to report to him; they exercised a fine independence of insubordination, recognising doubtless that the omnipotent Le Bœuf—who by no means loved Bazaine—would not take them severely to task. True to his convictions, Bazaine had insisted on a strict defensive, but Le Bœuf was to overrule this wisdom, and had influence enough to persuade the emperor out of the resolution he had taken on Bazaine's representations. To facilitate this Bazaine was ordered out of Metz before the emperor arrived on 26th July, and was hindered from access to the Imperial presence until misfortune on misfortune rendered it necessary to fall back on his counsels.

Frossard in command of an army corps, was lying on the Spicherenberg, within cannon shot of the frontier line running between the Spicheren and Saarbrück. He was an engineer officer, and had been the governor of the Prince Imperial, in which capacity he had gained the emperor's ear. He had conceived the notion of commencing the campaign, making its *début*, as he phrased it—as if the campaign had been an actress—by a sudden dash on Saarbrück. As a means to the end of resolute alert invasion such a scheme would have been practical ; carried no further, it was in itself a childish folly, a conspicuous confession of inability to do anything more. Bazaine was opposed naturally to such a stale-mate, but Le Bœuf was an advocate for the enterprise ; and the hope that his presence and that of his son in the field would have a good effect in Paris tempted the poor emperor to give his consent. Bazaine had a nominal co-operation prescribed to him on a flank ; he might have claimed the chief command, and probably would, but that they withheld from him the knowledge that the emperor and the Prince Imperial were to witness the little military promenade.

This occupation of Saarbrück was the sole attempt on the part of the French during the war at the offensive outside their own frontier. On this occasion they penetrated into the bowels of the land of the Teuton barely two miles, and then certainly not without impediment. Three French army corps took a greater or smaller part in the operation. The French force of some 60,000 men had opposed to it — what ? A German infantry battalion 800 strong, and two squadrons of Uhlans—in all, a force of barely a thousand men. This mighty host was commanded by one of the bravest and funniest of mortals, Colonel von Pestel. He had been ordered to retire and leave Saarbrück bare, but he begged hard to be allowed to stay on, promising faithfully to fall back when molested. In the meantime he took the offensive with a comic vigour. Every afternoon as he rode out past the little Bellevue tavern, on the low ridge intervening between Saarbrück and the loftier Spicheren, he would sing out cheerily, "Hurrah, I go to draw de shoots of de enemy! Come along!" If you went you found yourself engaged in a mental speculation, whether a target, inanimate object though it seems, has emotions, and if so whether its emotion when being fired at is one of serene beatitude. The Colonel's bearing, granting the former hypothesis, was conclusively in favour of the latter. Some of us were not so clear on the subject, and I suppose it was for the sake of having the opportunity calmly to analyse what our emotions were, that we occasionally went behind trees and waited there till the firing slackened.

Von Pestel treated his guests—who consisted of about half a dozen madcap newspaper correspondents—to this amusement for about ten days; alternated with a skirmish or two, in one of which, by the way, I saw the first man fall that met his death in the Franco-German war. At length, on 2d August, the Spicheren volcano erupted, and its red-trousered lava floods poured down towards Saarbrück. Von Pestel made a laughably good defence. Some outlying points were manned with stuffed defenders, with a live man or two among them to fire an occasional shot. He held the line in front of Saarbrück for about four hours, and then retired fighting in good order, only because his orders were not wantonly to sacrifice lives. As it was he lost about eight killed and twenty or so wounded, one of whom was the gallant Colonel Battye of the Guides, who afterwards fell so gallantly in Afghanistan. Some of us repaired Battye, whose ribs were stove in, with successive layers of brown paper made adhesive by starch, until he got up to the Mayence hospital, when the surgeons found our job so neat that they never interfered with it. General Bataille came down into Saarbrück and took up his quarters at the Hotel de la Poste; he was very pleasant and civil. His men permeated the town, and did a little mild looting. They drank a brewery dry, and kissed all the waiting girls in the Rheinische Hof, including Fraulein Sophie, the landlady's niece. A corporal, I believe, kissed the landlady herself. This was all the damage they did. On the night of 5th August they all went away back whence they came; and so ended the first and only instalment—about two miles long—of the march *à Berlin*.

The emperor and his son waited on the edge of the Spicheren till the firing was over. Prince Louis told me there was no truth in the ridiculous story about his picking up the bullets as they fell. As a matter of fact he was not actually under fire at all— neither he nor his father. When all was quiet they rode down the hill, across the valley, up the Kaltenberg, and looked down on Saarbrück from the edge of the Exercir Platz. The next time the emperor saw German scenery was when on his road to Wilhelmshöhe. Then the cortege turned and cantered by the "Golden Farmer" beer-house, back to Forbach, where the train was taken for Metz. Bazaine was most anxious to salute the emperor and his lad, and he came back from his flank operations to Forbach at a gallop, only to learn that the party had gone, and that the emperor had asked where he was without getting a satisfactory answer, whereat honest Bazaine was sore distressed.

Spicheren, Wörth, and all the early ruin, presage true of the wretched end, came bickering and crumbling about the Imperial ears. Bazaine, in the real stress of things, had got the handling of three corps, but the insubordination and confusion of commands hampered him at every turn. All he could do was to work—out there in the front, conducting the retreat, covering the ragged edges, trying to keep the men in heart as became a manly soldier. At length, in a paroxysm of worry, the emperor came out to consult with Bazaine—the man he turned to when he found Le Bœuf and the others like the crackling of the thorns under a pot. He brought that tough old buckram warrior Changarnier with him, and the place of rendezvous was Faulquemont, a foul little dunghill-village a couple of marches south-east of Metz. Bazaine was there in the midst of a disorganised horde of wearied and dispirited soldiers. His advice had a ring of soldierhood in it, but the wretched emperor, quivering with nervousness because of the Paris mob, would take no counsel that involved the uncoverment of Paris even in appearance. So Bazaine had to take up an abortive line of battle nearer Metz, and "give up this new hope of being allowed to make an effective diversion."

The blackness of the cloud overhanging the Empire grew denser, and the plot began that ultimately was to ruin poor Bazaine. To do him justice, the emperor did not devise the baseness; I question whether he ever had cognisance of it in its naked ugliness. Pietri telegraphed an urgent "confidential" to the empress that it should be insisted on that the emperor should surrender the command-in-chief to Bazaine. Mark the modern Iago!—"If misfortune should still pursue the army, Bazaine would then be the object of obloquy, and so take the onus of the responsibility off the emperor's shoulders." Bazaine was victimised accordingly. He did not know of the plot; but he recognised the eventuality, and being a loyal, honest man, accepted it as part of the duty of a subject to take the skaith from his sovereign. That burden of duty never troubled him; but he had a modest mistrust of his own intrinsic capacity for the post. There were two officers in the Army of the Rhine who were his seniors. So when he got the "letter of service" to take the command, he betook himself to the imperial headquarters, and told the emperor straightforwardly that both MacMahon and Canrobert were older and better officers than himself. MacMahon had other work reserved for him; Canrobert was equal to his Crimean antecedent of shirking responsibility in a tight place. "You are the right man," said the emperor to Bazaine, "and it is an order I give you to take the duties." Well, there was no more to be said, was there? I can conceive Bazaine saluting in silence and going right about face on his heel, as he was wont to leave the orderly room when a sergeant. The old war-dog was not the man to bandy words with his superior officer.

I have often wondered whether now, and again four days later as he drove away for Verdun, the emperor had a thrill of compassion for the simple steadfast man who had picked up the cross he had let fall. I would fain think so; and in the letters which he wrote to his old servant both after the capitulation of Metz, and when Bazaine lay under the sentence of death pronounced by the Trianon court-martial three years later, there are expressions which seem to have in them an undertone of natural tenderness. "I find," wrote Napoleon from his Wilhelmshöhe captivity, "I find one real consolation in the depths of misfortune into which I am plunged, in knowing that you have been always staunch to me." He could say no less to a man before whom loomed the fate of being stripped of everything that is dearest to the soldier—of reputation, of decorations that had been cut, as it were, from out the hostile ranks, of honours and of rank, because at a time when sacred oaths were as thistledown he had held himself bound to the allegiance to which his soldier-oath had pledged him.

A commander-in-chief in name, a buffer and a scapegoat in reality, Bazaine had toiled hard amidst many other discouragements to get the army out of Metz, and forward on the march of retreat towards Verdun. That army's rear the masterful Germans had struck at on the 14th August, and brought about the battle of Borny, as the French call it, or Courcelles, as the Germans name it, on the eastern face of Metz. A poor organiser, Bazaine was himself the moment that the war music began to make the air throb. He turned fiercely and skilfully at bay, and although the fight won the Germans the delay for which they had made it, Bazaine at least charged them a dreadful effusion of blood for the advantage which he had no alternative but to concede. A curious article might be written on the immunity from wounds in action of some generals, and the ill-fortune of others in becoming the billet for a bullet. No commander was ever more forward in the fighting line than Sheridan, yet he never got a scratch. Skobeleff, who many a time went at it with his own good sword, and in his white coat and on his white charger headed every charge with a recklessness that men called madness, had as complete an immunity as if he carried the charmed life

that his soldiers ascribed, and was wounded only in
the quiet trenches by a chance bullet fired into the air
a mile away. Wellington was but once hit, the bullet
that carried away his boot-heel scarce gave him a
contusion. Grant was never struck; Napoleon never
more than grazed. Of Sir Neville Chamberlain again,
one of the most distinguished officers of our Indian
army, the saying goes that he never went into action
without receiving a wound, and the gallant old man
has been fighting pretty steadily ever since the first
Afghan war. Bazaine was a man to whom Fortune
was not stingy in the matter of wounds. At Borny
there came to him the leaden reminder that he was
mortal, though this time it was but a gentle hint.
The fragment of a shell hit him on the left shoulder,
but it had been well spent, and, because of the protection of the epaulette, gave him but a contusion,
from which he had pain for several days, especially
when on horseback.

The fight over, the Germans forced back, and his
troops once more on the march through Metz and
across the Moselle, with their faces set eastward
toward Verdun, Bazaine bethought him of his master's
natural anxiety to know the situation. That master
was the white elephant of Bazaine and the army, but
in the countries where white elephants are they live
objects of sanctity. The imperial headquarters had
been fixed at the château of Longeville, a residence
on the left bank of the Moselle valley, lying among
trim, formal gardens, and nestled comfortably under

the guns of Fort St. Quentin, perched on the steep dominant hill behind it. Thither in the dead of night, struggling his way through the chaos of the retreating army jammed into the narrow streets of Metz, Bazaine hied himself, carrying his bruised shoulder from the battle-field. Of what followed I think it best to let the simple soldier-man tell in his own blunt, short, but surely not ineffective way: "I found his Majesty unwell and in bed,"—the malady that killed Napoleon a few years later was already debilitating him,—"and I was immediately admitted into his bedroom. The emperor greeted me with his wonted kind affability. I told him what had passed (about the battle, etc.), and I gave vent as well to my anxieties in regard to the next few days. The Germans, said I, were finding the routes free to them by which to travel to gain a position between the Moselle and the Meuse, and consequently athwart our line of retreat. I represented to the emperor that I was suffering physically; and, adding my fear that I could not endure the pain the contusion caused me when on horseback, I begged of him that he would relieve me from the command. His Majesty, touching my shoulder on the part where the torn epaulette showed where I had been struck, answered me with that kind humour that charmed all who came within its influence, 'This is nothing serious, dear Marshal, it is a matter of but a few days; and the blow you have got is but the token that it is you who are destined to break the spell of our ill-fortune!' These were his very words. He gave no hint that he had any other thought than to remain with the army."

At last, in this Longeville bedroom, I think we get a touch of human nature. Bazaine's heart was very full, it is clear; and his master's thick quilting of selfishness seems to have been pierced. Before the interview ended the Emperor impressed on Bazaine the necessity for the most studious caution. The falling man still nourished his delusions. "I wait," said he, "for answers from the Emperor of Austria and the King of Italy, who at the beginning of the war evinced a disposition to befriend us; for heaven's sake risk nothing by over precipitation, and avoid, above everything, any fresh reverse." And then, as Bazaine tells with a modest pride, the emperor bade him good-night with the final words, "I am leaning on you." One can fancy Bazaine leaving the chamber with a lump in his honest throat. How he felt about the future may be gathered from a chance colloquy. As he passed through the outer room the officers of the household, who sat watching, called out to him in the jaunty tone of such people —"You are going to fetch us out of this hole we have got into, are you not, Marshal?"—"I am going to do my best, gentlemen," replied the honest Marshal; "*tout mon possible;* none of us can do more, and there are none of us who would do less!" And so he went out into the darkness, and consoled his bruised shoulder with an hour or two's sleep.

This was on the night between the 14th and 15th August. What happened on the following morning was told me in Zululand by the poor Prince Imperial. He was asleep in the bedroom next to his father's. They will show you the two rooms still in a wing of the gray-fronted château with the Mansard roof. A crash awoke him with a start, and he was sitting up in bed bewildered, when the emperor rushed into the room : " Get up and dress—quick, my son, quick, Louis! the German shells are crashing through the roof." It was so. An audacious German horse-battery, seeing soldiery about the château, had galloped up to within range on the opposite side of the river, and had opened that " quick fire " at which the German gunners were so handy. As the prince looked out of window while he dressed hurriedly he saw a shell fall on the table in the garden, at which a group of officers of the battalion on guard were breakfasting, and when the smoke of the explosion blew aside three of the officers lay dead men. St. Quentin began to reply from its great siege guns, but a horse-battery is not a big mark, and the Germans stuck to their work with characteristic persistence. The carriages and baggage might follow ; Gravelotte was the rendezvous given ; but meanwhile the business in hand was to get from under that shell-fire. There was a hurried cup of coffee for Louis and his father ; then they and the suite went to horse, and the abominable German shells were soon left behind.

An inauspicious commencement, truly, of this 15th day of August—the poor harried emperor's fête day, of all days! The Imperial party pushed on towards Gravelotte how it might by the road cumbered with all the impedimenta of a disorderly retreat. Presently, about the village of Lessy, an absolute block was encountered. The road was bounded by heavy fences, there were three waggons abreast of each other hopelessly broken down, and a battery of horse artillery tangled up in the debris. Interminable delay confronted the Imperial party. But Prince Louis, during the early days in Metz, while as yet the Germans were afar off, had employed much of his time in riding around the adjacent country. He had mastered the "lie" of it, and gained a knowledge of the by-tracks. Quietly ordering some soldiers to make a gap in the fence on the St. Quentin side, he called out, " Follow me, father!" and led the way across country at a canter for a vineyard track, whose trend he knew. So the boy-guide conducted the graybeards down into the valley by Chatel, then up on to the ridge which in three more days was to be covered with corpse-mounds, past the auberge of St. Hubert, not then yet battered into dust and that dust made into mud by blood, down into the hollow of the Mance not yet then a ghastly shamble: and so up the slope between the poplar trees to the auberge of Gravelotte, standing in the angle where diverge the upper and the lower roads from Metz to Verdun.

Thither, at least as yet, came no German shells, and the hunted Napoleons could draw their breath. Thither, about one of the afternoon, came, too, the harassed Bazaine. Like Martha, the poor Marshal was "careful and troubled about many things." He found his master tramping up and down in front of the auberge. It was a way he had in trouble. I saw him doing just the same in the potato patch of the weaver's garden on the Donchery Road, during the interval when Bismarck rode away to King Wilhelm to know what was to be done with the man who had come to them from out the devilry inside Sedan. It must have been a poor place at the best, this roadside auberge, even before the shell-fire of the battle to which the village of Gravelotte gave its name had knocked it about. I knew it later well enough. I tried to get a place in it wherein to lie down on the night of the battle, but it was full beyond the threshold with wounded men. Later, during the siege, there used to dwell in it one of the cheeriest etappen officers I ever knew, who had a rare bin of local wine that resembled Muscat. As Napoleon stalked up and down, pondering uneasily, he was unconsciously making history, and just as unconsciously he moved in the heart of a scene waiting to be made historical ere many hours had passed. For over against him was the old church of Gravelotte, on the edge of whose graveyard the dead of the impending battle were to be used for breastworks. On its shattered wall was to rest the plank, sitting on which Wilhelm was to watch the stroke of the final blow wherewith he dinted in the long strenuous resistance that had held his soldiers at arm's length till after the summer sun had gone down on the red field.

Bazaine approached his master. Poor loyal old fighting henchman! Childish you may call this, in the throes of a climax so sombre; but does it not move you, nevertheless? "I complimented him on his fête day by presenting him with a little nosegay I had gathered in the garden of my last night's quarters." The emperor gave thanks for the present, and then, his trouble recurring on him, he asked in a loud voice, "Must I quit the army?" Bazaine, in surprise, bewilderment, and embarrassment, begged of him at least to wait events yet a little longer. So Napoleon turned to his people and said, "We will remain, gentlemen; but do not have the baggage unpacked." Poor Bazaine sometimes shows a rare incisive gift with that blunt, clumsy pen of his. "During this colloquy," he writes, "the soldiers, melancholy and beaten out, continued to defile along the road in front of the auberge. Not a single cheer, not one '*Vive l'Empereur!*' came from the tumbled ranks at the sight of that sovereign and his son so enthusiastically acclaimed but a few days before. The moral influence of the retreat had already so lowered the tone of the army!" Is it not a sombre etching bitten in deeply by a few strong strokes?

These two men, Emperor and Marshal, parted next day and for ever. I think Bazaine may be allowed to draw down the curtain in his abrupt, rugged fashion. "On the morning of the 16th August the emperor sent a galloper to fetch me. I lost not a moment, but rode alone at full speed to the Imperial quarters. I found his Majesty already in the carriage along with the Prince Imperial and Prince Napoleon. The baggage had been sent off under escort in the course of the night. General de France's cavalry brigade was already on horseback to escort the emperor. I had got no intimation in advance of those arrangements. I rode up to the carriage without dismounting. The emperor seemed in suffering and he said to me but a few words: 'I have decided to leave for Verdun and Chalons. Get you on for Verdun how best you can. The gendarmes have left Briey, because the Prussians are in it.'"

Bazaine does not record a farewell, so abrupt seems to have been the parting. Napoleon whirled away out of bad into worse, until what relief the very worst brings came to him after Sedan. An hour after the Imperial postillions had cracked their whips Bazaine was in the heart of the fierce mêlée of Mars la Tour, stemming all he knew, with his own sword-blade flashing through the dust of the hand-to-hand struggle, one of the whirlwind charges of the Brunswick Hussars. Ah! why did heaven deny him then a straight thrust from the beautiful "white weapon," to give him the good death a man so soldierly had surely earned!

SOCIAL AUSTRALIA.

I CAN picture a good many English readers smile with a supercilious humour of incredulity at the notion of "Society" in Australia. Among our many interesting traits, there is probably no smugness in the world comparable to the complacent smugness of our insular ignorance in regard to people and things as they obtain in the Australasian colonies. It is not very long ago that I heard an Anglo-Indian lady, embarking at Suez on a mail steamer that had come from Australia, call in shrill accents to her ayah: "Take my children immediately out from among those wretched convict brats!" When Sir Henry Parkes, then Premier of New South Wales, came among us three years ago, the belief was general that he was the Sir Harry Parkes of China fame, simply because few of us had ever heard of any other personage of the name.

I saw an envelope the other day, addressed by the editor of a well-known London illustrated paper to his special artist: "Sydney Exhibition, New Zealand." *Mea culpa!* I can claim to have been no less ignorant than my neighbours. For months after I had grown familiar with the geography of Australia by dint of the experience of travel in that continent, every mail brought me recurrent shame and confusion of face, because of an envelope, the legend on which, copied from the address I had left behind me on leaving home, ran thus: " Care of *Argus* Office, Melbourne, *South Australia*." The genial scoffer at the notion of the existence of " Society " in Australia has never been there ; superciliousness cannot be the attitude of the traveller who has enjoyed the graceful cordiality of Australian hospitality, who has had the honour of familiar acquaintance with Australian ladies in their own beautiful homes, who can reckon Australian gentlemen among the most valued of his friends.

The keynotes of the various pitches of home society are well defined ; each of the many pivots on which it turns are discernible to any one who takes moderate pains to investigate its phenomena. There is the social eddy of which Marlborough House is the centre. If the institution known as the " political salon " is not to-day in so great force as when as yet Cambridge House had not been converted into a club, it still is found in a degree in Arlington Street, in Grosvenor Place, under the roof of the Foreign Office, and beneath the façade of the Admiralty, as well as, in a modified sense, in some of the great country mansions with which the shires are studded. We have our old nobility and our *nouveaux riches;* and the social phase wherein a gradual blending between these elements is in progress, with curious under-contrasts of reluctance and eagerness. We have our "county families," our clerical coteries, our legal circles. Of such definite centres society in the Australian colonies is all but wholly destitute. True, each colony has its governor, who is the personal representative of the sovereign. But the colonial governor is an infinitesimal factor in colonial society. Nominally he is its official figurehead. But while his personal circle may be quite narrow and casual, his official circle has a radius of all but indiscriminate scope. It may roughly be said to include, or at all events to be potentially inclusive of, all the colonial world that is out of jail. I have known no colony to the society of whose capital its governor could be regarded as imparting any light or any shadow of its tone. When Lord and Lady Dufferin made the salons of Rideau Hall at once gay and graceful, they were the acclaimed arbiters of Canadian society; but this influence was a unique phenomenon, so far as my experience goes. I have known Colonial Government Houses the social influence of which, in the little area over which the ripple of that influence spread, was hurtful and deteriorating, because of the elements of petty intrigue and sour narrow caballing with which it was surcharged. But neither Ottawa nor Cape Town is in Australia; of whose Government Houses I simply record my impression that their society influence, if not their social influence, is of scarcely any significance.

Politics again, in a society sense, are as much at a discount in Australia as in America itself. In that sense few Australian politicians are held "presentable." The trade is regarded as rather a dirty one. "Its handicraftsmen may be very decent kind of people in their way," so says society in effect, "only their way is not quite our way. We have heard that they are not enthusiastically addicted to the use of soap and water; a large proportion of them, as we may have auricular evidence when we please, are dubious as to the use of the letter *h*. Their wives—well, we don't care to pursue this branch of the subject. Their boots—well, let us be equally reticent as to their boots. In effect, we don't care, except in the way of business, of course, to know those oratorical gentlemen, who have so glib a turn for personalities that make the parliamentary reports often very nasty reading." Of course there are exceptions. There are brave men who, being gentlemen, nevertheless have thought it their duty to enter the arena of colonial politics. That arena, it must be said, is fairly wholesome and clean-toned in South Australia, New Zealand, and Tasmania; and in New South Wales and Victoria there are venerable political persons still extant whose political conduct has never compromised their social standing. But, for example, in the membership of the Melbourne Club there are not six persons who sit in the Lower House of the Victorian Parliament; and these are members certainly not in virtue of their political position, but, I had almost said, in spite of it. As for Australian bishops, no doubt they wear on occasion lawn sleeves and purple aprons, if such be the episcopal insignia; but they exercise little social influence in virtue of their ecclesiastical position. As a dignitary the Australian bishop has no prestige. His comparatively meagre revenue comes out of a fund formed originally by subscription; he has no endowments; he is "my lord" but by courtesy. If he choose to call his house "the palace" he may, because it is a free country; but no halo surrounds it or him. Just before leaving Australia I had some pleasant intercourse with a bishop. I met him casually in Bowen, a decaying coast-town of Queensland. Assisted by a grinning black gin, he was carrying his trunk out of the bar of a public-house in which—I do not mean in the bar—he had spent the night. The gin's amusement was apparently caused by the episcopal gaiters. When his lordship and the lady had toted the trunk on to a cart, he remunerated the latter with a threepenny-piece, and taking a friendly farewell of the publican's wife, whose tone I thought rather patronising, he walked down to the jetty and took passage on the steamer on whose deck, as she wended her way northward, I had much interesting converse with him. His diocese is about the size of England. He makes his progresses through it on horseback, the nags being found by the scattered settlers. At first they used, in pure fun, to furnish him extensively with buckjumpers, and lie in wait to see the catastrophe ; but when they found that he sat a buckjumper as if the animal symbolised the arch-fiend himself, they took him to their hearts. I may add that he works harder than a bush hand, and that he lives on his private income, refusing to draw his official stipend from the Episcopal Fund.

Family, then, or money, surely these have social weight in Australia? Incidentally, yes ; but not imperatively. Good birth tells, doubtless, because good birth may be a *primâ facie* voucher for desirable qualities ; but certainly not in instances where that voucher stands discredited. And this outcome is cruelly common. For so long have the Australian colonies been used by the mother country as a sort of shoot for its well-born rubbish, and regarded as regions whence, because of their remoteness, there are comfortable obstacles to the embarrassing return of the ne'er-do-well scion of good family who has at last exhausted the patience of his relatives at home ; that good family pure and simple has become something of a drug, not to say a byword in Australasian communities. I could fill an article with examples of well-born emigrants whose ineradicable propensities, or whose purposeless shiftlessness has reduced them to the most sordid of Australian avocations. It was but the other day that I shook hands with a peer's son who is earning his "tucker" as a station cook in New Zealand. A Chinaman, aspiring to better things, had vacated the billet in his favour. Poor fellow ! the rough station hands, he told me, used to "curse his head off" because of his culinary deficiencies; and when he tendered me his hand, he made a humble apology for the greasiness of it. There is another reason for the feeble recognition accorded to family pretensions *per se*. Genealogies in Australia are by no means an universally favourite study. This is not difficult of comprehension in respect of communities that are comparatively new, yet that, spite of their newness, have had antecedents. The social *mot d'ordre* in Australia is, that a man is what he may make himself. *Only*, he must make himself, not alone wealthy, not only powerful—indeed, he may not make himself either; but he must make himself individually pleasant and meritorious, in a social sense, or rather, to speak more categorically, in some one or more details of the abstract social eligibility.

The truth is that society in Australia is founded and maintained on rational principles. It presents the curious yet intelligible paradox of being close and yet open. That is, anybody may aspire to it, anybody may cross its threshold experimentally, but only people who have socially meritorious attributes can remain in it and of it. The ineligible aspirants are sifted out by an all but imperceptible yet an effectual process. You can make a social position of a kind here in England, personally devoid howsoever of meritorious social attributes, by sheer dint of lavish expenditure, and by the judicious procurement of influential sponsors. You can be dry-nursed here, if you are willing to expend freely, into at least the vestibule of society, and a sorry dirt-eating and all-round humiliating process it is, reflecting credit neither on the aspirant nor on the sponsors, nor on what of society may degrade itself by becoming a party to the ignoble transaction. In Australia lavishness will help the aspirant but poorly. Sponsors will avail him so far as the *début* is concerned, only that these must not allow themselves to forget the responsibility which they owe to the society of which they are members. But the *début* made, sponsors will no whit avail to bear the neophyte up lest he strike his foot against a stone.

Socially, money will do very much in America; judiciously expended, I think it will do even more in England; in the way of sheer purchase of social recognition it will do curiously little in Australia. There was, indeed, a time there when, in a social sense, the monied man was regarded with actual suspicion. And for this there were some grounds. The original monied man might have had unpleasant antecedents, of which time had not yet effaced the memory. *Non olet* is not true of *pecunia* in Australia, although it is safe to predicate that with the lapse of years *non olebit*. But now there are a vast number of monied men in Australia, and the means whereby their wealth has come to them are known as reasonably savoury. They have therefore ceased to be regarded with suspicion. I do not think people at home have any idea how large. for-

tunes are in Australia, and how many of those large
fortunes there are. Once in South Australia I had
occasion to speak of a friend who had come from
that colony and taken up his residence in London.
I spoke of him as a very rich man. "Oh, no," was
the answer, "he is very well off, but we don't reckon
him a very rich man." "Why," said I, "I understood him to be worth a quarter of a million!"
"Well, I hope he is a little better than that," said
my interlocutor, "but still we don't reckon him here
as very rich!" I am not going to compile a roll of
Australian millionaires, because, for one thing, it
would take up too much space. But this I may
affirm, that two-thirds of them are not in society,
nor nourish any hope of ever being admitted within
that pale. If you find one of them inside it, he has
not crossed the palisade on the golden ladder; he
entered by the gate in virtue of his social attributes.
If these are unsatisfactory, you will find him outside
among the nettles; or again, it may be, far away in
the bush, a man content with himself, and caring for
none of these things. For it must be said that in
Australia there is no universal aspiration after the
flower-garden of society. But the monied aspirant
will not find that his wealth gives him social prestige.
There are Australians now in England who have
entertained Royalty and whose guest-lists have filled
columns of the *Morning Post*, yet who in their native
land have never, with all their efforts, got further
than the outlying fringes of Australian society.

I imagine that the reason why, in comparison with what obtains in England, money can give so trivial social preponderance in Australia is mainly this, that in Australia much money is really of so little practical applicability for social uses. The life of the well-off people is graceful, pretty, daintily-ordered, hospitable ; but it has a simplicity which incidentally makes it comparatively economical. There is no meanness, there is just the simple consuetude of the modest establishment. I will not say that the rich Australian does not know how to spend his income ; I had rather put it that each individual wealthy Australian, not from parsimony, but from fear of feeling himself a snob, is reluctant to take the daring initiative in a social revolution. It will not be his hand that will fire the train for an explosion, the only consequence of which he can definitely foresee is his own discomfort, in the disorganisation of the pleasant modest *ménage* that he has not failed to find amply sufficient unto him and his.

For my own part I recognise in this unwillingness to disturb the ancient social landmarks a fine equipoise of philosophical contentment. How often, both here and in America, have we watched the old-accustomed, far from joyless life sacrificed to foolish hankerings after another life, the hollow, spurious evanescent triumph of which compensates wretchedly for carking failures, for humiliations that degrade, for intrigues that deteriorate ; a life that exchanges serenity for feverishness, self-respect for sycophancy, everything that is true and good and honourable for so much that is false and mean and pitiful! The Australia of to-day is not Arcady, but it is yet more remote from being Babylon. The drift in the latter direction, I suppose, is inevitable sooner or later. I recognise the impulses that will set it forward in this ill-omened course ; but at least it is a refreshing experience to have known it ere the bad tide has perceptibly begun to make.

I remember hearing of an English duke with an income of some £200,000 a-year, who complained quaintly that after having met all the demands which his position claimed of him he had not £500 a-year "all to himself." In other words, he was simply forced by circumstances to live up to his income. When in Australia I had the pleasure to make the acquaintance of a resident gentleman possessing an equal income with that which pertained to—I will not say was enjoyed by—the English duke. I had the opportunity of ascertaining the annual expenditure of this wealthy Australian. It amounted—I take an average year—to just £35,000. Of this sum £20,000 had been expended in charity, subscriptions, and public contributions, which were not, as is the duke's expenditure in similar ways, virtually compulsory, but the greater proportion of which was in the fullest sense voluntary. His personal, family, and domestic expenses were covered by the remaining £15,000. He had a considerable family, and two sons were being educated in England. He maintained an adequate hospitality in a fine country mansion not far from Melbourne, and had, I think, two indoor men-servants. He bred racing stock, but had no horses in the trainer's hands. He had an ample stud of carriage-horses, hacks, and ladies' horses; carriages, coachmen, and grooms in sufficiency. I do not remember that he had any hobbies, unless the maintenance of a tenantry on an estate which would have paid him better as a sheep run may be called a hobby; and even if it were one, this only lessened his income, did not increase his expenditure. He was universally respected, his hospitality was regarded as profuse, and it was matter of common repute that his living expenditure was the largest in the colony; yet, taking the calculation at $7\frac{1}{2}$ per cent, he was living on the interest of his income. And I think if he had dared to spend much more freely, he would not have been held in so high general esteem. He told me in effect that he had neither the courage nor the inclination to be more lavish. To have been so would have been distasteful to himself and invidious towards others.

In a searching retrospect of my Australian experiences I can remember very few private houses where the *ménage* expenses gave evidence of exceeding £5000 a year. Of course I exclude expenditure in the gratification of special tastes. I do not reckon in the *ménage* a passion for rare wines at any cost, a taste for bric-à-brac or for pictures, a mania for gambling, or the maintenance of a large racing stable. But I include in my estimate all things legitimately and normally domestic — hospitality of the usual Australian free-handedness, equipages, education, and dress. I would exempt, of course, purchases of jewellery, and such unwonted expenditure as the cost of a great ball given to all the social world on the coming out of a daughter. There are many ways in which the Australian, like the rest of us, can skittle down his money. He may take poor Sir William Don's plan, and use £10 notes instead of the ham in sandwiches. He can get rid of it more surely still by taking shares in gold mines. He can pile his year's income on the wrong horse in the Melbourne Cup. He can lose £10,000 in a night at cards in the little room not far from the Melbourne Treasury Office. He can buy an overstocked sheep station just before a year of drought. He can attest with his purse his belief in a bogus lord. But if he would preserve the decorum of the conventional happy mean, he cannot easily spend much more than £6000 or £7000 a year on his pure domesticities.

There is one exception, perhaps, to this domestic thrift of the Australians. They crave for fine houses, and do not count the cost to get housed to their mind. Nor is it handsomeness and roominess merely in the structure that they desiderate; they will have elbow-room about it as well, even when they have to buy the land at a crazy figure by the foot. Thus it is that the suburbs of the capitals stretch away for miles outside the focus of streets, and that there are separate outlying municipalities in which there are not perhaps two dozen houses which do not stand inside their own pretty verdant and floral grounds. There is no expanse of water in the world whose shores are studded with so many picturesque and picturesquely situated mansions as are the beautiful broken edges of Sydney Harbour. And the Australian makes a point of owning his house; so that he pays no rent, and that, therefore, is not an item in the expenditure I have allotted to him. Nor does it include the wages of indoor men-servants, for the simple reason that the Australian does not employ indoor men-servants. There may be three or four private houses in Victoria where "a man is kept;" there is but one such house in all South Australia. I do not believe there are more houses in New South Wales than in Victoria, if so many; there is not an indoor man-servant in Queensland outside Government House, if we except the Kanaka boys whom the sugar planters import for agricultural purposes, and make house-servants of them in the face of the Act of Parliament. Now this is not, as some Australians will tell you, that indoor servants are not to be had. Money will procure men-servants as it will other luxuries, and the colonial governors, who are not reckless spendthrifts, can always supply themselves. The truth is that the Australian does not like men-servants. Having himself a full consciousness of manhood, it gives him discomfort to be domestically waited on by one who in the act seems to him to be resigning something of his manhood. It is because of this spirit, as I imagine, that no Australian gentleman to my knowledge has descended to the use of a valet.

But pretty houses are expensive luxuries in the Australian capitals, because of the high price of land and the cost of labour and of building materials. From this cause and others, if there are no high pinnacles in colonial social expenditure, it must be said that the mean of that expenditure is rather a tax on the resources of the weaker brethren—of people, for instance, with fixed salaries. It used to be said of households in Chowringhee, the Anglo-Indian quarter of Calcutta, that there was but one scale of expenditure, and that at the rate of £3000 a year. It resulted that the people whose incomes did not reach this figure had to run into debt, the liquidation of which absorbed their surplus for years after their incomes exceeded it. There is more elasticity in the Australian scale, and the social requirements are far less exacting. Yet to live in an Australian capital abreast of their fellows, to maintain a position that shall bring home the force of no mortifying contrasts, is a feat not to be undertaken by a family of narrow income. For the poor gentleman with incumbrances, for the half-pay married officer with little private fortune, for the family bent on retrenchment, I really know no region of the Australian colonies having any social attributes that are to be recommended. It is all very well for the single man, on whom no reciprocity is incumbent. A young friend of mine in Melbourne, who, as a single man, had been wont to have a very joyous time on a precarious £600 a year, perpetrated matrimony just before I left on an assured £1500 a year. But he realised with something like awe how warily the altered household would have to be guided. Now I need not point out how fair a competence is £1500 a year anywhere at home, except in the metropolis, and how far it will go even there when judiciously dealt with.

A weakness of the Australian character is the hunger after titles and decorations. Toward the close of the Servian war, so cheap did the Russian officers hold the Servian decoration of the "Takovo Cross," that they used to tie the bauble round their dogs' necks, and have the animals trot behind them thus adorned. The "C.M.G." seems to me about as cheap a piece of trumpery as the Russian officers regarded the "Takovo Cross." But the Australian, though while he is without it he affects to sneer at the "C.M.G.," and links the initials to a derogatory legend, grasps it and wears it when the Colonial Office throws it to him. He would intrigue for it yet more eagerly than he does, if only his wife could be a "C.M.G." as well as himself. But as in heaven there are many mansions, so there are successive grades in the titular Elysium of the Australian.

The " C.M.G." is recognised as but the first rung of the ladder. Its utopian apex is a baronetcy, but that distinction is very rare of attainment. A knighthood or the K.C.M.G. is, however, within reach. The latter is the reward of the politician who has held office sufficiently long to have matured by courtesy into a statesman. For the knighthood there is an understood tariff. It comes as the result of a gift of £20,000—a larger sum will make the thing a greater certainty—for the behoof of some meritorious public object. The surest mark for such a donation is the Colonial University ; a shot of equal charge at a working man's college or a picture gallery has been known to miss fire. But it is worthy of note that those much-coveted distinctions carry with them little intrinsic weight. Sir This and Lady That may be in society, but not because of the handle to their names ; if they are not within the pale on their merits no title will open the wicket, any more than money will.

Social Australia has been reproached for its lavish love for a real live lord. The admission must be made that it does nourish this sentiment. At first sight the predilection looks like sheer snobbery, and I am not prepared to deny that it has in it a taint of this atrocity. But it is far from being all snobbery, as I venture to think. The Australians have a tender affection for the "old country." They glory in the hoar age of Britain, its solidity—perhaps even its stolidity—the fixed order of things that obtains in the country of their origin. The peerage they abstractly worship as a shining exemplar of all those time-encrusted institutions. When a lord comes among them they take delight in him as a symbol, just as when they come to England they make haste to visit the Tower and Westminster Abbey. He may be yesterday's mushroom, but they set him down as titularly an ἄναξ ἀνδρῶν, the head of an historic house, come of a race that is among the pillars of the old State. In this there is, rather than snobbery, a simplicity in which I recognise something touching. But it must be frankly said that this feeling, which is not all ignoble, too often degenerates into another, which is ignoble without redeeming feature. Thus, the victims to it render themselves liable to be imposed on by spurious lords. They have been known to invent a lord, in the teeth of the poor creature's feeble remonstrances; with the natural result that they have suffered for the over-zeal of their ingenuity. All that I have to say in mitigation is simply this, that everywhere new communities have their fantasticalities.

The well-accredited visitor to Australia may lay his account with having what the Americans call "a lovely time." His hosts—and all the colonies will be his hosts—will strain every nerve to make him enjoy himself. Australian hospitality is proverbial the world over, and it has in it a cordial freshness that imparts to it a special charm. If he be a true man, he will leave no colony without realising that he is leaving behind him in it many warm and genuine friends. He need not be a very susceptible person to find that, with the friendships he has left, he may have left his heart as well. Australian ladies have a characteristic bright airy piquancy. They sparkle as perhaps not even the American lady sparkles. Their "manner"—one finds one asking oneself bewilderedly how or whence they get it; for you will find the damsel of a remote bush township as graceful, frank, debonnaire and winsome, as is the Melbourne girl who may have spent half a dozen years in European residence and travel. One of the finest ladies I have ever met, in every shade of inflection of that term, was never outside the colony of Victoria in her life, except for a short visit to New Zealand. Australian ladies read. I fancy Gordon and Gotch could supply some startling statistics in regard to the number of high-class reviews and periodicals they export to the Antipodes. I am happy to say that I never met a blue-stocking in Australia; but I have had the honour of converse with many Australian women of high culture and deep thought on subjects, superficial thought on which is as the crackling of thorns under a pot. But you do not find yourself oppressed by untimeous volunteered franknesses of this sort; you have to seek that you may find. To sum up with a curtness and rough generalisation for which apology is due— Australian ladies are fairly accomplished; in modern languages they are somewhat weak; in music very good, occasionally exceptionally so. They all sing, and many sing well. The most exquisite flower-painter I know lives under the Southern Cross, and her gift is real genius. Victoria can boast of an amateur actress in whom also I ventured to recognise something of the sacred fire. In physique they are taller, slighter, more lithe, shapelier, than their congeners at home; their colour, save in Tasmania, is seldom brilliant. The expression is full of vivacity; the eyes nearly always good, and the head and feet shapely, although not, as are those of American ladies, exceptionally small. They dance divinely.

Australian gentlemen are manly cordial fellows; more pronounced and less reserved than are our people at home. The tone is a trifle more brusque, but it has the genuine ring in it. I think, perhaps, that they have even more prejudices than we have—I do not mean personal prejudices; and they are certainly freer-spoken in the enunciation of them. They are wholly without one attribute that is a discredit to so many Englishmen—the affectation of being idlers because of an absence of necessity for being workers. "Have you a leisure class?" asked an Englishman of an American. "What is that, anyhow?" interrogated the citizen of the Union. "A class who can afford to have no avocation," explained the Briton. "Why, certainly," responded the American with alacrity, "*we call them tramps.*" It is much the same in Australia. The only people who let themselves afford to have no specific object in life are the "sundowners," as they are colonially called; the loafers who saunter from station to station in the interior, secure of a nightly ration and a bunk. Bar the "sundowner," every Australian man has his avocation, and would think shame of himself to ape a sorry pride of not being industrious in it. He works like a man, and he plays like a man—sometimes like a boy. He is more speculative than is the business man who is his home correlative; and he therefore may experience greater vicissitudes of fortune. But he has an elasticity and a versatility that are more American than English; and so copious are the opportunities of Australia, that if fortune frowns to-day she may smile to-morrow from ear to ear. In all Australian life there remains still a large out-of-door element comprising occasional hard exercise, the recoil from which has a tendency to make men burly, if not portly. Theirs is a ruddier, sturdier manhood than is ours, even in the towns. In culture, in refinement, in manner, the Australian women are the superiors for the most part of the Australian men; but I think this is so in all communities of which the civilisation has not attained to an exceptional degree of finished organisation.

Australian social life is simpler all round than is the same life with us. Early rising is almost universal; and that pronounces against habitual late hours. In Australia there is nowhere any such institution as "Afternoon Park," far less "Morning

Park." Nowhere is there any out-of-door society resort like "the Row." A principal street in each town is affected as a promenade by the women of a secondary social position—a ceremonial which is currently styled "doing the block;" but ladies are not addicted to "doing the block." Afternoon receptions are infrequent, and the men cannot find time for much afternoon calling. Ladies, however, have their "days," and afternoon tea is as much an institution in Australia as at home. Lawn-tennis is perhaps even more so. There is a great deal of dinner-giving; and in the season—which in Australia begins with the winter, culminates about the Melbourne Cup epoch in the end of October, and wanes as the hot weather approaches in late November— there is much dancing. Many of the big suburban houses have regular ballrooms; and it is a common practice among ladies who have not, and who do not care to disorganise their own drawing-rooms, to give their ball at public rooms hired for the occasion. Even in the height of the season there is no "going on" from one house to another as with us. It is not often that there are two *funçions* on the same night in the same set; such clashing, which in a society comparatively small would hurt both, is avoided by arrangement. When Australian people go to a ball, they go with the intention of remaining at it till it is time to go home. There is a good deal of theatre-going: although "theatre parties," which are so pleasant a phase of American social life, are only as yet in the first stage of inception. And there is a great deal of marrying. The Australian marries young—much younger than the Englishman who is wise. This is partly because the former finds himself in a position to do so earlier than does the latter. And again, the conventionalities in Australia do not define what one may style the marrying platform with so stern rigour as do those which exercise sway at home.

The decorum of social life in Australia is marked and beautiful. There are very few domestic scandals; and still fewer exposures. Domesticity is a virtue of which neither men nor women are ashamed. Society savours wholesomely and sweetly. One finds in Australia no ladies having a reputation for reckless utterances, no elaborately fictitious *ingénues;* no men who have a celebrity for their dexterity in innuendo and for the nasty subtilty of their *doubles entendres*. There may be those who will aver that the clean, wholesome flavour of Australian social life is but superficial. I have heard men adventure such insinuations, and have had my own opinion concerning them. Personally I am not one who cares to plumb the depths in such matters, if there be any depths; but this is obvious to all, that the tone of conventional decency is rigidly accentuated, and even if this were all, it is surely something. But as an honest witness, and as a man who holds dear many who live within the seas that wash Australian shores, I record my deepest conviction that this is not all. I imagine one may answer for the female element being as pure as it is sweet and gracious. A man who has lived for some years in the world acquires, I think, the intuition to discern good women, and to detect, or at all events to suspect, the others, if there should be any. As for the gentlemen, for aught I know some of them may have private affairs of a loose description, but if so they must keep those strictly private if they care to remain within the social pale. No man in Australia who would keep his place in society could dare flout social public opinion by flaunting a Lais in the face of day on the box seat of his mail phaeton, or on the lower cushion of his dogcart; nor be seen at the theatre in the box of such an one. That drawing-rooms should be feverish with the story of the elopement of a man's mistress with that man's friend; that ladies should be conversant with the ill-flavoured details, and profess their sympathy with the poor bereaved one, are casual traits of a social condition, of the existence of which anywhere I do not believe it would be possible to convince those poor primitive, untutored outsiders away in the Antipodes. You have, of course, a natural pity for their simplicity of innocence; you smile, no doubt, at a community still in these latter days susceptible to the obsolete emotion of incredulity about anything bad; and yet somehow there may pierce faintly through the thick atmosphere of your cynicism a feeble sunbeam of surprised respect for a community which cannot bring itself to believe that such things are!

MACGAHAN.

BELONGING to the same craft and working together in the same fields during the Franco-German war, the Paris Commune, and the Spanish Civil war, MacGahan and I yet never met until the spring of 1877. His early work was done for an American newspaper, and he first began to be spoken about in English journalistic circles as the hero of that most remarkable and daring exploit in all the annals of war correspondence, not excepting poor O'Donovan's romantic journey to Merv—his ride through the great desert of Central Asia in pursuit of the column with which Kaufmann was marching against Khiva. In this tremendous venture, to use a familiar phrase of his own land, he "took his chances" with a singular recklessness; and those chances included not alone death in half a dozen shapes, but the risk of punishment by Kaufmann for his daring violation of the sweeping prohibition against correspondents. For four long weeks of constant travel from Orenburg, he and his staunch comrade Schuyler journeyed across the level frozen steppes of Russia and the broad snowy plains of Turkestan, enduring a cold ranging from 20° to 30° below zero. Kayala, that entering wedge of the Russians into Central Asia, he reached only to find that the Russian column he had expected to overtake there was long gone, and that between him and it there intervened some 300 miles of desert and hostile country. And Kayala he found, too, a Russian who diplomatically had too much concern for his safety to sanction his persistence in the stern-chase. But MacGahan was not the man to be balked by the craftiest of Russian officers. He evaded the strategic obstruction at Kayala, and pressing on to Fort Perovsky, he there bade adieu to his friend Schuyler, and went out alone into the wilderness, in among the fierce Girghis of the Kyril Khum desert. Seventeen days ride through this region brought him to Khala Alta, to learn that Kaufmann was far away, and to listen to the stern mandate of Colonel Weimarn that he could not be allowed to follow that chief. How with equal daring and cunning he dodged Weimarn, and to quote his own words, "plunged out into the darkness" with the Oxus for his goal, quailing not at the knowledge that besides the danger of the desert there lay before him the task of running the gauntlet through the hostile Turkomans hovering around the Russian march, need not be told in detail; has he not with equal modesty and brilliancy described those experiences in his volume, "Campaigning on the Oxus"? The Cossacks, sent from Tashkend to intercept and bring him back, galloped after him in vain. They dared not follow him beyond Alti Kuduk when they learned the risks that had not daunted him, and they desisted from their pursuit on the grim assurance from MacGahan's friends at Alti Kuduk that ere they could set out, he must be either "with the jackals or with Kaufmann." He escaped the jackals, and verily he had his reward for his courage and fortitude After many days of hard riding, after many days of scanty black bread and scant water, the glittering Oxus lay at his feet, and its valley was echoing to the roar of Kaufmann's cannon. Well might he write, in his modest, cheery fashion, "As I sat on horseback watching the contest there was a sense of difficulties overcome and dangers passed, which, with the exciting scene before me, was well calculated to put a war correspondent into good humour."

Kaufmann accepted him with cordiality, and promptly hailed him as "Molodyetz," the Russian for brave fellow; and his little army, with the Russian glowing admiration for reckless personal bravery, took MacGahan to its bosom. The emperor sent him the decoration of the St. Stanislaus; and thenceforward he was the accepted comrade of every Russian officer and soldier. During the Russo-Turkish war I met many of the old Khivan men. Their first question was ever, "Do you know MacGahan?" and then came the warm tribute, "Ah, he indeed is Molodyetz." In the Russian army in those Bulgarian days it was next best to being MacGahan himself to be MacGahan's friend. It was good to see him and an old comrade of the Khivan campaign meet. There was no work for MacGahan that day, be the crisis what it might ; but long interminable gossip with the old war chum about Kaufmann, Skobeleff, the Turkomans, and the desert. It was in Khiva where begun the lifelong brotherhood—for their mutual regard was closer than friendship—between Skobeleff and MacGahan. The two men had a curious resemblance in character, and even in certain respects in personal appearance.

MacGahan's work in the exposure of the Turkish atrocities in Bulgaria, which he carried out so thoroughly and effectively in 1876, produced very remarkable results. Regarded simply in its literary merits, there is nothing I know of to excel it in vividness, in pathos, in a burning earnestness, in a glow of conviction that fires from the heart to the heart. His letters stirred Mr. Gladstone into a convulsive paroxysm of burning revolt against the barbarities they described. They moved England to its very depths, and men travelling in railway carriages were to be noticed with flushed faces and moistened eyes as they read them. Lord Beaconsfield tried to whistle down the wind the awful significance of the disclosures made in those wonderful letters. The master of sneers jibed at as "coffeehouse babble," the revelations that were making the nations to throb with indignant passion. A British official, Mr. Walter Baring, was sent into Bulgaria on the track of the two Americans, MacGahan and Schuyler, with intent to disparage their testimony by the results of cold official investigation. But lo! Baring, official as he was, nevertheless was an honest man with eyes and a heart; and he who had been sent out on the mission to curse MacGahan, blessed him instead altogether, for he more than confirmed the latter's figures and pictures of murder, brutality, and atrocity. It is not too much to say that this Ohio boy, who worked on a farm in his youth and picked up his education anyhow, changed the face of Eastern Europe. When he began to write of the Bulgarian atrocities, the Turk swayed direct rule to the bank of the Danube, and his suzerainty stretched to the Carpathians. Now Roumania owns no more the suzerainty, Servia is an independent kingdom, Bulgaria is tributary but in name, and Roumelia is governed not for the Turks but for the Roumelians. All this reform is the direct and immediate outcome of the Russo-Turkish war. But what brought about the Russo-Turkish war? What forced the Czar, reluctant as he was and inadequately prepared, to cross the Danube and wage with varying fortune the war that brought his legions finally to the very gates of Stamboul? The passionate irresistible pressure of the Pan-Slavist section of his subjects, burning with ungovernable fury against the ruthless Turk, because of his cruelties on those brother slaves of Bulgaria and Roumelia; and the man who told the world and those Russian Slavs of those horrors, the man whose voice rang out clear through the nations with its burden of wrongs and shame and devilry, was no illustrious statesman, no famed *littérateur*, but just this young American from off the little farm in Perry County, Ohio. Therefore, it is that I say that MacGahan it was who, having brought about the Russo-Turkish war that hounded the Turk from the regions which his hoof defaced, has his rightful place in history as the force that brought about the changes which the Treaty of Berlin made in the political geography of Eastern Europe.

When travelling in Bulgaria with MacGahan in the war time, we would occasionally enter some village which he had previously visited during his investigations into the atrocities. It was touching to see how the people thronged about him, fondly treating him as their liberator, and kissing his hands with a devotion that was thoroughly sincere. It is absolutely the truth that there was a large faction in Bulgaria on both sides of the Balkans preparing to agitate for the offer to MacGahan of the chiefhood of the future principality. The idea was of course a piece of quixotry, and the specific clause in the Treaty of Berlin was scarcely needed to secure that the chosen ruler should be one belonging or attached to a princely family, apart altogether from the circumstance that MacGahan was in his grave before that treaty was drawn up; but that there were Bulgarians who were seriously eager for MacGahan as their ruler, proves how strong was his hold on the people in whose behalf he had wrought and written so fervently.

With the prestige of his Bulgarian correspondence MacGahan was master of the situation when he went to St. Petersburg in the beginning of 1877, to watch and record the preparations for the war which the Czar declared in the April of that year. He could do anything he liked with the authorities of the Imperial bureaux. The stiff reserve of the Russian Foreign Office dissolved before his frank, easy manner. I have often noticed how much better than the British correspondent the American man gets on with continental functionaries, both civil and military. The habitual attitude of the British official is of that character, that there ever is the *a priori* feeling in the non-official person of the abstract impossibility of any true accord with him. The former has the air of occupying an entrenched position against all non-official comers; and the latter realises that if he is to achieve anything in their business intercourse—socially the English official can be and often is delightful—the advantage must be won at the point of the bayonet. When the non-official Briton has occasion to come into contact, otherwise than socially, with foreign officialdom, he cannot easily rid himself of the associations of his insular experiences. He goes into a foreign bureau with the same sensation he was wont to have on the Whitehall threshold, of being about to struggle with beasts at Ephesus; he expects to be slighted with supercilious civility, if not to be maltreated by actual discourtesy. It is fortunate for him if his perceptions are acute enough to effect an early change in the mental attitude second nature presents to him in relation to foreign officials; it is odds indeed against his ever shaking off the repulsion which force of experience has ground into his being. And there is this to be said, that if he cannot accomplish this feat —if he cannot rise to the realisation that all officials are not of the recognised type of British officials, he is likely to lose much, as well in smoothness of intercourse as in the actual results of that intercourse. However much he may educate himself out of his repugnance to the official person, he will always find himself at a disadvantage in his intercourse with that individual, when he compares himself with the American citizen. That happy child of the West has never gone forth from the "departments" of his native capital, gnashing his teeth and panting for some kind antagonist who will oblige him with a fight; strange as the statement may seem in English ears, American officials from cabinet ministers to vice-consuls experience no reluctance in accepting the humiliating consciousness that they are the servants, and not the masters of the public. Thus the American quits home free from the settled conviction that the official in virtue of being an official, no matter of what clime, regards him as a natural enemy. MacGahan went farther; he actually started into intercourse with officials on the premiss that they were friends. His experiences had been exclusively Continental, and thus he had escaped the rude shock of disillusionment. I never saw such a fellow for making himself at home among high officials. In his manner there was no flavour of impudence or presumption. I question whether of that word, indeed, he understood the meaning. It was as if he in the character of a man, and a Republican man, had reasoned the matter down to bare principle. "I am a man," seemed to me to be his attitude, "and I am a man who honestly and legitimately, for a specific purpose of which you are aware or which I shall be glad to make you aware, want something. That something—be it information, be it a passport, be it what it may—you can give me best, therefore I ask you for it. It is immaterial to the logic of the position I virtually put, whether you are an office messenger or the chancellor of an Empire, a lieutenant or the commander-in-chief." The Russians being a people among whom etiquette is not stringent, among whom a private soldier calls the emperor by his Christian name, and a grand duke styles a peasant "brother," fell in easily with this republican directness, and failed to see that anybody was any the worse for it.

Thus it was that MacGahan lounged around St. Petersburg, popular, a genial power among genial people, and getting to know all that there was to know without condescending to intrigue. This is what a common friend wrote to me after MacGahan's death, about this period of his life: "With his indomitable coolness and quaint imperturbability, Mac-

Gahan had amazing success in gaining his point. In a discussion with the War Office people in St. Petersburg before the declaration of the war, some difficulties were started about authorising his presence with the army in the capacity of war correspondent MacGahan did not bully or lose his temper. He smiled in his easy way, and quietly said, 'Oh, very well, I shall go to the Chancellor and get his sanction to go with the army in another character. I will claim as the ambassador of the English Opposition.' The authorities were not in earnest. The difficulty was merely a technical one, as MacGahan knew well enough ; and he slid it out of the way by a bit of jocular swagger, the quaint fun of which took from it the attribute of serious impertinence. MacGahan could do anything he liked with Ignatieff, calmly made love to Madame Ignatieff, rather patronised Prince Gortschakoff, and nodded affably to the Grand Duke Nicholas."

All this was before I knew MacGahan. From April to December 1877 our lives were so blended that there is an inability to speak of MacGahan without speaking of myself as well; what of seeming egotism may occur, I trust will be excused as unavoidable.

When the Russo - Turkish war was declared MacGahan was already with the Russians and I was ordered to join them. Both were to undertake duty as representatives of the same paper and in the same field. MacGahan and I had never met. It was not certain how we should assimilate, and the most whole-souled co-operation is needed for dispositions and operations whose object is the production of an adequate record of the progress of a great campaign. There is nothing in my experience that tries the temper like war correspondence; nor any pursuit so prone to engender jealousy and ill-feeling among the men engaged in it. Essentially they are rivals, and the rivalry is, equally essentially, of the keenest and quickest kind. One is constantly torn between comradeship and one's duty to one's paper. In the nature of things, it is difficult for a man with exceptional advantages to strain all his powers to the utmost and so score, and yet be beloved by men whose natures do not permit them to be thus energetic. Still less is it easy for the energetic man against whom fortune may have a spite, to be cordial with the fortunate easy-going man whom he meets complacently riding away from a fight that is over and done, to reach which in time the luckless energetic man has galloped a hundred miles straight on end. In the friction of competition expedients which their successful deviser thinks fair enough, may become dodges in the eyes of his fellows who had not happened to think of them. I have an old comrade with whom I have travelled many a thousand miles in the pursuit of peaceful journalism, with never a shadow between us; and we have both been thankful that fortune never sent us campaigning together, in the mutual apprehension lest as rivals in that field there should have been the rupture of our long friendship.

In the farewell interview with the manager of the newspaper, I could not but discern that he was troubled lest MacGahan and I might not hit it off. Not knowing MacGahan, I was not aware how sweet was his temper; and although I was conscious that the equability of my own is such that to disturb it is more than one man single-handed can accomplish, I was anxious to have a definite understanding which of us, in case of a conflict of opinion, was to have the right to decide. That was vested in me as the *ultima ratio*, but only to come into force if circumstances made the disclosure an absolute necessity. So far as I was concerned I am sure MacGahan went to his grave without the knowledge that, in the last resort, the control of our dispositions was in me. We never had a moment's friction. Often we differed. Then we argued the points out, and the man whom the other convinced loyally gave in. From the very first there was as strong, close affinity between MacGahan and myself as ever, I believe, subsisted between two men. Women may love each more—that is a matter about which I cannot speak; but I do not believe that any two men loved each other more than MacGahan did me and I did MacGahan.

We met first at the railway station of Jassy, the chief town of Moldavia, when I was on my way to Kischeneff, the headquarters in Bessarabia of the Russian army commanded by the Grand Duke Nicholas. I was in the heart of a difficulty about baggage with a batch of stupid Moldavian porters, when a shortish, thick-set man, with calm clear eyes, short, dense brown beard, and singularly small hands and feet, came up to me with a limp, and asked in a singularly pleasant voice whether I was not an Englishman, and whether my name was not Forbes. I replied in the affirmative. Then he simply said he was MacGahan. We confronted each other for a short space in silence, looked each other deliberately over, gazed steadfastly into each other's eyes, and then, as if by a simultaneous impulse, clasped hands. The grip was a symbol of a friendship that was never to falter. MacGahan had an ankle set in a plaster of Paris cast. He told me how at a recent review at Kischeneff, riding a wild young horse belonging to Prince Tserteleff, the beast ran away and fell with him, breaking one of the small bones about the ankle-joint. At the inaction compelled by such a mishap I should have fretted myself half to death. But MacGahan did not know how to fret. His nature was of the sunniest serenity. He accepted the trouble with a genial heroism that kindled my most fervent admiration. I never saw him ruffled, although I once heard him threaten to shoot a man. He announced his intention in a bland drawl; he pulled out his revolver with a sweet smile; and when the hulking ruffian backed down, he resumed the thread of the interrupted conversation with a calm deliberation, in which there was not so much as the quiver of the voice. "He'd get along all right," he said, "in spite of the broken bone; he never *had* cared much about walking, and now he'd simply ride all the more." There came a time when he could not even ride; and even so he was not to be hindered from his duty. He accompanied Gourko's adventurous raid over the Balkans soon after the crossing of the Danube, and in a narrow place in the Hankoi Pass his horse slid over a bank and fell on his rider, so that the half-set bone was broken again. But the indomitable MacGahan declined to be invalided by this misfortune. He quietly had himself hoisted on to a gun-carriage, and so went through the whole arduous expedition, being involved thus helpless in several actions, and once all but falling into the hands of the Turks. No word of his lameness, or of the hardship and danger he had to incur by reason of it, ever found its way into his correspondence, the absence of egotism in which is only equalled by its brilliancy. He limped cheerily all through the campaign, and would have been lame for life had he lived to be an old man. But in spite of his lameness the Russians called him the "Cossack Correspondent," so dashingly alert were his movements.

As for his life, so for his livelihood, he was true to the motto of his country, and "took his chances." When the campaign began he and I together bought for him in Bucharest, besides saddle horses, a waggon and team, stored the vehicle with supplies, and engaged for him a trusty coachman. With it he duly travelled down the Danube, left it behind when he crossed the great river, and never once saw the vehicle again until after the fall of Plevna, six months later, when he kept by it for two days, and then finally lost it for good. His wretched coachman was a standing joke among the correspondents; a forlorn wandering Jew ever in vain search after his meteoric master. At all sorts of unlikely places poor Isaac would turn up, following some phantom trail, with the melancholy stereotyped question, "Have you seen my master?" followed by a request for a little money to keep himself and his horse alive. For aught I know Isaac and the waggon may be haunting Bulgaria to this day. MacGahan never had any clothes except what he stood up in, and a clean shirt, which he had probably washed himself, in his saddle-bags. Yet he had the wonderful attribute of always looking clean. Other men, scorched by sun, and caked with layers of Bulgarian dust, looked disreputably dingy and travel-soiled; but MacGahan seemed exempt from the sun-blisters that gave most people the aspect of suffering from confluent small-pox, and it seemed as if the dust would not clot on him. He "took his chances," in an eminent degree, as to rations. From his own resources it was rare that he saw a sure meal ahead. Wherever there was a Bulgarian hut or a Russian regiment he was all right for food, such as it was. I have often seen him standing among the privates supping soup out of the company kettle with the huge wooden spoon one of the men had lent him. He was an adept at roasting eggs in the ashes of a Bulgarian hearth ; and when nothing to eat came in his way he went without with a light heart. On one occasion, before Plevna, his imperturbable coolness stood him in good stead in the matter of " proviand." He, his comrade Millet, and Prince Schahofskoy, were eating together under the shade of a tree within range of the Turkish fire. There was about food enough for one, and all were very hungry. A shell burst among the branches of the tree, and Millet and Schahofskoy left off eating. Then came a spattering of bullets that brought the leaves down about their ears. Millet and Schahofskoy hurriedly jumped up and sought a safer spot. Mac-Gahan sat still and serenely finished the victuals.

When, as soon as the passage of the Danube at Simnitza-Sistova had been secured, it became known among us that Gourko was to attempt a dash across the Balkans, the question had to be settled whether MacGahan or myself should accompany that expedition. It was sure to be one of extreme interest and daring adventure ; and it was clear, as soon as we began to talk the matter over, that both of us had set our hearts on going with it. It was MacGahan who went, and his gratitude for the sacrifice he saw I was making consoled me for what I was conscious I was losing. But I must own in candour that I yielded to him not altogether actuated by the motive of giving him pleasure. The man who went on the Gourko expedition might have his own communications compromised, and certainly must lose touch of all other occurrences within the theatre of war during his absence. Now, besides the raid across the Balkans, there were understood to be impending a march on Rustchuk to the left flank, and an advance on Plevna on the right. Arrangements for having those operations covered had to be made, and the general organisation of correspondence seen to. Thus early had I realised that, although MacGahan was head and shoulders above me in descriptive power—in what may be called the pure correspondence part of the war correspondent's work, I was his superior both in organisation and that faculty which I have never been sure whether to define as prognosis or as presentiment. So my sacrifice was partly to MacGahan, partly to a sense of duty. I was well rewarded. No line of correspondence ever came back from the men who went with Gourko; they were as dead till he re-emerged from his trans-Balkan excursion. But frequent despatches came through from him to the Imperial headquarters, and these Ignatieff placed at my disposal, so that in effect I who had remained behind was the newsman of the expedition. Yet again, during the trans-Balkan absence of Gourko and MacGahan, I had seen fighting away on the east flank almost under the shadow of Rustchuk, and had witnessed the crushing repulse of Schahofskoy and Krüdener's attempt on Plevna—a repulse that altered the whole face of the campaign and quite effaced the interest of Gourko's operations.

The friendship between Skobeleff and MacGahan

was as the love of David and Jonathan. They had become sworn comrades in common peril during the Khivan campaign, and throughout the Russo-Turkish war MacGahan always tried to be with his friend. After MacGahan's death I met Skobeleff in Paris, and he burst into tears when we met, for I brought MacGahan vividly to his mind. We had a quiet evening together, and the brave Russian spoke with deep tenderness of the man who had grown so close to his heart, and whose death had poisoned for him the honours which his brilliant fighting genius had so deservedly brought him. During the fighting before Plevna in September, which lasted during six days of almost continuous rain and fog, MacGahan was as usual with his friend Skobeleff on the extreme left of the Russian flank, against the "Green Hill" and the "Khrishin" redoubt. Skobeleff actually carried the latter redoubt, and maintained his position there during two days of constant ruthless fighting, until with passionate reluctance he was compelled to evacuate it, because the imbecility of the headquarter staff refused him reinforcements. MacGahan's description of Skobeleff, as he led the remnant of his division back from the position he had held on to with so heroic persistence, is the sublimest piece of word-painting, the most luridly vivid "picture of battle," with which I am acquainted in any language. He tells of him with features haggard and distorted, blackened with powder, his eyes bloodshot, his lips dry and scarred, his voice reduced to a hoarse whisper, his clothes torn and bloody, his Cross of St. George twisted round on his shoulder, in his hand his broken sword, and a few hundred battered broken men mournfully following their balked leader. Talking over this description with me later, MacGahan gave a curious illustration how narrow are the confines of the sublime and the ridiculous. He told me that after writing of Skobeleff's blackened and scarred lips, he had added, " and with his tongue hanging out of his mouth." This he erased on glancing over what he had written, not that it was not true, but because he discerned, and rightly, that it verged on the ludicrous. Skobeleff was one of the mourners at poor MacGahan's funeral, and Frederick Villiers, who was living with Skobeleff in his camp at the time, told me that for days after the young general remained prostrated by grief for the loss of him whom he called his dearest friend.

Those six days of constant exposure before Plevna in September broke me down. I took malarious fever, and after a critical time in Bucharest was invalided home to England. I returned to Bucharest early in September, just in time to receive there, and to straighten out for the telegraph-wire, MacGahan's brilliant despatches recounting Osman Pasha's final desperate attempt to break out of Plevna, and telling of the surrender of the Turkish army that followed on its frustration.

A few days later MacGahan himself turned up in Bucharest on a few hours' hurried visit. I was sitting with Colonel Mansfield, the British Consul, when he came in. He was still limping, looked thin and worn, and wore the sheepskin coat of a Bulgarian peasant. We went back to the hotel, and that was our last evening together, though we promised each other pleasant days in the future that was never to come for him, poor fellow. He returned to the scene of action next day, and presently, through deep snow and bitter cold, set out with Skobeleff to cross the Balkans by the Trojan Pass, and afterwards to accompany the army on its march to the Sea of Marmora. He might have been alive to-day but for his devotion to the duty of friendship. He was under orders for Berlin to attend the Conference, when Lieutenant Greene, the United States military attaché with the Russian army, sickened of typhus fever. MacGahan undertook the task of nursing him as he lay ill at San Stephano, and so delayed his departure and sacrificed his life. He caught the infection from Greene, and died in Constantinople after a few days' illness. They buried him in the little cemetery of the foreigners close to the clear waters of the Bosphorus, but his country recently claimed the ashes of as noble a son as ever country had, and he lies now with his kin in the Ohio graveyard. Frederick Villiers and Frank Millet, the former an Englishman, the latter a New Englander, both of whom had commenced and finished the campaign with him, helped to lower him into his far-off foreign grave, around which stood weeping mourners of a dozen nationalities, and over which his loving and constant friend, Lady Strangford, placed a stone with an inscription as true and beautiful. Another friend, who while life remains will never forget him, his wisdom, his sagacity, his frank courage, his loyal manliness, his cheery lovableness, his noble genius, puts this poor stone on the cairn to the memory of MacGahan.

WHERE WAS VILLIERS?

BEFORE I let my little story answer this question, it is expedient that I explain—who Villiers is. Villiers, then, to begin with, is one of the best fellows in the world. He is the war artist of the London *Graphic;* and he has been my staunch comrade in several campaigns, and on not a few battle-fields; and since I went on the shelf he, yet young, has seen fighting enough to constitute him a veteran twice over. He came to me first in the middle of the Servian war, with a letter of introduction from a dear friend of both of us. His face was so ingenuous, his manner so modest, his simplicity so quaint, that I adopted him as "my boy" before our first interview was over. We loved each other from the first. Whenever, afterwards, the war-tocsin sounded, it was the signal, too, of a letter or a call from Villiers, to know when I was setting out; it went without saying that he and I were to go together. Thus it fell out that he came to share most of my field experiences in the summer and autumn of 1877, when we were campaigning with the Russian army that had marched from the Pruth down to the Danube, and had crossed the king of European rivers into Bulgaria, to drive the Turk across the Balkans, and finally to follow him up as he step by step fell back, fighting hard, till at length the minarets and domes of Constantinople greeted the eyes of the hardy children of the "great white Czar."

Near the end of July in that year Villiers and myself were with the advance posts of that portion of the Russian army which was commanded by the Cesarewitz (now the emperor), and which was engaged in masking the Turkish fortress of Rustchuk, lying, as it did, dangerously on the left flank of the Russian line of advance. We were happy enough, but things were too quiet for both of us, by a great deal. It was lazy, idle work, lying in the tent all day long, gossiping with Baron Driesen, while Villiers and dear old General Arnoldi drew caricatures of each other for lack of any better occupation. So we determined one morning to ride back to the emperor's headquarters in Biela, and find out there whether something more stirring elsewhere was not to be heard of. We did not mean to abandon altogether the army of the Cesarewitz, but only to quit it for a short holiday; so we left our servants and waggon behind us, and started with only our saddle-horses, carrying each a blanket and a few necessaries on the saddle.

At Biela we found General Ignatieff living in a mud-hut in the rear of a farmyard occupied by the emperor's field-tents. He advised us to strike westward across Bulgaria, in the direction of Plevna. Something worth seeing he said in his vague, diplomatic way, was soon to happen there. Prince Schahovskoy—nobody ever spelt the name right, and I believe the owner himself never spells it twice the same way—and old Baron Krüdener, two generals commanding each a nominal army corps, were massing their forces with intent to assail Osman Pasha behind those formidable earth-works that he had been so skilfully and sedulously constructing around the little Bulgarian town on the banks of the Osma. If we made haste we should reach the vicinity of Plevna in time for the engagement. Ignatieff was so courteous as to furnish us with a letter of recommendation to the prince with the unspellable name; and, full of eagerness for the excitement, we rode away on our lone cross-country journey that same afternoon. It was a journey of about eighty miles, as far as we were able to reckon, and the country had been made somewhat desolate by the ravages of war. We travelled by the map, and without a guide, asking our way of peasants as we went along. This method was not an entire success, and we wandered about deviously. For one thing our acquaintance with the Bulgarian language was strictly limited; for another, peasants were not always to be found when we wanted them; and for a third, the Bulgarian peasant has very vague ideas both as to distances and as to the points of the compass. He reckons by hours, and with most irritating looseness; his hour is as elastic as the Irish mile or the Scotch "bittock." "How far to Akcair?" I would ask. "Two hours, *Gospodin!*"[1] would be the reply. "What direction?" A wave of the hand to the right, and a wild, indiscriminate, unintelligible howl, would be the lucid response. We ride on for an hour, and encounter another peasant. "How far to Akcair?" "Three hours, *Gospodin!*" "What direction?" A wild, indefinite wave of the hand to the left, and a howl as indescribable as that emitted by the gentleman we had previously interrogated, would be the reply of this second exponent of local geography. There was a road, indeed, but it had never been travelled on, having been made as a job and being overgrown with weeds and grass. Besides, it had an awkward habit of breaking short off at critical points, to be found again, at a few miles' distance, in a wholly unexpected and irrelevant sort of way. Turkish roads are as aimless and eccentric as are all other things in that land of polygamy and shaven heads.

Nevertheless, on the evening of the second day, tired and hungry, we reached Poradim, where Prince Schahovskoy had his headquarters. I knew him of old to be a grumpy man—he was the only distinctly discourteous Russian I ever had the misfortune to meet. We waited on him to ask for permission to abide for a time with his command, and I handed him General Ignatieff's letter. "I cannot help myself,"

[1] *Gospodin*—a term of address corresponding with our "sir," or the French "monsieur."

said he; "you bring me an injunction from headquarters that I am to do so." And then, rising, he said, "Gentlemen, excuse me, I am going to dine."

It was more than we had any chance of doing, famishing as we were; but I was glad of the begrudged sanction. I had met an old comrade of the Servian campaign on Schahovskoy's staff, who made us welcome to his tent. He had gone on a reconnaissance, and we lay down to sleep on empty stomachs; Villiers, who has not the faculty of long abstinence from food with impunity, was positively sick from hunger. Early next morning I went foraging, and succeeded in achieving some raw fresh eggs, which I placed by his head, and then awoke him. "I give you my word," said the lad, "I was dreaming about raw eggs"—and he turned to and sucked them with a skill that proved he might give his grandmother lessons in this accomplishment.

There was no forward movement this day, but a long council of war, from which old Krüdener went away gloomily, predicting defeat; for he had remonstrated against the attempt which was to be made, and which was to be carried out only in obedience to peremptory orders from the headquarters of the Grand Duke Nicholas, the commander-in-chief of the Russian army. Failure was a foregone conclusion from the outset.

This council of war would have been a very interesting spectacle to any one unfamiliar with the *personnel* of the Russian army. On the windy plain, outside the tents constituting Schahovskoy's headquarters, had gathered representatives of all the types of Russian officerhood. Here was the gray-bearded, hard-faced old major who, without "protection," had fought his sturdy way up through the grades, with long delays, much hard service, and many wounds. He had been an ensign in the Crimea, and afterward was forgotten, for nobody knows how many years, in some odd corner of the Caucasus. He is only a major, poor old fellow; but he has half a dozen decorations, and, please God, he will gain another to-morrow, if he has the luck to stand up. He is as hard as nails, and would as soon live on biscuit and "salt-horse" as on champagne and French cookery. There is little in common between him and the tall, stately, grizzled general by his side, who is an aide-de-camp of the emperor; a *grand seigneur* of the court, yet who has never forsworn the camp; a man who will discuss with you the relative merits of Patti and Lucca; who has yachted in the Mediterranean, shot grouse in the Scottish highlands, and gone after buffalo on the prairies of America; who wears his decorations, too, some of them earned in the forefront of the battle, others as honorary distinctions, or marks of Imperial favour. He can gallop, can this young hussar in the blue and red; he can cut the sword exercise; he can sing French songs; he would give his last cigarette either to a comrade or to a stranger like myself; and in his secret heart he has vowed to earn the

Cross of St. George to-morrow. Till the very end of the war I never took quite heartily to Lieutenant Brutokoff—the very opposite of the swell young hussar I have described. The first time I met him, I knew that I disliked him down to the ground. His manners—well, he had none to speak of—and his voice was a growl, with a hoarseness in it begotten of schnapps. He did not look as if he washed copiously, and he was the sort of man who might give some colour to the notion that the Russian has not yet quite broken himself of the custom of breakfasting off tallow candles. But he turned out not a bad fellow on further acquaintance, and would share his ration with a stray dog.

Before daybreak on the last day of July the whole force was on the move to the front. Krüdener had the right, Schahovskoy, with whom we remained, the left attack. There was a long halt in a hollow, where was the village of Radisovo, into which Turkish shells, flying over the ridge in front, came banging and crashing with unpleasant vivacity. The Bulgarian inhabitants had stayed at home and were standing mournfully at their cottage doors, while their children played outside among the bursting shells. Gradually the Russian artillery came into action on the ridge in front.

About midday Schahovskoy and his staff, which we accompanied, rode on to the ridge between the guns. The Turkish shells marked us at once, and amidst a fiendish hurtling of projectiles we all tumbled off our horses, and, running forward, took cover in the brushwood beyond, the orderlies scampering back with the horses to the shelter of the reverse side of the slope. Then we had leisure to survey the marvellous view below us—the little town of Plevna in the centre, with the Turkish earthworks, girdled by cannon smoke, all around it.

After an artillery duel of three hours, the prince ordered his infantry on to the attack. The gallant fellows passed us, full of ardour, with bands playing and colours flying, and went down into the fell valley below. For three hours the demon of carnage reigned supreme in that dire cockpit. The wounded came limping and groaning back, and threw themselves heavily down on the reverse slope in the village of Radisovo, in our rear. The surgeons already had set up their field hospitals, and were ready for work.

Never shall I forget the spectacle of that assault made by Schahovskoy's infantrymen on the Turkish earth-works in the valley below the ridge of Radisovo, on which we stood. The long ranks on which I looked down tramped steadily on to the assault. No skirmishing line was thrown out in advance. The fighting line remained the formation till, what with impatience and what with men falling, it broke into a ragged spray of humanity, and surged on swiftly, loosely, and with no close cohesion. The supports ran up into the fighting array independently and eagerly. Presently all along the bristling line burst forth flaming volleys of musketry fire. The jagged line sprang forward through the maize-fields, gradually falling into a concave shape. The crackle of the musketry fire rose into a sharp continuous peal. The clamour of the hurrahs of the fighting men came back to us on the breeze, making the blood tingle with the excitement of battle. The wounded began to trickle back down the gentle slope. We could see the dead and the more severely wounded lying where they had fallen, on the stubble and amidst the maize. The living wave of fighting men was pouring over them, ever on and on. Suddenly the disconnected men drew closer together. We could see the officers signaling for the concentration by the waving of their swords. The distance yet to be traversed was but a hundred yards. There was a wild rush, headed by the colonel of one of the regiments. The Turks in the work stood their ground, and fired with terrible effect into the whirlwind that was rushing upon them. The colonel's horse went down, but the colonel was on his feet in a moment, and, waving his sword, led his men forward on foot. But only for a few paces. He staggered and fell. We could hear the tempest-gush of wrath —half howl, half yell—with which his men, bayonets at the charge, rushed on to avenge him. They were over the parapet and in among the Turks like an overwhelming avalanche. Not many followers of the Prophet got the chance to run away from the gleaming bayonets wielded by muscular Russian arms.

But there were not men enough for the enterprise. It was cruel to watch the brave Russian soldiers standing there leaderless,—for nearly all their officers had fallen,—sternly waiting death for want of officers either to lead them forward or to march them back. As the sun set in lurid crimson, the Russian defeat became assured. The attacking troops had been driven back or stricken down. For three hours there had flowed a constant current of wounded men up from the battle-field back to the reverse slope of the ridge on which we stood, with the general, his staff and escort, and down into the village behind, into what seemed comparative safety. All around us the air was heavy with the low moaning of the wounded, who had cast themselves down to gain some relief from the agony of motion.

The Turks spread gradually over the battle-field below us, slaughtering as they advanced ; and the ridge on which we stood, that had for a brief space been comparatively safe, was again swept by heavy fire. Schahovskoy, who had been silently tramping up and down, and gloomily showing the bitterness of his disappointment, awoke to the exigencies of the situation. He bade the bugles sound the "assembly," to gather a detachment to keep the forepost line on the ridge, and so cover the wounded lying behind it. The buglers blew lustily, but only a few stragglers could be got together. "Gentlemen," then said Schahovskoy to his staff, "we and the escort must keep the front ; these poor wounded must not be abandoned!" They were words worthy of a general in the hour of disaster. We extended along the ridge, each man moving to and fro on a little beat of his own, to keep the Bashi-Bazouks at bay. It was a forlorn hope — a mere sham of a cover; half a regiment could have brushed us away; but it was the only thing that could possibly afford a chance for those poor sufferers, lying moaning there behind us, to be packed into the ambulances and carried away into safety.

Villiers had been ill and weak all day, and the terrible strain of the prolonged suspense and danger had told upon him severely. His mother, as we quitted London, had with her last words confided him to my care. Now, in his work, as in mine, a man has to take his chance of ordinary casualties. But the ordeal which was now upon us was no ordinary risk. It was known that I had been a soldier in the British army, and I could not go to the rear while the men with whom the danger of the previous part of the day had been shared were now confronting a danger immeasurably greater. But with Villiers it was different. He was game; and it was only by pointing out to him that he could not be of much use up here, while he could be of important service helping the surgeons with the wounded, that I persuaded him to leave the fire-swept ridge, and go back, down into the village behind us, where there was less direct risk. At length he went, and the responsibility for him was off my mind. I promised to join him when we should be relieved, or when night, as we might hope, should bring the dismal business to to a close.

We were up there till ten o'clock, and I do not care to write more concerning that particular experience. Some dragoons relieved us, and so, following the general who had lost an army going in search of an army which had lost its general, we turned our horses, and, picking our way through the wounded, rode down the slope.

But where was Villiers?

I could find him nowhere. There was no response to my shouts. I could find no surgeon who had seen him; every man was too busy to take much heed of a casual stranger. "Well," thought I, after my vain search—"Villiers is somewhere, doubtless. He may have ridden off farther to the rear; he can not surely have taken harm. Anyhow, it seems of no use for me to linger longer here; I must follow the general and his staff."

We had a bad night of it, dodging the enemy's marauders; but of that I need not now tell. At last came the morning. Ay! and with the morning came the horrible tidings that in the dead of night the Bashi-Bazouks had worked around the flank of the thin Russian picket-line we had left on the ridge, had crept into the village of Radisovo, and had butchered the wounded lying helpless there, with most, if not all, of the surgeons left in charge.

The news thrilled us all with horror; but for me

now the question, "Where was Villiers?" became agonising in its intensity. Away on the Bulgarian plateau there, the memory came back to me of the pretty house in the quiet London suburb, where the lad's mother, with a sob in her voice that belied the brave words, had told me that she let her boy go with an easy heart, because she knew that he would be with me. And now there came ruthlessly face to face with me the terrible duty that seemed inexorably impending, of having to tell that poor mother there was but one grievous answer to the question, "Where was Villiers?"

I would not yet abandon hope. I rode back toward Radisovo till the Turkish sharpshooters stopped me with their fire, quartering the ground like a pointer. Far and near I searched; everywhere I sought tidings, but with no result. Every one who knew anything had the same fell reply, " If he was in Radisovo last night he is there now, but not alive!" It was with a very heavy heart, then, that, as the sun mounted into the clear summer sky, I realised that professional duty with me was paramount; that I must give up the quest, and ride off to Bucharest, to reach the telegraph office, whence to communicate to the world the news of a disaster of which, among all the journalists who then haunted Bulgaria, the fortune had been mine to be the sole spectator.

It was a long ride, and I killed my poor, gallant horse before I had finished it. But next morning

I was in Bucharest, and, heavy as was my heart, writing as for my life. The day had waned ere I had finished my work, and then I had a bath and came out into the trim, dapper civilisation of Bucharest, with some such load on my mind as one can imagine Cain to have carried when he fled away with Abel's blood burning itself into his heart. There came around me my friends and the friends of Villiers, for every one who knew my young one loved him. Kingston, the correspondent of the *Telegraph*; Colonel Wellesley, the British military attaché; Colonel Mansfield, the British minister to the Roumanian Court; and a host of others, were eager to hear the news I had brought of the discomfiture of Schahovskoy, and not less concerned when they heard of the dread that lay so cold at my own heart. We held a consultation—a few of the friends of Villiers and myself. We settled that I should give a day to fortune before I should adventure the miserable task of telegraphing heart-breaking tidings to the lad's mother. Most of that space I slept— for I was dead beaten, and I think that Marius must have fallen asleep even amid the ruins of Carthage.

On the evening of the next day Wellesley, Kingston, Mansfield, and myself were trying to dine in the twilight, in the garden of the hotel. Suddenly I heard a familiar voice call out, "Waiter, quick— dinner; I'm beastly hungry!"

It was Villiers!

The question was answered. I sprang to my

feet on the instant—my heart in my mouth. So angry was I at the fellow's callousness in thinking of his dinner when we were sobbing about him—so tender was I over him in that—thank God!—he was safe, that as I clutched him by the shoulder, and, I fear, shook him, I scarcely knew whether to knock him down for his impertinence or fall on his bosom and weep for joy at his deliverance. So quaint was the spectacle,—his surprise at my curious struggle of emotion, my attitude of wrath with which a great lump in my throat struggled,—that the others afterward insisted the situation should be commemorated by a photograph, in which we two should re-strike our respective postures.

Villiers had been asleep in an ambulance waggon, to which his horse had been tied, when the Bashi-Bazouks had entered the village. A young surgeon had sprung on the box, in the very nick of time, and had driven the vehicle out of the village just as the hot rancour of the fanatics had surged up close behind it. It was the nearest shave—but it had sufficed to bring him out safe, and he had got to Bucharest in time to shout for his dinner and to save me the misery of telegraphing to his mother that I had a sad answer to the question, "Where was Villiers?"

WOLSELEY:

A CHARACTER SKETCH.

ONE day in the month of August 1871 a fierce sham fight between two divisions of the British army was raging on the slopes of the "Hog's Back," a long ridge stretching from near Aldershot towards Guildford. The recently concluded Franco-German war had startled England into a fitful spurt of anxiety for increased military efficiency; and we were making the first of our few and soon abandoned experiments in autumn manœuvres. Staveley's men had swept the ridge clear of their opponents, and were driving them handsomely down into the undulating valley beyond. On the road which runs along the ridge I had been chatting with General Blumenthal, whom I had known as chief of staff to the Imperial Crown Prince, and who was among the foreign officers who had come to witness our essay in the game assiduous practice in which had helped to give the Germans the triumph which the Treaty of Versailles had consummated. Blumenthal had been strictly non-committal in his replies to my efforts to obtain his opinion as to the handling of our troops, and had parried my questions by laconic encomia on the fineness of the weather. I had given Blumenthal up in despair, and was riding down the slope to follow the fighting-line, when I was addressed by an officer in staff uniform, mounted on a wiry chestnut horse. I had previously noticed this officer riding about alone, apparently quite idle, quite at his ease, and outwardly an unconcerned and unattached spectator of the day's doings. He was of youthful aspect, yet the double row of medal ribbons athwart the left breast of his staff frock-coat indicated that he had seen an exceptional amount of service,—at that time our officers were much more sparsely decorated than they are now,—and I remember having casually wondered who this lonely, smiling veteran might be. He revealed himself in his accost. "My name is Wolseley—Sir Garnet Wolseley—and I am happy to make your acquaintance." I was proud as well as happy to make his; for he had long been one of my heroes. It was not until later that poor "Lucknow" Kavanagh related to me on the spot the story of Wolseley's daring at the capture of the Motee Mahal, but no man conversant with the Mutiny record could be ignorant of the audacious gallantry which he displayed throughout Lord Clyde's operations for the second relief of Lucknow. And if, in the late summer of '70, the attention of most men had been concentrated on the stupendous struggle then being enacted in eastern France, the student of military operations had not failed to follow Wolseley and his trusty followers in their adventurous expedition by river and lake, through forest and over portage, from Thunder Bay to their goal at Fort Garry. Yet there was something between us to which what I take leave to regard as a just pride in my profession, forced me to allude on this threshold of our acquaintance. I had been reading Wolseley's *Soldier's Pocket-book;* and the spirit which pervades that work, not less than its multiplicity of accurate detail, had filled me with admiration. But the author had permitted himself to make one statement at which I own my blood had boiled. I did not feel aggrieved at his aspersion of war correspondents as "the curse of modern warfare." If that were true it was not our affair, but the affair of those who permitted our presence with armies in the field; and from the purely military point of view I was not then, nor am I now, quite sure that I was not with him in my inner consciousness. But my back went up when reading on I found—". . . Newspaper correspondents, and all that race of drones, are an incumbrance to an army : *they eat the rations of fighting men, and they do no work at all.*" This was a calumny. "Curse" or no curse, the war correspondent is assuredly no "drone." Whether for good or harm, he is a permitted person in the field ; he is there as the servant of the public for whom he toils harder than any soldier ; to whom rest and ease are strangers ; and who faces danger and meets death in the line of his duty with a courage as gallant as that shown by any soldier who ever wore uniform. The Nemesis of unfounded aspersion has overtaken the author of the *Soldier's Pocket-book*. He has lived to thank once and again for arduous service rendered him the men whom he sneered at as "drones."

When we met on the "Hog's Back," and Wolseley made shift to bury this hatchet by a compliment, he was illustrating a phase of his many-sided character. Wellington had marched and conquered from Torres Vedras to the Garonne without the aid of that military functionary known as "Chief of Staff." But that functionary had reached the dignity of a personage among the conquerors of the campaign just ended. Kaiser Wilhelm had been inspired by Moltke; the Crown Prince enjoyed or endured Blumenthal as his *adlatus;* Prince Frederick Charles had been assisted by the saturnine Stiele; the Crown Prince of Saxony by the sententious Schlotheim. Our military authorities are nothing if not imitative. So, experimentally, a chief of staff in the person of Wolseley had been sent charged nominally with the function of aiding Staveley to cope with Hope Grant in the mimic campaign among the hedgerows of Hampshire. There was a sort of understanding that the Horse Guards were lukewarm in regard to the innovation, and had adopted it merely in deference to the weight of public opinion. Staveley assuredly did not relish it, and gave the embodiment of the innovation the coldest of cold shoulders. Now, there are men who would have wrestled against this treatment, and who would have struggled for the right to perform the as yet somewhat undefined duties appertaining to the appointment. Wolseley can fight for his own hand as well as another—better indeed, and to more purpose, than most—when real occasion demands; but he is a man of supreme tact and perfect temper, and he knows when it is worth while to make a stand, and when it may be better policy to accept the situation. This was a time for the latter line of conduct. A combat about straws is a waste of power. Staveley would give him nothing to do, and Wolseley did that nothing with a characteristically serene nonchalance. And so it was that I met him riding about the Hog's Back alone, a blithely idle man, with a contented smile on his handsome face, and a cheery willingness to smoke a cigarette under a tree, when the commander whose right hand he was nominally, was fumingly falling into the patent trap which wily old Hope Grant had set for him. Ever since that day I have had the honour of Wolseley's friendship.

Sitting quietly listening in a club smoking-room to "outsider" officers fulminating against Wolseley as a charlatan and a "duffer," I have often wondered whether the vituperators quite realised that the object of their abuse, comparatively young though he be, is more of a veteran, in the true military sense of the word, than almost any other soldier who wears the Queen's uniform. In that sense, a soldier is a veteran in proportion as he has taken part in active service. The lad of twenty-three, who at the age of eighteen had marched out from Coimbra in May 1809, and who in the summer of 1814 embarked at St. Jean de Luz on his return to England, was in the military sense of the term more of a veteran, although a soldier for less than six years, than the oldster who had grown gray in an interrupted round of home service. When I met Wolseley first, in 1871, he had been but twenty-one years a soldier; but then he had been campaigning and fighting almost without intermission all that time; and into the years that have elapsed since 1871 he has crowded five campaigns more. He cannot indeed count wounds with Alick Elliot, who got fourteen sabre-slashes to his own share in the ten minutes of the heavy cavalry charge of Balaclava, or with grand old Sir Neville Chamberlain, to whom during all his fighting career an action without a wound would have been a startling novelty; but a man who is short of a piece of his thigh, who has not much more than half of a shin-bone to congratulate himself upon, who has lost the sight of an eye, and been honeycombed all over from head to foot by a shower of stones knocked out of a gabion by the bursting of a shell, need not feel any anxiety on the score of not having received his own share of personal damage at the hands of the Queen's enemies.

It is no part of my purpose in this sketch to detail Wolseley's biography, but a short outline of his earlier career may not be unacceptable to the reader. He joined the 80th Regiment in 1852, while yet a lad of nineteen. The old family connection was manifest in his choice of a regiment, for the 80th is a Staffordshire corps. He did not soldier long with the Staffordshire knot on his coat collar; but his first regiment came under his command when he was sent out to Zululand, where also he found under him the 90th, the regiment in which he had won promotion and glory in the Crimea and India. When he was gazetted to the 80th, it was on service in Burmah, where Sir John Cheape was conducting what is known as the "Second Burmese War." Sir John was operating against a certain Burmese chieftain, who owned the euphonious name of Myat-Loon, and also the reputedly impregnable stronghold of Kyoult Azein, situated in the heart of a dense jungle. The outworks of this stronghold had to be taken by storm, and Wolseley, only just joined, volunteered to lead the storming detachment. His handful of the 80th was conjoined in the operation with a little band of Madras Infantry under the command of Lieutenant Taylor. Taylor and Wolseley raced for the honour of being first inside the enemy's works. Neither won, owing to circumstances over which neither had any control. Both were simultaneously wounded, and strangely enough in the same place. A gingal ball struck Wolseley on the left thigh, tearing away a mass of muscle and flesh. Taylor suffered similarly, but with the more lethal addition that his femoral artery was severed. He bled to death on the spot. Wolseley slowly recovered, but he will bear to his grave the furrow of the gingal ball. When at home convalescent he was promoted to a lieutenancy in the 90th, then in the Crimea. After a short spell of trench service with his regiment, Wolseley was selected for duty as acting-engineer of our right attack, and filled this post through the long cruel winter. He was gazetted a captain in the end of 1854, but the promotion was cancelled. And for what reason it would not be easy to guess. Because of Wolseley's youth! He had not been too young to earn the promotion, but the authorities thought a lad of twenty-one-and-a-half too young for a captaincy! Wolseley, justly incensed, threatened to resign if deprived of the promotion he had won, and the authorities cancelled the cancellation. He was thanked in despatches for his services in the capture of the Quarries, and took part in the first unsuccessful assault of the Redan. When engaged in his engineer work in the trenches in August 1855 Wolseley was all but shattered by a shell that killed the two sappers who were assisting him. The shell burst in a gabion that had been packed with gravel, and the explosion simply "stuck Wolseley full of stones." Jagged bits of pebbles were embedded in him all over from head to foot. There was not a square inch of his face that had not its stone; his left cheek was all but torn away, his eyes were closed (to this day he is blind of one eye), and part of the bone of his left shin was carried away bodily. Fortunately he has been able to keep the eye left to him pretty wide open. He was picked up for dead, but astonished the surgeons who were speaking of him as quite gone by cheerily mumbling that he was "worth a dozen dead men yet." This wound, or rather this broadcast area of wounds, temporarily invalided him, and so he missed being present at the capture of the great fortress of the Euxine. He had got mended, however, by 1857, and started with his regiment for service in China. The 90th was one of the regiments with this destination which Lord Canning's swift steamers contrived to catch *en route*, and divert to India to aid in the quelling of the great Mutiny that had broken out with so fell an unexpectedness. The gallant "Perthshire Greybreeks" were included in the column which Sir Colin Campbell led from Cawnpore to the second relief of Lucknow. From the Dilkoosha Sir Colin had sent the "Black Watch" down the slope on the Martinière. The 93d and the Sikhs had made a ghastly shambles of the once beautiful Secunderabagh garden. Peel's men of the *Shannon*, were slogging with their ship's guns into the massive structure of the Shah Nujeef, preparatory to carrying it by escalade out of the branches of a tree which grew against the wall of the shrine. Wolseley, with his two companies of the 90th, was sent to the left to carry the "Mess House." The way to its compound wall was across the open. Wolseley's fellows took with them a couple of light guns. So fierce was the Sepoy fire that, to use Wolseley's own quaint colloquialism, "the bullets dropped off the tires of the wheels like peas off a drum." The Mess House was carried with a rush, Wolseley with his own hand, in the midst of a hailstorm of bullets, pulling down the flag of the mutineers from the staff in its roof, and planting in its place the British banner which he carried. Beyond the Mess House lay the palace known as the Motee Mahal, the last rebel post separating the relieving force from their environed fellow-countryfolk. Wolseley led his detachment forward to the assault of the Motee Mahal, which in its turn was taken and cleared after hard fighting and severe loss. This operation consummated the relief. Between the Motee Mahal and the steam-engine post lay only Mr. Martin's house, which the rebels had evacuated. Young Moorsom ran the gauntlet, and the connection was established. It was Wolseley who greeted the forerunner of the besieged.

Wolseley took part in the hard fighting which brought about the final reduction of Lucknow, and in the energetic marching and fighting all over Oude, whereby the late Sir Hope Grant contributed so greatly to the stamping out of the great revolt, on the final extinguishment of which Wolseley found himself a brevet lieutenant-colonel at the age of twenty-six. Quick promotion certainly, from ensign to lieutenant-colonel in eight years; but every step in rank had been honestly won at the point of the sword. From India in 1860 he went to China on the staff of Sir Hope Grant, was with the advance party at the storming of the Taku Forts, and took an active part in the operations which culminated in the surrender of Pekin and the destruction of the Summer Palace. At the close of this war he was despatched on his first non-military mission, an expedition to Nankin to gather all available information in regard to the Taepings, and condense it into a report. He had scarcely returned to England when the "Trent affair" occurred, and he was among the staff officers sent out to Canada in advance of the expeditionary force which was sent across the Atlantic as a consequence of that complication. There followed for Wolseley nine years of hum-drum colonial staff work—the dreariest occupation for a man keen for active soldiering. Although in 1865 he had got his brevet colonelcy, the prospects of distinction were dim, and I believe that he had serious thoughts of leaving the service and taking up the profession of civil engineer, for which his acquirements and experience adequately qualified him. But there was no more thought of this self-obliteration when in 1870 there was assigned to him the command of the Red River Expedition. That service entailed no bloodshed, because when Wolseley's riflemen and militia had hurried across the Manitoban plain up to the stockade of Fort Garry, it was found that the malcontent half-breed Riel and his adherents had fled and dispersed; but it did entail, if it were to be a success, careful organisation, steady, arduous labour, constancy of purpose, and shrewd knowledge of men. From Thunder Bay inland nearly 500 miles of boating and portage had to be accomplished, and there was no rum in the ration. Not a man was lost from start to finish, and where before Wolseley's arrival the half-breeds in their scattered huts were defying Canadian rule, there stands to-day a Canadian city with a population of 25,000 souls, the capital of a vast and prosperous province.

Wolseley's later work, his conduct of the Ashantee expedition, his administration of Natal, his occupation and organisation of Cyprus, his service in Zululand and the Transvaal, his Egyptian campaign, and the more chequered and more arduous duty on the Nile on which he has been more recently engaged, it would be superfluous to summarise. That work has been done in the face of the people of to-day, who have followed every phase of it, and who have based on it their appreciation of the ready, versatile, self-reliant man to whom no task that may be set him, however arduous, comes amiss.

In our first essay in autumn manœuvres Wolseley's *rôle*, as I have said, was a supine one. In the more extended manœuvres of the following autumn the Salisbury Plain campaign, when he held the appointment of A.A.G. on the staff of Sir John Michel, the commander of the "southern army," he played a more prominent part, and had the opportunity of showing his tactical ingenuity and wily daring. Those manœuvres were more like real warfare than any sham fighting I have ever seen, and incidentally involved something in the nature of a test competition between the "new school" and the "old school" of our staff officers. Michel had all the new lights in his force—Wolseley, Valentine Baker, Evelyn Wood, and others. Sir Robert Walpole, who commanded the "northern army," had for his subordinates a group of able "Conservatives," some of whom have distinguished themselves in actual warfare before and since. The issue was fought out at the "Battle of Amesbury." The "northern army's" duly assigned duty was to cover the roads to London against an invader approaching from the south-west, which invader was represented by the "southern army." The former was drawn up in the early morning with its back to the river Avon, looking out westward toward the latter, which had camped for the night on the plain near old Isaac Day's racing stables. Hostilities commenced by a demonstration on the part of Valentine Baker's cavalry on the front of the northern army. To all appearance Baker was engaged in covering the deployment of the mass of the army to which he belonged for a frontal attack on the northern army, standing there expectant in position. All the attention of that army was centred on his evolutions. That attention he held for two long hours and the northern artillery had come into action against him. Suddenly, from the edge of a wood on a knoll right in the rear of the northern army, flashed out a cannon shot. The northern army was taken in reverse. Baker's cavalry evolutions had been a mere ruse to distract its attention while the mass of the southern army was crossing the Avon by a bridge lower down, and marching on to the ridge in its rear, into a position actually cutting off the northern army from the roads to cover which had been its allotted task. The operation was as neat a piece of tactics as one could well hope to see, and Wolseley was the contriver of it. The contention of the northern experts was, I remember, that if there had been actual instead of sham war, the turning movement could not have been carried out, and that even to attempt it would have been insanity. With this argument I could not bring myself to concur. I hold that what of daring enterprise is practicable in peace manœuvres, when men's blood is calm, when their faculties of observation are undisturbed by the distracting influences of actual battle, is infinitely more likely to succeed when the air is full of flying lead, and the turmoil of the fray is straining equanimity. This I hold true of a tactical operation only; the strategy of an actual campaign, antecedent to the clash and bicker of the battle, must be as wary as can be the strategy of any peace manœuvres.

It has never been my good fortune to accompany a force on campaign under the command of Lord Wolseley, and I write, therefore, under some disadvantage. But the expedition which he conducted from Malta to Cyprus when he went to organise the British administration of the latter island, was at least of a semi-military character, and the opportunity offered of watching his methods as well as a commander as a civil organiser and administrator. His leading characteristic struck me as equanimity. There were many temptations to irritation, in the defective commissariat arrangements, in the characteristic obstructiveness of the Turkish authority whom we were dispossessing, in the hazy indefiniteness of the situation generally. But Wolseley, decisive, nay, incisive when occasion demanded, never betrayed a sign of temper. That he was energetic, one could discern, not less than that his powers of hard work—and of fruitful hard work—were exceptional; but there was no gustiness in the energy, and he slid through his hard work with apt, bright dexterity. He never fussed; and he never entangled himself in the labyrinth of trifles. The absence of all friction in his administrative methods stood accounted for partly by his own idiosyncrasy, partly—a phase, indeed, of the other reason—because of the perfect organisation and thorough inter-working of his staff. I travelled out from home with Wolseley and his staff. The latter had been gathered together hurriedly, but its members met, blended, and set to work in the saloon carriage between Dover and Calais, as if they had stepped into it out of a department in which they had been co-operating for years. While they settled minor points of detail, their chief meanwhile slept serenely, easy in the perfect assurance based on experience, that his subordinates would deal with these as he would desire they should be dealt with. It was clear to me thus early, and the impression but grew in distinctness, that Wolseley was the man who decided, who decreed, the centurion who said, " Do this ;" and that he had recruited for the fulfilment of his behests a set of men on whom he could rely as intelligent and devoted executants, and to whom therefore he could and did confide the functions assigned to each, reserving himself as the chief, unhampered by a multiplicity of details, for the big work of resolving and directing. In all this he was making no experiment. He was sure of his " machine ;" it was of his construction ; he had selected every cog and pinion of it ; and had tested its efficiency both in parts and as a whole.

That machine was the congeries of staff officers which outsiders, as they gnash their teeth, designate as the " Wolseley Gang." The outsiders do not deny the efficiency of the gang as a working instrument ; their grievance is that it should always consist of the same men. There are as good men, they angrily contend, outside the gang as those who are inside the favoured pale ; why should Wolseley always lead the same officers on to appointments, opportunities of distinction and rewards, instead of giving other men—the " outsiders " themselves, inferentially—an opportunity to win tricks in the game? Wolseley makes no specific reply, but his tacit answer is unimpeachable. "I know these men of mine," he says in effect, "and they know me. I selected them originally because of my discernment of character, not at the behest of interest or from the dictates of nepotism. We have worked long together; their familiarity with my methods and my just reliance on them, relieves me of half the burden of command. And again, it is obvious that I must ever, as more important commands are assigned me, be widening the pale of the 'gang.' I never see a man doing good work in the quiet efficient manner that I like, that I do not recruit him into my following. I am always on the alert for capable men, since they are not so plentiful; and, oh! outsider, if you should fulfil my requirements, your turn may come to-morrow." Further, contends the outsider, somewhat inconsistently, the credit of Wolseley's success is due, not so much to his own merits, as to the attributes of his followers. They forget the legal axiom—*quid facit per alios, facit per se.* That intuitive discernment of character by which Wolseley recognises the capacity of a man for his own purposes, is an attribute second to no gift that a commander can possess. Nor can any one who has had opportunities for watching the professional intercourse between Wolseley and his long-accustomed supporters, fail to note that his is ever the unquestioned and unquestionable master-mind.

Wolseley's attitude in habitually using the services of the same men is simply that of David in regard to the unaccustomed accoutrements. "I cannot go with these, for I have not proved them." In his curt incisive fashion the Duke of Wellington defined his line of conduct when an officer who had not previously served under him, solicited a staff appointment for the Waterloo campaign. "However flattered I may be," wrote the duke, "and however I may applaud the desire of an officer to serve under my command in the field, it is impossible for me to take upon my staff officers with whose characters I am not familiar in preference to those to whose services I am so much indebted, particularly if the latter desire to serve again." It is not easy for the most censorious to challenge the discriminating acumen of Wolseley's selections. It would be superfluous for me to emphasise the merits of Redvers Buller's military character, although perhaps I happen to know more than do most men how much, once and again, that fine officer's acute discernment, fearless masterfulness of nature, and ruthless promptitude have served us. Wolseley read Buller's capacity already in the Red River expedition, when the latter was but a lieutenant, and when as yet his comrades had no suspicion of his merits. It was in the course of a casual ride along the line of communications on a section of which Herbert Stewart was drudging as a somewhat forlorn captain, that Wolseley chanced upon that noble soldier, recognised the manner of man he was in the course of the day's intercourse, and then and there enlisted him into his special service, thenceforth till the hour of Britain's misfortune by his glorious yet premature death, to be one of the foremost and trusted members of the "gang." Young Maurice he took out of the battery in which he was serving and placed in closest relations to him as his private secretary, actuated by the fine motive that the young lieutenant had beaten himself in the competition for the Wellington Prize Essay.

In the course of our Cyprus experiences I accompanied Lord Wolseley when he circumnavigated the island in the Helicon despatch boat. We were approaching Limassol, concerning which all that was known, and that vaguely, was that the admiral some time previously might have landed there a small party from the squadron. As we ran into the jetty, there was visible a gleam of scarlet; we landed. The chief was received with the "present arms" of a fine army of six marines, under the command of a lieutenant. That officer stepped forward with modest confidence, and in reply to a question put from the general, made his succinct practical report. I do not pretend to strict accuracy in its reproduction, but it ran somewhat on the following lines: "I was landed here with twelve marines a month ago, with general instructions to make the best of things. There was a detachment of Bashi-Bazouks in the place, who were extremely truculent. I had to attack this force, which I routed and dispersed. The Cadi and other Turkish officials were insolent and obstructive, so I have got them in irons in the jail with six of my force doing duty over them. The Moullah preached against us in a manner I regarded dangerous, so I put him into a gang which I had impressed to cleanse the streets which I found in a filthy condition. I have begun to collect revenues out in the district; the accounts and proceeds you will find in the Kaimakhan. Limassol is now clean, quiet, submissive, and I believe becoming well affected." Wolseley looked straight at the officer, and asked him if he had seen any service. He replied in the negative, but added he had found opportunity, between tours of duty, to eat his terms and pass as a barrister. Within the week the Marine lieutenant was appointed magistrate at Nicosia, and he now, I believe, occupies a seat on the judicial bench of Cyprus.

The keynote to the constitution of that group of devoted adherents who have come to be designated as the "Wolseley Gang," I take to be its completeness for the functions which it has to perform as a composite whole. In each of its constituent elements, its compounder, if I may use the expression, has discerned some specific attribute, of which, when the occasion calls it into requisition, he shall take astute and purposeful avail. As a whole, then, it is *totus, teres, atque rotundus*, an engine effectively adapted to a wide range of potential uses. The individual units of that whole do not strike one as by any means, one and all, men of exceptional general military ability. Some of them, indeed, may be called dull men. But never a one of them but has his speciality. One has a genius for prompt organisation; another a rare faculty for administration. A third has a winning manner and a good address, a fourth is the scout of scouts. You may wonder what Wolseley can see in so and so, that he has them always with him. Watch events long enough, and time will furnish you with the answer. This man, perhaps of no great account for ordinary purposes, has a strange gift, when there is doubt in regard to some line of action, of defining the right course in a single rugged, trenchant, pithy sentence that carries conviction; him, one may see, Wolseley keeps just to help him to make up his mind. This other man has seemingly no attribute at all, save inertness, a love for gazing on the wine when it is red, and the cultivation of strong language. But he too has his gift. Arrange for him a plan of attack, set everything in order, tell him that all is ready, and that he may go to work. Then you can discern for what Wolseley has enrolled him in the gang. He draws his sword, he lets a roar out of him fit to wake the dead; he becomes a veritable god of battle—a lambent thunderbolt of war; he radiates from him the mysterious irresistible magnetism that inspires men to follow him, ay, to use the rough soldier-phrase, "through hell and out at the farther side." The deed done, the conqueror wipes and sheathes his sword, mops his forehead, sighs for a big drink, and is conspicuous no more till he shall be wanted again.

There is to be said that no one of Wolseley's

special men have belied the discrimination which selected him, at all events while remaining under the inspiration of the chief who recruited him. One or two there may have been who have shown unwisdom when placed in independent positions, yet others, although rarely, have failed to earn approbation under other leaders. But this is but a tribute to the force at once of Wolseley's influence, and the acumen of his discernment of character. He can inspire his subordinates, he can allocate them to duties in the fulfilment of which they earn credit and contribute to the success of him their master. The "gang" as an aggregate is a weapon of extraordinary and diverse force; break it up and its parts are but the withes of the faggot, with here and there a stick of exceptional stoutness.

The "gang" proper, his personal following, Wolseley recruits, so far as my observation goes, purely on the principle of recognition of attributes he desiderates. But he is an ambitious man. He realises how strong against him are professional jealousies; and I, for one, hold that he is fully justified in striving by every legitimate expedient, to strengthen his cords and to enlarge his borders. If he may haply give pleasure in high quarters by offering a command to a personage, or if by a similar offer he may draw the sting of a hostile critic, is this blameworthy—rather is it not dexterously natural? Then again, he is mindful of early comradeships. That he is generous in regard to later rivalries stands revealed in the fact, that he desired the command of the Suakim force should be offered to Sir Frederick Roberts.

I do not conceive that there can be any impertinence in an honest attempt to define, according to one's lights, Lord Wolseley's place as a commander. It is not a matter open to doubt, that just as Providence creates this man with a great faculty for mathematics, that one with a gift for invention, yonder one with innate powers to sway his fellow-men by the force and charm of his oratory; so Providence occasionally creates a man with a genius for war. How frequently is a question impossible to answer approximately because the born soldier may, by chance or force of circumstances, live the life of a bargee or a coal-heaver, of an Edinburgh advocate or the manager of a London Dock Company. In the actual outcome the "heaven-born soldier"—the inspired leader of men, is a phenomenon of exceeding rarity. The warfare of the last thirty years has produced, in my humble judgment, but two men of this type, Stonewall Jackson and Skobeleff. Two other men have approximated to the character—Sheridan and Prince Frederick Charles; and there are elements in the nature of Redvers Buller which indicate him a man falling little short of the lofty ideal. But it follows from the rarity of the heaven-born soldier, that successful military enterprises are habitually effected by men who lack the grand inspiration, and who may be designated as simply more or less exceptionally able soldiers. Of this order were Lee, Grant, and Sherman, Gourko, and perhaps Radetski. Moltke is a master of the art of war, and his skill, supported by the fighting qualities of the Prussian soldier, brought first Austria and then France prostrate at the feet of his master. But his task at the least was simplified by the absence of any chiefs of inspiration from high commands in the armies of either worsted power. It may safely be averred that Moltke has never found himself pitted against an opponent of real military genius. His abler subordinates, with the exception of Prince Frederick Charles—such men as Goeben, Werder, and Manteuffel—were men of similar, and no higher attributes than their great director-general; the ruck of the German generals were no more than intelligent men, well versed in their profession; acting habitually in the precepts of the Moltke tuition, and accorded a range of discretion that produced self-confidence without rashness. With none of those types are the relative conditions such as to admit of Wolseley's easy comparison. The heaven-born soldier is he who achieves startling successes with apparently inadequate means, who darts on his enemy at unawares, who stands indomitably between that enemy and the prize that has seemed to be to his hand. To prove himself in such supreme crises has never fallen to Wolseley's lot. No more has fortune ever prescribed to him the task of planning the strategy of a great campaign, of swiftly modifying the details of a great strategic plan in compliance with sudden emergencies, of playing with great armies as if they were pawns on the chess-board. In civilised warfare he has held no command, whether subordinate or independent. He has never even been pitted against quasi-disciplined and fairly-armed antagonists of any fighting prowess, as was Gough against the Khalsa hosts; Colin Campbell against our mutinied Indian army. For opponents worth the name Wolseley has had never any other than savages, possessed indeed of savage valour, but equipped with little else than barbaric armament.

On occasion he has had to contend against exceptional natural obstacles, and those he has conquered with skilful and gallant constancy. It must be added that he has lacked no appliances which the resources of a wealthy nation in the van of civilisation could contribute. His every requisition—and he has requisitioned with a free hand—has been met. He orders a railway—a railway is sent him. The world is harried for mules to constitute his transport, and the wharves groan with the multifarious supplies he has indented for. That he is wise and right to avail himself of the lavish appliances the nation is fain to supply at his bidding, goes without saying; but it is not to be denied that they smooth his path to success. Wellington was stinted of everything by a grudging government, from men and money to supplies and munitions; tinned provisions were unknown to him, and jams and marmalade undreamt of; he had to feed himself, improvise his own transport, raise his own money; but he cleared the Peninsula and marched to the Garonne. One need not multiply instances within Lord Wolseley's earlier personal experience of successful operations carried out with hardly a tittle of the resources which have ever been so freely at his command. Putting out of reckoning his most recent enterprise, failure in which occurred mainly because of circumstances outside his control, it remains that, thus equipped, Wolseley has been set to do nothing that he has not done promptly, neatly, cleanly, adroitly. He has fully answered every call that has been made upon him, and that without apparent strain. It would be absurd to assert that he has been tried very highly; but I remember using this expression before the Nile campaign was begun: "It seems a fair augury from that past to which Wolseley has ever been equal, that he is likely to prove equal to any future that may come to him."

The races are mixed in Wolseley, and the cross accounts for the curiously varied traits which his character discloses. His family is a cadet branch of the old Staffordshire Wolseleys, who still hold their property in the Midlands and who are Anglo-Saxon. The branch from which he springs has been domiciled in Ireland from the time of William III., and intermarriages with Hibernian families have brought it about that quite half the blood in Lord Wolseley's veins is Celtic blood. It is from that he gets his audacity, his *élan*, his buoyancy, his debonair aplomb, his strain of mostly well-timed recklessness, his alert dexterity, his *finesse*, the adroit suppleness which occasionally astonishes his friends, his warmth of heart. The Saxon blood in him gives him his steadfast constancy under conditions however depressing, his solid strength to hold his own against hostile intrigues, his calm manliness, his almost unparalleled equanimity, his cool steady rancour against those who have done him despite, his unfaltering fidelity in friendships. Wolseley is a man who must have risen, no matter what avocation he had chosen to pursue. That from boyhood he had a special predilection for the military profession is true; it does not conclusively follow from this that he has a special genius for war. So far as his career has revealed itself he makes war well, just as he would have done well any other duty that might have fallen to his lot; simply as he would have gained a reputation for success in delicate missions if he had been a diplomat, or attained to the position of a director of the Bank of England had he been a merchant. If he had been a boot-black he would have started a "Boot-polishing Company, Limited," with himself as managing director; if he had gone into patent medicines he would have out-advertised Professor Holloway, and secured the testimony not of an Arab sheik but of an emperor, in favour of the efficacy of his pills. No adverse conditions could have held Wolseley down; no native obscurity could have kept him mute, inglorious. And it may be added that he could have touched nothing which he would not have adorned.

THE AMERICAN GENTLEMAN
WITH THE MOIST EYE.

HE was a tall lean square-shouldered man, whose rather fine head had a plaintive droop on the chest, as he sat there wrapped in abstraction. There was a fresh colour on his long yet square-chinned face, the expression of the lower part of which was that of alert resolution; but in the high narrow brow, hollow at the temples, and in the full blue eyes suffused with moisture, over which fell the shadow of the long brown eyelashes, there was a suggestion of emotional dreaminess. I remember how, as I looked at him, there recurred to me the memory of some of Bret Harte's characters—" Kentuck " for instance, or " Tennessee's Partner." The face as a whole expressed manliness, quaintness, humour, and sensibility.

My own seat at table in the saloon of the good steamer *Tasmanian*, of the Northern and Southern Hemispheres Connecting Link Line, one day out from her Australian port of departure, was at a side table near the door; but as dinner was being finished, I moved to one of the central tables, for a chat with a friend and his wife. It was opposite to the latter where was seated the tall lean man with the drooping head and the moist eye.

I noticed that he raised his head and glanced somewhat shyly, as it seemed, across the table at the lady. She had whispered to me that the face had interest for her, and I suppose the glance revealed to him some expression of that, and perhaps also some suggestiveness of sympathy. He looked across once or twice more, just sweeping us men with that slow limpid glance ; and at length, after a preliminary cough or two, he nervously addressed the lady. After the little stammer over the first word he was fluent enough, although very deliberate, as is the manner of Western men.

"M-madam," said he, "I guess when you look across the table you see a mighty soft fool. Yes, madam" (reflectively). "I left 'Frisco in the last outgoing steamer, proposing to make a six months' tower in Australia for behoof of my health ; I hed been sick with dyspepsy. Well, I hed gotten down there to Sydney ; and I admired to see what a fine location it hed gotten ; and concluded to strike inland after spending a day in taking in the city. But that same night, madam, as I lay in my lone bed down in that there city, I fell athinking on my little wife to home up in 'Frisco. My heart began for to yurn on the poor woman, as hed been left lonely for the first time sin I took her from her mother seven years back. 'Guess you'll start out a laughin' right in my face when I tell you as I never slep'd a wink of sleep for longing to be consoling her and remorse for having quit her. Bright and airly next morning, madam, this 'ere great soft galoot was in the steamboat office, buying a ticket home to the little woman by the next steamer. My Australian tower was through in six days, madam, and the outside edge of it was Paramatta, fourteen miles inland from Sydney. I don't mind yer laughin' at me, strangers, ef yer so minded ;—I spend the balance of the time when I'm not thinkin' about her, softly cussin' myself for the darnedest fizzle as ever left the port of San Francisco. But I don't go back on it—not a nickel ; no, sir " (fixing me rather with that wonderfully eloquent blue eye), "no, sir, I don't weaken on it, not one continental. Fac" (with a little burst of shy radiance that somehow reminded me of a rainbow), " I'm kinder proud on it!"

Then his eyelids fell, the head went down on the breast, and he slid into a reverie, the wistful sweetness of which was to be discovered in the face. Our lady murmured a few words of interest and sympathy —a little incoherent perhaps, and sadly conventional, for she is a timid little woman who does not quite know what to do with herself when moved. But the moist-eyed man seemingly neither heard nor heeded. Her husband, a blunt colonist, threw out a vaguely malicious hint that the little woman in 'Frisco might not welcome with exuberant rapture this precipitate and premature return of her lord, who indeed might find her very much not at home (the gentleman is of Irish extraction). But as little did our *vis-à-vis* heed the jibe. He sat the very presentment of happy abstraction.

The man interested me, and I did not lose him in the general ruck of passengers. Later the same evening he gave me a surprise. I found him in the smoking-room, a glass of grog on the table in front of him, a little circle of eager disputants around him; he himself voluble, argumentative, and indeed vociferous. He was on politics—American politics. A Republican of course, to the core of the marrow. Yes, he had been an office-holder, he had held a position in the San Francisco customs during Garfield's administration, and had gotten "fired out" when Arthur's Presidency had given the call to the Stalwarts. But this was a mere incident. What he wanted to discuss were general principles. To believe for a moment, forsooth, that the democratic ticket would carry the next presidential election! Why, he'd take the stump himself to bust the head of that bar'l in! He'd been on the stump before—and so on *usque ad nauseam*. He was constituting himself a nuisance, especially to the British and Australian section of the smoking-room, which numerically was greatly in the ascendant; and so we hooted him down with threats that he would be turned out if he didn't quit "those confounded American politics."

He subsided, and drank his grog in silence thenceforth. I noticed a little Chicago drummer with a yellow moustache, deliberately "taking in" the gentleman with the moist eye—it was moister now, as the two sat confronting each other, and at length the drummer moved across and took a place next to my uxorious friend. The drummer recommenced politics in a low tone, praising the other highly for his principles and the eloquence with which he had supported them. He backed his profuse flattery—a Chicago drummer always works with a trowel—by having the other's glass replenished. The moist eye grew yet more moist, its owner seemed to beam; and at this crisis the drummer by an easy divergence abandoned the topic of politics, and significantly observed that he had noticed his friend had spoken of having been an officer in the San Francisco customs. A nod was the response. Then the drummer's voice waned lower, and I caught but occasional words, such as "dutiable articles," and a mysterious phrase which I may have overheard erroneously, but which sounded like "twirling the elephant's tail."

For several days, except at meal times, I saw nothing of the moist-eyed gentleman; but once, when I was looking down through a grating into the baggage-room, I noticed him pottering around in a curiously leisurely fashion among the trunks. If I gave the matter a thought at all, I have no doubt I believed him, in his own deliberate sentementous way, engaged in searching for his own baggage.

One evening in the smoking-room, our friend, who, since his previous discouragement in that peculiarly frank-spoken Tabaks-Parlement, had been very quiet and retiring, broke out again into eloquence. This time he lifted up his voice to pronounce a glowing eulogium on the British nationality. He avowed himself born a Welshman, and, although expatriated in tender years and admitted to American citizenship as soon as he had attained the statutory age, he was not the man, like Stanley, to deny the land of his nativity. I own that I found a difficulty in reconciling this claim to Welsh extraction with a statement he had made in the course of his confidences to "Madam," to the effect that he had been "born and raised in Keokuk, Iowa," but these little discrepancies, I was duly sensible, may occur in autobioloquial observations without seriously affecting the veracity of the average human animal. The eloquence of the moist-eyed man, if diffuse, was decidedly stimulating, and stirred the enthusiasm of the Britons and Australians. They are jocund friendly creatures in the smoking-room after the steward has answered the bell a few times; and at the close of a cheer for Queen Victoria, in which the Americans joined with a "tiger," an Australian jeweller, kindled into hospitality by his loyalty, called for champagne round. The champagne inspired quite a spasm of international *rapprochement*. Patriotic songs set in— "Britannia rules the wave"—most of the Britons had been deadly sick for the first two days, "Hail Columbia," "The Red, White, and Blue," "The Star-Spangled Banner." The attempt at "Yankee

Doodle" was scarcely a flowing triumph, since no one present appeared to know any words to that air which complied with the requirements of the strict propriety always maintained in the smoking-room of an ocean steamer, as indeed in every part of such a vessel; and the impromptu concert fitly concluded with "God save the Queen." Presently the smoking-room thinned. The American gentleman with the moist eye remained, leaning back in seeming slumber, the Australian jeweller was still on hand, fidgeting about as if there were something on his mind; I sat smoking silently in my own dark corner. Presently the jeweller awoke the American with a touch on the shoulder, and sat down beside him. The cautious Australian murmured some words of which I caught "false bottom"—"are they very sharp?" The American spoke out like a man. "Guess I know some of the boys—see you right though, partner!" and then followed hot toddy.

Two days after this episode the unusual spectacle was afforded of the moist-eyed man having afternoon tea *tête-à-tête* with a lady in the most retired corner of the great saloon. "Madam" and I had both disseminated the quaint tale we had been told at the beginning of the voyage, and the big blue-eyed man with the far-off expression so often on his face was regarded with no little kindly interest. Then it became pretty well known that he had been in the 'Frisco customs employ, and that he was a civil, pleasant-natured, softish sort of fellow generally.

His entertainer at the four o'clock tea refection was a gaunt, withered, little grig of a Scoto-New-Zealand woman, who called herself Mrs. Lorne, and professed to be a widow, both of which pretensions were considerably inaccurate. She had "corralled" the moist-eyed man on the subject of her baggage, about which, ever since she joined the ship at Auckland, she had been betraying nervousness among her intimates. At least I gathered this had been her little game from the frank hearty remark the moist-eyed man made as he stood up from the tea-table. "Don't ye skear worth a cent, madam, don't ye. Colonel O'Driscol, the boss on the jetty, is an old-time crony of mine. I'll say one word to the colonel, and you're through as slick as an eel!" whereat the bogus-widow Lorne blushed and looked half pleased, half confused.

Among the passengers who joined the *Tasmanian* at Auckland was a droll little American from Fiji, a hard-bitten beachcomber style of old reprobate, with a keen zest for liquor. The old fellow professed lightness of purse, and arranged with the people of the ship that he should occupy one of the state-rooms in the "second cabin" department, which was quite empty, having the run of the first-class saloon for his rations. "Fiji" had a good thing of it with that six-berthed state-room all to himself; and he improved his opportunity by having all his baggage, of which he had no inconsiderable quantity and some of which looked suspiciously unlike "personal effects," stowed in the state-room to keep him company. From his first day he went at the drink, but, even in an advanced state of cocktail, the queer gnarled old stick maintained a curiously saturnine demeanour. The American gentleman with the moist eye drank with him industriously, standing treat with quite a reckless freehandedness, and getting, to all appearance, himself into a more mixed temperament than "Fiji" ever exhibited. But the American gentleman had a marvellous faculty of swift self-recuperation. I spoke to him once or twice when he seemed very far gone; he drew a long breath, shook himself, looked at me out of those wonderful blue eyes, whose limpidness no alcohol seemed to affect, with the original quaint contemplative gaze, and replied with deliberate coherency. And, stranger still, no sooner had we parted than he had visibly lapsed again into hiccoughs, incoherency, and other ugly testimonials to insobriety. One afternoon, while both the gentlemen were liquoring up as usual, the moist-eyed man complained vehemently to the assistant purser of the heat of his berth, which it seemed was adjacent to the engines. He explained in proof of this complaint that he always kept a bottle of grog on tap in his state-room for his friends, who, when they came down to partake of a convivial glass with him, growled because the liquor he gave them was lukewarm. "Why don't you come aft my way?" cried "Fiji," with a hiccough, and on this genial hint, which probably had been drawn from "Fiji" by the mention of the moist-eyed gentleman's facilities for refreshment, the latter effected a transfer of residence. I am bound to say that this added propinquity did not seem to inspire in the room-mates any practical admiration for total abstinence. One night "Fiji" evacuated the smoking-room more than commonly disguised. Next morning I overheard him fulminating at his steward for not having secured his baggage by lashing it. The trunks, he said, had gone adrift during the night because of the roll of the ship; which struck me as strange, for she had not been rolling more than her somewhat emphatic wont. He grumbled consumedly that the wax on the seal of a special little trunk had got smashed in the fall. "I sleep like a dead whale," he grunted across to the moist-eyed gentleman, who had begun to sputter and yawn in his bunk over the way; "but darn it, I wonder the muss among the baggage didn't rouse you up!"

"Boss," replied the moist-eyed one genially, "I guess I sleep like a dead whale as has been resurrected, got tired o' the bother of keepin' alive, and gone dead again for good!"

"Great Scott!" exclaimed "Fiji," as he scrambled for his raiment, "seems to me that defunct insec' has been gaily friskin' around my pants. They're right out from under the pillow where I stowed 'em last night, an' dog-goned ef my keys ain't loose in the spitbox!"

"Blow your pants!" retorted the moist-eyed gentleman, "don't you feel like washin' down them 'ere cinders a' stickin' in your ventilator?" and with that he passed over the grog-bottle.

The pair continued inebriate, and at length their names were given to the bar-tender, a measure which stopped the supplies. I heard the moist-eyed gentleman, one evening, complaining touchingly of thirst to a little American Jew-with-a-dash-of-the-Cockney, who was one of the passengers, and who was travelling up from Australia professedly in the buggy interest. The Jew volunteered to procure drink if the moist-eyed man was ready with the compensation. The latter, I noticed, got strangely soon affected. I supposed that the old debauch was not yet quite dead in him. It was then that the little Jew, taking him aside, imparted to him a secret, which I overheard. The Hebraic worthy had two trunks stuffed with "dutiable goods," on which he was most anxious to make no contribution to Uncle Sam's revenues. Far gone as he was, the moist-eyed man was promptly equal to the occasion. "Ask for Colonel O'Driscol on the jetty, an' *square him*. I know he can be got at. Besht thing, before you come ashore yourself, send on to the wharf a little note addressed to the colonel, with twenty-five dollars an' your card enclosed; and then strike him as soon as you land. You'll find him hunky, you bet. That'll pass you along as easy's slipping off a log. Only, never give a soul a hint I gave you the inside track!" "All right, pardner," was the philosophic comment of the astute Hebrew,"guess the lot on you roosters understand each other, kinder—eh?" The moist-eyed man winked and hiccoughed, and Mr. Moses retired to rest in the pleasing consciousness of not having wholly wasted his friendly offices in circumventing the bar-tender.

At Honolulu the *Tasmanian* embarked a large draft of passengers for San Francisco—rather a mixed lot. A large number of these had to take their meals in the empty second saloon, the table seats in the chief saloon being all previously occupied. Two nights after leaving Honolulu, while dinner was being served in the latter apartment, the gentleman with the moist eye compromised himself by a miscellaneous resort to strong expressions uttered by no means in a subdued key; and was summarily ejected by the chief steward, who characterised him in allegorical language as having been "as full of drink as the Baltic Sea." At the subsequent court-martial in the captain's cabin he received the mild sentence of modified ostracism to the second saloon, where there were neither ladies nor a bishop, and whose denizens were not nasty particular over a little mild cursing, so long as the gentleman displaying this weakness was not backward in desiring to ascertain practically the form of poison held in highest esteem by his convives. If he committed himself beyond bearing in this society, however, added the captain, with a sternness that struck me as being a little forced, he was to be relegated to the outer darkness of the steerage. There was much good fellowship in the second saloon, where the moist-eyed man speedily found marked favour ; and sooner or later, as I noted during occasional visits to that bower of jollity, most of the Honolulu folks had whispered confidences of an apparently satisfactory nature with him, in regard to the idiosyncrasy of the customs inquisitors on the San Francisco quay. These confidences had a uniform sequel in the shape of copious libations, not at the expense of the moist-eyed gentleman.

For myself, I observed with unfeigned sorrow and no little amaze all those evidences of a fallen nature on the part of a man by whose simple and touching manifestation of a purer and better spirit I had been so much touched at the outset of the voyage. But as I grieved because of the feet, or rather stomach of clay, and very porous clay at that, which disfigured the golden head, I found one consolation, in that I recognised this man with the moist eye as a type. He became to me more and more identified with the Bret Harte character—this Pacific slope man with the chronic crave to see them " put up," with the callous disregard of high principle, with the propensity to grisly oaths ; and yet withal, with the strange holy streak of exquisite genuine tenderness. At the end of the voyage I thought him more like " Kentuck" than I had done at the beginning.

As the *Tasmanian* steamed by Alcatraz Island it was an open secret among a good many of the passengers that the moist-eyed gentleman was to scramble on to the wharf by the first cable, and give a quiet significant intimation to "Colonel O'Driscol" and the "boys," that in certain specific instances a perfunctory inspection would be highly appreciated and not be quite barren of complimentary recognition. As he stood in readiness for the acrobatic feat, I noticed his vest pocket considerably bulged by quite a little packet of letters, which I had reason to believe all bore a superscription to "Colonel O'Driscol." The moment came, and we saw him slip off the cat-head down the hawser on to the jetty with an agility which was much admired by all spectators ; some believing that he was thus urgent that he might clasp to his bosom the little wife to whom he had hurried back, others commending his alertness to execute the genial and delicate commissions he had undertaken. He disappeared into the interior of the shed, and we saw him no more.

Half an hour elapsed before the gang-plank was practicable, and then the passengers streamed down into the shed. The baggage began to be rapidly debarked. I happened to be near the little American Jew-with-a-dash-of-the-Cockney. He asked a Customs officer where he should find "Colonel O'Driscol." "Yonder he is !" replied the man steadily, pointing to a tall man with a gold-lace cap, who was standing behind an enclosed desk with his back to us, busied with some papers on a nail on the wall. The Jew approached and touched the tall man on the elbow.

"Colonel O'Driscol, sir!" he uttered in a confident tone.

The colonel remained engrossed among his documents.

"Colonel O'Driscol, sir!" repeated the Jew in a tone that had a little ring of perhaps not unjustifiable peremptoriness.

"At your service, sir!" said the colonel, as he turned sharply round; and from under the visor of the gold-lace cap there beamed upon the Jew from under their long brown lashes a pair of moist blue eyes. The Jew gave one gulp of wild astonishment, then staggered back, and sat down in silence on the floor of the shed. He was too much discomfited even to swear.

Very few witnessed this little scene, most people being engrossed in the work of getting their baggage together. The colonel sat down and bent his head over his desk. Presently little Mrs. Lorne came jauntily sailing up to the desk.

"Colonel O'Driscol!" she sweetly said.

"At your service, madam!" replied the colonel, raising his head.

Mrs. Lorne gave a little shriek; but she was a woman, and a woman is always nimbler in a tight place than a man. She rallied with surprising quickness, and spoke with low emphasis.

"Colonel," said she, "there is a lady in the case, and I know that you are a gentleman!'

"Yes, madam," responded the colonel with a

gallant bow, "and I don't go back on my word—to a lady"—the last three words with a curious deliberate intonation. "Here, officer, just open this lady's grip-sack, and then chalk her baggage, and call a porter for her. Good morning, Mrs. Lorne!" concluded the gallant officer with ineffable sweetness and grace.

Mrs. Lorne didn't hang around much. The same afternoon I noticed the American Jew and the Australian jeweller, each tramping around the city in the close society of a gentleman in uniform. It appeared they were looking for bail, in default of which they would have to "go across the bay." "Fiji," in blank despair of bail, had gone to the cells direct from the quay, where, according to rueful testimony, trouble did not cease until nightfall.

There had been a good deal of smuggling into 'Frisco by the steamers of the Hemisphere Line, and a smart officer had been sent out to the Antipodes to "shadow" a cargo of passengers. The colonel's tender story about the little wife was a pretty invention to avert any suspicion that might have attached to a man who went out in one steamer going back in the next. The captain was in the secret. I subsequently heard O'Driscol was a very temperate man. I think he ought to have been an actor.

INTERVIEWED BY AN EMPEROR.

THIS is the age of interviewing. Monarchs have no immunity from the irrepressible gentleman with a note of interrogation between his teeth, and his open tablets in the palm of his hand. The Emperor of the Brazils was put through the interview-mill extensively during his stay in Paris. The Shah of Persia in vain tried to evade the ordeal, and King Tawhiao was paraphrased by the flowery young man from the *Pall Mall Gazette*. M. de Blowitz "cornered" the Sultan in the interests of the great journal, and as he told the tale, must rather have disquieted the successor of the Prophet. During my term of active service as a journalist—I am now in the Chelsea Hospital of that craft—I never interviewed an emperor, or even tried to—since in my time this business had not yet been imported into British journalism. I am mournfully conscious now that I missed great opportunities. But for feebleness of initiative I might have gone down in history as among the pioneers of the science of interviewing. I have seen two emperors under fire, and was the witness of the surrender of a third as a prisoner of war. Why, oh why, did I refrain from confronting Kaiser Wilhelm as he stood by the churchyard wall on the day of Gravelotte, and insisting on knowing his emotions as the French shell burst among the ranks of his soldiers on the field at the gable of the auberge? When the late Czar stood with folded arms and drooped head on the gallery of that "observatory" in the tent behind which his staff were lunching, while Turkish shells from the Gravitza redoubt were crashing among huddled masses in the hollow in front of him, what an effect was missed when absurd scruples of decency restrained me from challenging him to express his sentiments on the situation! I am a prey now to remorse because, when I was at Sandringham during the Prince of Wales' illness, I did not insist on penetrating into the sick-room and, on being allowed to watch for an interval of consciousness, to exact from his Royal Highness his opinion as to the efficacy of the hop pillow. I blush now for my culpably scrupulous colleagues who were in St. Petersburg when the late emperor was assassinated, that no one of them had the "enterprise"—that is the word—to get at the expiring monarch and obtain his moribund impressions on the subject of explosive bombs. Were I in the trade now, no absurd regard for self-respect would deter me from making and improving opportunities for the gratification of the natural and proper curiosity of my circle of readers. But alas, I belonged to the dark, decent ages. I never interviewed anybody, except

Sir Samuel Baker and a shipwrecked mariner who had strange notions on the subject of cannibalism. It was the other way about with me—it befell me once to be interviewed myself, and that by no less a person than the great White Czar himself.

It was in the summer of the Russo-Turkish war. Bulgaria swarmed with the soldiers of Muscovy; big, flat-faced, broad-shouldered fellows, with high cheekbones, small fishy light-blue eyes, and hair like tow; and swarthy little Cossacks from the Caucasus, with Arab profiles, deep-sunk dark eyes, and a set propensity to kill and spare not. Events had not gone prosperously for the worthy unselfish crusaders who had marched so many dreary versts on the emprise to emancipate from the "unspeakable Turk," the infinitely more unspeakable Bulgarian. The campaign up to the arrival of Todleben in front of Plevna after the terrible mischance of September is fraught with a curious usefulness for the military student. The more closely he investigates its details, the more lessons will he learn what to avoid. The story thus far contains but three creditable pieces of work—the crossing of the Danube on the part of the Russians, Skobeleff's capture of Loftcha, and Osman Pasha's prompt entrenchment of the invaluable position into which he had casually drifted at Plevna. Gourko's early raid across the Balkans had been spiritedly conducted, but the outcome of it as an operation had been worse than useless. A golden key is a weapon not strictly of a military pattern, yet greatly affected by the Russians in war-time; it has its merits, but there is always a risk that after all it will not turn in the lock, and when this happens the consequences are serious. It is all the more aggravating when the mischance is brought about by the sheer folly of one who might have been trusted, surely, not to spoil a delicate combination by indiscreet disclosures. The Russian army of the Lom in the end of July was echeloned along the road to Rustchuk, waiting for the word to surround that fortress. It had not an entrenching tool, nor a siege gun; but the place of every division had been allotted to it in the planned environment that was to precede but by a day or two an effort to carry the place by a *coup de main*. On the morning fixed for the commencement of the movement, it was abruptly countermanded. The golden key had stuck in the lock. The Turkish Commander of Rustchuk had been bought; the *coup de main* was simply to have been a decorous if somewhat sanguinary blind to his treachery. After a respectable slaughter the place that, resolutely held, only a long regular siege could have reduced, and that subsequently mocked Todleben's efforts, was to be surrendered, with, as the result, an unspeakable relief to the Russian left flank. But when everything had been settled and the little arrangement was on the eve of execution—there is some evidence indeed that the Rustchuk Pasha had been paid the price of his treachery—there came a sudden miscarriage. A high official, away in the Imperial headquarter, had been so complacent over his diplomatic cleverness, that he had incautiously let fall some hints of what that policy was about to result in. Turkey had unofficial friends even in the Czar's headquarter camp, and a courier to the Hungarian frontier sent a swift warning telegram to Vienna. From Vienna the Seraskerait were significantly notified, and for once acted promptly. The Rustchuk Pasha was summarily superseded; a new man succeeded him who was not to be bribed; and this news reaching the Grand Duke Nicholas' headquarter was the cause of that sudden order which gave pause to the army of the Caesarewitch on the very morning on which its movement was to have commenced. Henceforward for many weeks that army was condemned to lie in enforced inactivity among the pleasant villages beyond the Jantra. Nor had the Russians better fortune on their other flank. Schahovskoy and Krüdener, after a long and desperate struggle, had been hurled backward from Osman's earthworks on the eastern face of that gallant soldier's Plevna position, and had left the maize-fields strewn with the corpses of valiant men who had known as little how to advance dexterously as how to retreat when all hope of success had died away. Gourko had come back from his abortive raid across the Balkans, and had gone to Russia to bring up the guard cavalry. The whole Russian advance, paralysed by Osman Pasha looming dangerously there on the right flank at Plevna, was in a condition of arrestment until the reinforcements, that had been hastily summoned from every province of the great Empire, should cross the Danube and fall in to strengthen the thinned ranks. Everywhere depression prevailed throughout the hosts of the Czar. It was strange to the foreigner with what vigorous freedom officers and men alike allowed themselves to comment on the blundering that had brought a great and brave army to this ignoble pass. Stranger still were the outspoken criticisms of superior officers—even of those who, being on staff-service in one or other of the headquarters, might have been expected to preserve a discreet reticence.

It was an especially sombre time—this period of inaction—in the headquarter of his Majesty the Emperor. He himself, worn by anxiety, wrung by disaster after disaster, was out of health. There was friction between his headquarter, lying there in the hot hill-slope over against the Bulgarian village of Gorni Studen, and the headquarter of his brother the Grand Duke Nicholas, the commander-in-chief, whose tents encircled a farmyard on the edge of the village. No wonder that relations should have been strained. Nicholas had nominally the supreme command; he and his subordinates Niepokoitschitsky and Levitzki, were responsible to Russia and to the military world for the strategy of the campaign. The Russian emperor in theory was but a simple spectator, whose presence in the field was to stimulate the enthusiasm of the soldiery, and keep warm Russia's fervour for the war. But it could not be that the head of the State in the field with his army was to retain, even nominally, this irresponsible relation to it and to events influencing its fortunes. Bluff Nicholas on the top of his hill would freely damn that inconvenient encampment over the way; while some of the light-hearted young people in the over-the-way camp made no concealment of their belief that Niepokoitschitsky was an obsolete old ass, and Levitzki an abstruse theoretic incapable.

On those rival headquarters, already tormented by mutual jealousies and full of concern for the precarious position of an army whose position was so vicious with both its flanks in chronic danger, a new and terrible anxiety was to fall. So long as the Russians could cling on to that crest-line of the Schipka which had been so gallantly won by Skobeleff and Gourko, they held the key to that Roumelia which lies south of the Balkans, and might stretch the hand yet further, across its rose-valleys and fertile slopes, to where the Bosphorus washes the city that has been Russia's goal for many generations. The Schipka position lost to them, they were definitely confined inside the limits of Northern Bulgaria, and would have to fight hard to recover the lost command of the Balkans. Yet with that shiftlessness which was the characteristic of the Russian military dispositions in the earlier months of the campaign, the all-important position on the Schipka Pass had been allowed to remain very weakly held, and quite without adequate support. Of its defenders portions had indeed from time to time been withdrawn for one or the other purpose, until about the middle of August the lines of St. Nicholas and the other fortifications comprising the defensive position on the saddle of the Schipka Pass, remained defended by but some twenty weak companies of infantry under the command of General Stolietoff, a large proportion of which force consisted of Bulgarian legionaries, of whose character under the strain of hard fighting the estimate was not high. In the Russian headquarter it was known that Suleiman Pasha was on the march northward from Adrianople at the head of some forty battalions of excellent troops withdrawn from the Montenegrin frontier, but the belief was persisted in that Suleiman's object was to reinforce or co-operate with Mehemet Ali against the Russian left flank in the Lom country ; and not even an attempt he made to force the Hankoi Pass occasioned any apprehension that his objective might be an attempt to recover the Schipka. At length, in the third week of August, suspicions of his design began to penetrate the stolid intelligence of the headquarter ; and tardy dispositions were made for strengthening the feeble force holding the all-important position. But these could not take that immediate effect the emergency so urgently demanded. In the hand-to-mouth fashion of dealing with difficulties as they cropped up, the commands had been quite dislocated, and battalions and brigades of different corps jumbled together in the most chaotic way. The troops that should have stood at Drenova and Gabrova to support the actual garrison of the Schipka had been withdrawn and scattered; a brigade out to Elena on the eastern side of Tirnova to patch a hole there; another away south to Selvi to confront threatening Turks from the Loftcha quarter; a great detachment drawn in around Tirnova to be in the hand lest trouble should come from the Hankoi direction. So when, on the 21st of August, Suleiman's Turks came swarming out of the valley and surged up the steep slope on the crest of which stood Stolietoff's scant array, the succours were far off for which that gallant chief, careless of himself, was urgent, because of his realisation of the importance of the position the guardian and defender of which he was with so inadequate a force to do his bidding.

I had been reconnoitring about the Plevna forepost line trying to form some before-hand estimate of the chances for that renewed assault which was expected to be made before the end of the month. As on the morning of the 22d August I rode into the Imperial headquarter at Gorni Studen, gloomy faces met me on every hand. The news had come that Stolietoff had been attacked in force on the Schipka position on the previous morning, and that with his scanty force he could not prevent the Turks from pressing round his flanks with the obvious intent to cut him off. His prayer for assistance had come, but it would be almost too good a result to hope for that he could hold out till the succours, march they ever so hard, could reach him. The Czar was walking up and down that private walk of his in the little garden at the back of his quarters, his head drooping on his breast, his shoulders bent, his whole attitude eloquent of discouragement. Ignatieff even was grave and curt of speech as he outlined for me the situation in his tent under the mulberry tree, and the accustomed frank buoyancy of Adlerberg was quenched in the gloom of the situation. I waited only until my horses had eaten and rested, and ere midnight I was riding up the steep ascent into the rock-perched town of Tirnova. By sunrise on the following morning I was on the road that leads from Tirnova to the foot of the Schipka.

As I rode onward up the lovely valley, through the thick woods whose dense foliage shaded from the blistering sunrays, by wimpling streams on which were gurgling millraces, by fountains bubbling from out hoary walls, and through vineyards where the heavy masses of dark green foliage but half hid the pale green clusters of grapes just beginning to soften into ripeness—the whole line of road from Drenova to Gabrova was a mass of infantry and artillery marching forward in urgent haste. As we neared the latter place, which lies bosomed in a deep river-gorge at the foot of the steepsided mountain which is called the Schipka Pass, the sound of the near cannonade filled the glen as if it had been not a mere sound borne downward on the wind, but was actual solid substance. In the quaint tortuous streets over whose rugged pavement hung the projecting timber-fronted houses, the people were clustered under the pale moonlight in anxious, silent groups, through which ran a visible shudder as a louder crash accentuated the dull ominous roar. For miles beyond Gabrova the valley we had traversed was cumbered with the scattered bivouacs of the miserable fugitives who had fled across the mountain chain from out the path of the fell Suleiman, as his ruthless Bashi-Bazouks had come surging up through the fair and fertile rose-gardens that sweeten with their fragrance the picturesque plain which skirts the southern fringes of the Balkans. Scared women huddled under the trees, praying aloud that the good God would strengthen the arms of the soldiers who tramped by them hurrying on to reach the scene of strife. The poor creatures might well pray. For between those helpless, cowering fugitives—between the pale townsfolk of Gabrova and utter and ruthless destruction, there intervened but that comparative handful of Christian fighting men, clinging desperately to the rocks up there on the sky line within actual view. It had been in the very nick of time on that afternoon when all hope was withering from the breasts of Stolietoff and Derozinski—when they had telegraphed to the Czar a message of loyal devotion and farewell—that General Radetski had come clambering up to their succour at the head of a battalion of riflemen mounted on Cossack ponies for the greater expedition. But the crisis was scarcely the less intense for this scant reinforcement. If Radetski could not hold his own in that eyrie till Dragomiroff's division, which I had overtaken in the valley, should struggle up to where he and his valiant comrades were confronting the fierce Turkish assaults, not Tirnova itself, forty miles in the rear, was safe for four and twenty hours.

When the ideal war correspondent shall manifest himself to an admiring world, among his attributes will be found the ability to do without sleep altogether. But that great creature's less gifted precursors cannot afford to fly wantonly in the face of nature. They must sleep, and he is the wisest man who knows how to sleep strategically. What avails it a man that he should have kept awake for a week watching events, when nature peremptorily refuses to be denied just at the moment when it is urgent that he should be riding at best pace, or writing as swiftly as his pen will travel? The war correspondent is a failure who only sees battles; the complement of the reason of his being is that he shall describe what he has seen, and get that description printed in his newspaper with the least possible delay. To accomplish this when the conditions are arduous, it is imperative that he should economise his powers to the best of his ability: however thrifty he may be with them, he will find himself an old man while yet middle-aged. He must risk something to gain that modicum of rest and sleep which will enable him to endure strain and keep awake when the call comes for him to put forth every exertion of which he is capable, if he would succeed in accomplishing the great *coup* for the achievement of which the ambitious war correspondent lives his professional life. In my first campaign I should have been physically incapable of falling asleep while those gusts of firing came borne on the wind, as they soughed down through the trees on the foothills. I could not have stopped to eat or drink in Gabrova, but would have been climbing in the moonlight to reach the side of stout old Radetski. But experience had brought some discernment, and I knew the Turks had little ardour in night attack. So my comrade and myself snatched a few hours' sleep in Gabrova, and ere the summer sun had risen we had ridden up the narrowing glen of the Jantra, and were climbing the steep ascent of the Pass itself. Already the fighting, in which there had been a lull during the small hours, was recommencing with eager virulence. The Russians were firm on the central "saddle" of the Pass, where were the lines of the fortifications, such as these were; but the Turks were masters of the parallel ridges on either flank, and what they were vehemently striving for was to join hands in the rear of the Russian position, and so surround and isolate it and its defenders. Over and over again they had been all but successful; and meanwhile, on their bare exposed ridge between the two fires, the Russians, all but wholly destitute of cover, were falling fast. Some of them had been in the struggle for three long hot days of incessant fighting, and were quite beaten out with fatigue, heat, hunger, and thirst ; for there was no water in the position, and the company cooks had been shot down while they tried to boil the soup-kettles.

I am not going to describe here this long summer day's desperate fighting. Suffice it that as the shadows of the evening were falling on the blood-splashed rocks and on the scattered dead that lay about among the boulders, the Russians had succeeded in carrying at the bayonet-point one of the two flanking positions whence the Turks had been so mischievous. There had been ample work— perhaps one may say, too, ample risk—in trying to be of service to wounded men, for those who like Villiers and myself were not engaged in the grimmer task of fighting. We had helped to carry the wounded Dragomiroff behind a precarious shelter, and to bind up his shattered knee until he should reach surgical assistance when he had been carried through the fire to the dressing-place lower down— for the fine old chief would have no surgeon called away from his work there among the wounded soldiers. Radetski, grimed with sweat and dust, had come back from one of the attacks, and was leaning panting against a rock, a quiet smile on his grim, genial face. "It seems to me, general, as if you would be able to hold on now," I remarked to him, recognising how much more freely he breathed, now that at least the double lateral pressure had been relieved by the success of the attack to which the Jitomer regiment had followed the commander of an army corps. "With the help of God I will," was the reply. "So you are going, are you? Well, you can tell them what you have seen. And you will come back, say you? Please God"—and here he crossed himself—"you will find me here when you come back, dead or alive!"

I had known the stalwart old fighting chief ever since he had crossed the Pruth four months previously, and had discerned what a steadfast, earnest soldier he was. It had seemed to me that, although on the morrow, and for many morrows probably, there would be a renewal of stubborn fighting, yet that this day's gain would enable the Russians to keep hold of the Schipka position against all that Suleiman could do to dislodge them, assuming, as I had warrant for assuming, that the leader could lead, and that his men could fight. Pondering these things, I walked back to where my horse was fastened behind the picket-house wall, gave Villiers the crust of bread and the butt end of sausage that remained in my provision-holster, shook hands with the staunch comrade with whom before and since so many strange experiences have been shared; and then started on the long ride of 180 miles to Bucharest, on the other side of the Danube, the nearest point at which the telegraph-wire was available. A moment such as this was is the crisis of fate in a war correspondent's career. I had seen fought a desperate fight, and believed it won—not only the fight itself, but the issues turning upon the result of it. Then hey for the telegraph office with all speed! But, again, what if it were not won? What if the wish had been father to the thought, both with Radetski and myself? What if to-day's battle had been a drop in the bucket compared with the morrow's, which I should have lost by thus prematurely riding away? And not only lost that, but should have committed myself to the conviction which its result might falsify! Again, should I tarry, and there be no very serious work on the morrow, should I not have lost a precious day? For so kind had been fortune that of all the army of war correspondents pervading Bulgaria in those days, Villiers and I were there alone on that momentous day. But there were rivals and colleagues eager to act on Prince Frederick Charles' standing order of marching on the cannon thunder, and there were among these men whose ears were so keen that they heard the cannon thunder an amazingly long distance away. Never soldier or civilian rode harder or blither to where the bullets were flying than poor MacGahan, once his foot was in stirrup. America was on her mettle, and even a French correspondent had been seen outside a *café*, and with a saddle-horse tied by a halter behind his travelling carriage. As for the Russian correspondents, they positively revelled in getting wounded, and their great ambition was to smoke cigarettes with an air of easy unconcern in the heart of the very hottest fire they could conveniently find.

Well, there was no time for prolonged deliberation. I had seen what I had seen. I had drawn my conclusions as a man with something of a military eye, and possessed of some of that experience which enables its possessor to read a battle-field through the blurred fog of slaughter, confusion, and chaos. "Yes, I'll back myself. I have the feeling of being right"—I muttered to myself as I tightened the girths and mounted my horse for the long solitary night ride.

On such occasions a man never rides so fast as he had calculated on doing. I had laid out relays of horses on the way up: three between Gorni Studen and Gabrova, besides the one I had ridden up on to the Pass, which was a pony I had borrowed in Gabrova. I reckoned the distance from Gabrova to Gorni Studen to be about ninety miles; and at the latter place I had a fourth horse, which would carry me to the Danube, beyond which, in Roumania, there need be no more riding. But Roumanian and Bulgarian horse-tenders are perverse, and are hard to rouse; then a horse had to be fed ere he was fit for the road, or a shoe was loose and I had to drive in a nail to hold it in place. At the outset I had experienced hindrance, having been apprehended in Gabrova by a Russian picket commanded by a drunken corporal, who had some hazy idea that I might be a spy. He could not read, so my papers were of no service, and there was difficulty in finding an officer. A couple of roubles ultimately set me free, after having been kissed by the corporal and each individual of his little command. It was about eleven o'clock when at last I was able to ride out of Gabrova, after having eaten for the first time that day a crust of cheese and a morsel of black bread. Steadily through the soft beautiful night I rode, listening to the cool splash of the water over the millwheels, and breathing the scent of the balsam and the thyme from the cottage gardens, fringed by willows whose trailing tresses laved themselves in the stream. The sun rose on me long before I had reached Tirnova; and in fact it was not until noon was past, that, dead-tired and faint from want of food, I rode into the irregular square of tents which constituted the camp of the officers on the staff-service of his Majesty the Emperor. With none of these had I any concern, save with Colonel Wellesley, our military attaché, whose grooms were taking charge of the horse on which I was relying to carry me down to the Danube, and to whom it was my duty as a British subject to communicate the information of which I was the bearer.

Just as I rode into the square General Ignatieff came out of Prince Dolgorouki's tent, and met me full face.

"Ha, Mr. Forbes, where from now, you great galloper?" was the general's jovial greeting. I had gained some little reputation among the Russian headquarter people for hard riding when news had to be carried fast.

"From the Schipka," was my reply. "I saw a battle there all day yesterday, and left Radetski at eight last night."

"The deuce you did!" returned Ignatieff bluntly. "Why, we have no tidings so late. You have beaten all our orderlies! Come into my tent and tell me the story."

It meant delay, and delay was of all things just then what I could least afford, when I grudged every moment that kept me from the telegraph-wire. But I had been obliged to the general for many a kindness, and it would have been neither grateful nor seemly to have excused myself.

"And you think," was his comment, as I concluded a narrative which I made as short as I decently could—"you think that Radetski can hold on, that the Schipka is safe?"

"For what my conviction may be worth, general," was my response; "I prove it best in the fact that I am here. I shall commit myself to it in the telegram, to despatch which to the *Daily News* I am hurrying to Bucharest."

"Well, your belief is dead in the face of all our opinions here. You know your own business best. Pray heaven you may be right, and all our experts wrong!"

It was time for me to say a word to protect myself; it seemed from the general's tone as if there was a risk that I might be committed to a false position.

"Remember," said I, "you have asked me for my opinion, general. I did not bring it to you as a volunteer. Now that you have got it, I beg of you to take it simply for what it may be worth."

And with this I left General Ignatieff, and went across the square to Colonel Wellesley, to whom, while I was eating, and while his groom was getting my fresh horse ready, I gave a succinct summary of the situation according to my lights. But my conversation with our military attaché was abruptly interrupted.

"Hi! hi! Mr. Forbes! Where are you? I want you at once!" was the summons that presently reached me in General Ignatieff's strident tones. "Oh, come along! make no delay! I have related to the emperor the information you have given me, and he at once commanded me to go find you, make you his compliments, and express his desire that you will come and relieve his anxiety by telling him all you know."

This summons from the great White Czar himself was no doubt complimentary, but it was also embarrassing. I was in a great hurry, for the *Daily News* was more to me than were all the emperors of the habitable globe. And then the state I was in! I do not profess to have been brought up among emperors; but I may claim, nevertheless, the possession of some sense of decency, and I knew that a man ought to wait on an emperor in his Sunday clothes. I hadn't seen any Sunday clothes, or proper Sundays either, for three months; and I was conscious that my personal appearance was flagrantly disreputable. I had been wearing clothes, originally white, for over a fortnight, night and day. The black of my saddle had come off on to them with great liberality; and they were spotted down the front with poor Dragomiroff's blood, which had been trickling when we had helped to carry him out of the fire. I was all over about half an inch thick with dust, while the dust on my face was cheerfully relieved by fiery sun-blisters, and by a stubbly beard of about a week's growth. I had not washed for three days, and I altogether felt myself a humiliatingly dilapidated representative of that Great Empire on which the sun never sets. But Ignatieff was peremptory, and insisted that the emperor in the circumstances would by no means stand on ceremony. He told me that he had ventured to rouse his Imperial master from sleep to communicate to him the intelligence which I had brought; and he presently ushered me through the Cossack guard into the dingy alcove which was to form the hall of audience. The Imperial residence was a dismantled Turkish house, the balcony on the upper floor of which, where we found the emperor impatiently striding to and fro, was enclosed with curtains of plain canvas. There was not even a carpet on the rugged boards. A glimpse into the bedchamber, whence the emperor had emerged, showed me a tiny cabin with mud walls and a little camp bedstead standing on a mud floor.

The emperor, who was quite alone, received me with great courtesy, shaking hands, and paying me a compliment on the speed with which I had travelled. It was about the worst period of ill-fortune to the Russian arms, and the harassment of anxiety and mischance was plainly telling on his Majesty's physical condition. He carried himself with rounded shoulders; he was gaunt, worn, and haggard; his voice quivered with nervousness, and was fitfully interrupted by the asthma that affected him. A few months later, when Plevna had fallen, and that tardy success had revolutionised the situation, I saw his Majesty in St. Petersburg—a veritable emperor, upright of figure, proud of gait, arrayed in a splendid uniform, and his breast covered with decorations. A glittering court and suite thronged around the stately man with enthusiastically respectful homage. The dazzling splendour of the Winter Palace formed the setting of the sumptuous picture; and as I gazed on the magnificent scene I could hardly realise that the central figure of it, in the pomp of his Imperial state, was of a verity the self-same man in whose presence I had stood in the squalid Bulgarian hovel—the same worn, anxious, shabby, wistful man, who, with spasmodic utterance and the expression in his eye as of a hunted deer, had asked me breathless questions as to the episodes and issue of the fighting.

The Schipka Pass had been in Russian possession for quite a month, and it was not unreasonable to assume that a sketch of the position there was, as a matter of course, in the Imperial Cabinet. I asked for the plan, since with its help my task of explanation would be so greatly simplified. But it seemed that there was no such document; and I ventured to say that I could get along much more satisfactorily if I had a sheet of paper on which to jot down some rough explanatory outlines. The emperor said at once, "Ignatieff, go and fetch paper and pencil." Ignatieff went, and there remained the emperor and myself alone together, standing opposite to each other, with a little green baize table between us. The thought that drifted across my mind as we stood there looking into each others' faces was, that, emperor as he was, no consideration that the world could offer would tempt me to change places with a man so oppressed by ills. And I noticed, or thought that I noticed, what flicker of thought darted into a corner of his mind. As we so stood, he listening to me talking, there came into his face for a fleeting moment a strange, troubled expression, which seemed to reveal the sudden thought—"What a chance for this man to attempt my life!" It was a mere quick shadow, and had passed away ere Ignatieff came bustling back with a sheet of foolscap, on which I rapidly outlined the positions, explaining the details as I proceeded. It would be superfluous to recapitulate what was almost a purely technical conversation, which, interspersed by the emperor's eager questionings, lasted for about half an hour—considerably longer than pleased a man who was devoured by an eager anxiety to be hurrying along the road to Bucharest. Under any other circumstances there would have been no tediousness in the interview; for the emperor caught up every point with the alertness of a trained military intelligence. I believe that what I told him gave him some comfort. He expressed the same hesitation to accept my view of the situation as Ignatieff had manifested; although he had been eager enough to know what that opinion was.

"Mr. Forbes," said he—he spoke in English—"you have been a soldier?"

"Yes, your Majesty," was my reply.

"In the artillery or engineers, doubtless?"

"No sir," said I, "in the cavalry of the line."

The emperor said, "I had not known that your cavalry officers are for the most part conversant with military draughtsmanship?"

I replied that I had served the army not as an officer but as a private trooper; I know not whether thus conveying to his Majesty the impression that the honest British dragoon is habitually skilled in plan-making.

When at length I was permitted to take my leave, the emperor addressed to me some words which gave me a natural glow of great pleasure. As they had reference to certain conduct of my own, the reader will readily understand the delicacy and reluctance with which I allude to them; nor certainly would I cite them but that the expressions used by the emperor illustrate with what dignity and gracefulness he could acknowledge service that commended itself to the tender-heartedness he felt for his gallant soldiers. "Mr. Forbes," said the Czar, "I have had reported to me the example which you showed when with our forces on the sad day before Plevna, in succouring wounded men under heavy fire. As the head of the State I desire to testify how Russia honours your conduct by offering you the Order of the Stanislaus with the 'crossed swords,' a decoration never conferred except for personal bravery."

The emperor sent me across to the camp of his brother on the opposite hill, and the commander-in-chief detained me yet another hour, because of his anxiety to learn every detail in my power to communicate; but there was a recompense in the courtesy by which, recognising how worn I was, he spared me further riding by sending me down to the Danube in one of his own carriages. There followed quickly on my heels to Gorni Studen ominous news as to the condition of affairs in the Schipka, and indeed one afternoon the position was reported utterly lost. I was exposed to much perverse obloquy simply for having given my opinion when it was asked for. When on returning to the Imperial headquarter I called on Colonel Wellesley, that friendly countryman advised me to leave the camp at my early convenience, if I would avoid listening to angry reproaches. General Niepokoitschitsky, he added, had gone up into the Balkan country, on the errand of "taking up new positions in the rear of the Schipka"—and, added the colonel significantly—"you know what that means." The commander-in-chief, who had been bluffly gracious to me three days before, now cut me dead with an angry scowl, and Ignatieff was very much the reverse of cordial. Smarting under a sense of injustice I started the same afternoon to revisit the Schipka; for I had never faltered from my conviction in regard to it. Between Drenova and Gabrova I met General Niepokoitschitsky, on his return to headquarters from that position. He stopped me as I was passing him with a silent salute, for I was very sore with all Russian staff-officialism, and gave me pleasure by telling me that results had borne out my estimate of the situation; that the Schipka was perfectly safe, and that he would not fail to do me justice on his return to the headquarter. Six days after that evening when I had left Radetski among the carnage, I climbed once more the steep slope of the Schipka, to find the staunch old warrior serenely drinking tea on the summit. "I told you," was his greeting, "that with God's help I meant to remain here; and here I am, by His protection, alive and well. But we have been fighting ever since you left." And, indeed, the old man was drinking his tea under a dropping fire.

SOME ASPECTS OF AMERICAN SOCIETY.

I.

FORTY years ago there was scarcely any " society " in the United States, in the current conventional sense of the term. Boston had maintained its intellectual and cultured circle ever since the pre-revolution days. The " Knickerbockers," as the old Dutch families of what was once New Amsterdam had come to be called, kept up a rigorously exclusive cliquehood in New York, where Washington Square was then far " up town ; " and isolated detachments of Gentile brokers and merchants were making futile efforts to sap up to the knickerbocker entrenchments. Philadelphia had its brotherhood of quiet well-to-do religious folk, mostly of Quaker origin, although some had begun to fall away from that creed. Baltimore had its " first families " of the old cavalier blood, braced by some more recent intermarriages with British nobility, and yet further equivocally elevated by occasional alliance with an Imperial stock whose imperialism had been a thing of the past since the lightning bolt of Waterloo shattered it into fragments. In Virginia, with its headquarters at Richmond, there was a good deal of ancestral patricianhood; and Charleston, the capital of South Carolina, had its annual season, when the planters who traced back to good old houses of England, came in to their town-houses and associated at stately dinner-parties and well-ordered assembly balls with the newer English families who had made their homes in the beautiful city under whose shady esplanades the waters of the Ashley and the Cooper meet. New Orleans had its miscellaneous jumble of Creoles, families of the old Spanish blood, Britons, and live modern Americans from the North contrasting curiously with the American planter families of the South. But forty years ago, when already land lots in Melbourne were being sold by the foot, a few pioneer shanties dotted the plain over which Chicago now spreads its populous streets and magnificent avenues. San Francisco was then a straggling row of "greaser" fishermen's huts lying under the shadow of the old Franciscan Mission whence the great capital of the Pacific took its name; the original fishing hamlet was known as Buena Yerba, because of the fertility of the patch of garden ground behind the sand of its beach. Detroit was a mean little place inhabited chiefly by lumbermen and Franco-Indian half-breeds, whose dwellings clustered around the mouldering fort that had been French, then English, and was now American. Washington was a mere caravansérai of the Federal legislation; and the wooden houses inhabited by departmental clerks sparsely studded the "magnificent distances" along which are now ranged the stone and brick palaces of a city that twenty years hence will be the finest capital in the world. Westward of the Missouri, where now a population denser than that of the oldest Australian colony make Kansas and Nebraska the wheat granaries of the Union, spread the wide range of Indian territory which the white pioneer was forbidden by law to trespass upon. Denver is a city but of yesterday, but forty years ago the sites of Topeka, Atchison, Leavenworth, and Omaha—cities of hoar antiquity in trans-Missouri chronology—were pastured over by the buffalo. The vast and now closely settled region of which the great cities of St. Paul and Minneapolis are the local centres, lay unexplored save by the Jesuit pilgrim carrying the cross through the Indian tribes, and the trappers and hunters who had for the most part thrown in their lot with the red men of the West. The West! why, Ohio, now reckoned an Eastern Middle State, was forty years ago reckoned by New England as "the West." Quebec was gay with its English garrison and its French-Canadian belles, and there was something of the tone of a capital in Montreal; but as yet there was no "season" in New York; and Newport, to-day a mixture of Cowes, Homburg, and Biarritz, was a commonplace trading town dwindling into decay.

It may be accepted as the old-world assumption, that the foundation on which the structure known as

"Society" is founded is the existence of a leisure class. This was true of a state of things when the class lines were acutely defined, when dress defined grades in life, and when the merchant lived above his shop. But except in Germany, in Russia—in the former of which the shibboleth to social position is the prefix of "von;" while in the latter there may be said to exist no recognised class at all beyond the "tchinovnik," or noble, and the "moujik," or peasant—the assumption indicated is illusory and fallacious. The *haute finance* of Paris out-dazzles in the same salons the *haute noblesse*. In England the bands of innumerable intermarriages girth the merchants and banking castes with the squirarchy and the nobility. No, it is not the existence of a leisure class which brings about what is called "society." The most potent factor seems to me the attainment on the part of a community of an adequate proportion of cultured and refined gentlewomanhood, whose means are sufficiently easy to afford exemption from the drudgery of the household. Lavish wealth is not, or need not be, among the needfuls; indeed, save under favourable counter-conditions, it may in the abstract be regarded as detrimental, as tending toward a vulgarisation of society by ostentatious display. But there must be means enough to give ease, to contribute to amenities, to admit of entertainments, to let appointments and dressing be tasteful.

American society has much to contend against. It is almost in the nature of things that it should be imitative of the institution in Europe, and I am among those who regard a moderate original as preferable to a bad copy. But its worst foe lurks in the grass of its own paddock, in the guise of wealth, as stupendously large as phenomenally swift won. Forty years ago a hundred thousand dollars were accounted a large fortune in the United States, and probably John Jacob Astor was the only millionaire, and he but a dollar millionaire. To-day there is certainly at least one man in the United States possessed of upwards of one hundred million dollars; there are at least a dozen more who would each "boil down" for twenty-five million dollars; and there are an indefinite number—certainly over a hundred —the clear assets of each of whom range from five to twenty million dollars. It may be easier for a camel to pass through the eye of a needle than for a rich man to enter the kingdom of heaven; but it is easier for an elephant to wriggle through the same diminutive orifice than for the new rich man to escape a taint of snobbery. Yet I am sure we are forced by weight of circumstantial evidence to believe that the camel must often perform the seemingly impossible feat; and there are few among us not possessing acquaintances who inferentially prove that the camel must not unfrequently accomplish his exploit of self-compression. And this apparent paradox I advance with the sincerest conviction, that while there are more new rich men in America than in any other country in the world, there is in America amazingly little snobbery. This, as it seems to me, stands accounted for because of a variety of reasons; partly, probably, from the universality of fair education; more, perhaps, because of the intuitive sense of proportion, which is a characteristic of the American idiosyncrasy —an innate mental equipoise, so to speak; yet most of all it comes of an alert elasticity of intelligence, which gives it to a family that they develop with their rise, that they catch easily the tone of novel surroundings, and that a composed serenity is their normal frame of mind.

It was the great Civil War, spite of all its slaughter and horrors, that may be said to have commenced the crystallisation of American society. The war wiped out the South in the social as in every other sense, for ten years at least. I found Charleston three years ago just beginning languidly to raise its head in a social sense; Augusta and Wilmington are still all but dormant. The war took away out of the North that Southern social element which was so bright, so sparkling, so refined, and so overbearing. But there remained this for the great strenuous spreading North, that the danger, the bloodshed, the patriotism, had been blending coteries into communities. Then fortunes were being made with magic speed by contractors, producers, and commission people; and when the triumph followed the surrender at Appomattox Court House everything, society included, "boomed" with a great boom. There followed years of prosperity in business for almost every interest, colonisation ran with rapid footstep, mining operations in which capital was invested returned colossal rewards—the old "placer" diggings had made no great individual fortunes—internal commerce advanced by leaps and bounds. America was being griddled crisscross-wise with railways; and the making of and speculating in those enterprises, if they broke many, enriched more. But it was a feverish era, and there was little settled solidity in anything. Socially the Republic was indeed active, but still chaotic and uncouth; these were the days of shoddy and petroleum. "Society," in the true sense, has no affinity with yeast, and the social life of America was still then in the fermentation stage.

The financial crash of '73 came, and the inflation collapsed into abject flatness with a suddenness that was startling. The distinction between a sound old country and a windbag new country showed itself in forcible contrast. Take one illustration. In London no theatre closed its doors because of "Black Friday." Overend Gurney's and a score more banks, closed theirs; but there were people enough in London to furnish theatrical audiences—people who leant serenely on the funds or on solid land, and to whom the bicker in the City was as the sough of a far-off storm, whose devastation could involve no bark of theirs. But by the end of the week in which the American crash fell, no theatre remained open in all New York. It was as if Wall Street were the gasometer, and when it exploded the lights went out all over the city. The whole community was so hard hit that there remained of it unscathed, free from care or worse, not members enough to furnish audience for one place of amusement. Italian opera battled longest with the sudden adversity, and succumbed only to the argument furnished by a house in which there were more people on the stage than in the auditorium.

No such universal crash could befall America again. There is feverishness still, and always will remain in a company whose people have impulses so speculative. To this day there are few people possessed of any means in any urban community of the United States, who do not more or less concern themselves with the ups and downs of the stock and share market. The "ticker" streams its tape of quotations into the consulting room of the physician, the bureau of the hotel proprietor, the private room of the lawyer, the office of the merchant. It would be a surprise to find ten men in a hundred average middle-class Londoners who could tell you the latest price of Brighton A's or " Eustons"; there are not twenty in the five hundred male inmates of the Fifth Avenue hotel ignorant of the quotations at the "last board" for New York Centrals or Union Pacifics. But the speculativeness now is for the most part on the wave-edges and tossing crests of the great sea of population. That sea has depths now of still steadfast waters. Vanderbilt has sixty million dollars invested in United States Government Securities; others less wealthy follow suit proportionately. People of means are content with four per cent interest on the bulk of their fortunes, and amuse themselves in speculation merely with what they call their "pocket-money." Society all over the States stands organised on a comparatively firm and permanent basis, as contrasted with the old-time "here to-day and gone to-morrow" series of spasms.

There are three principal social centres in the Union, although there is no considerable place not in its first youth that cannot lay some claim to attribute of a distinctive society of its own. The three great centres are New York, Boston, and Washington. Of these New York society is the largest in a numerical sense, the gayest, the most variously ramified, the most lavish, the most indiscriminate about its fringes, the fitfullest, and the most piquant. It scintillates with dazzling brightness and sparkle. It is full of curious transient fads that can scarcely be called fashions. It costs— yes, it costs consumedly. It has a wonderful lambent kind of charm for a person fresh to it; and it is not so very hollow, so that satiety does not soon come sneaking in with that insidiously unpleasant *cui bono* suggestion which makes Dead Sea apples of so many pleasant things. The lavish expenditure of New York society has a graceful picturesqueness that goes far to disguise the chink of the multitudinous dollars. If the dinner courses are tediously elaborate, the wines somewhat ostentatiously rare, and the menu a monument of costliness, the dining-chamber is a model of chaste grace. The serpent of extravagance lurks on the table, but its folds are hidden under blossoms and foliage. The elaborated viands are served on a board that is a joy of beautiful flowers; the glass is quaintly artistic; there is a winsome daintiness in every appointment that screens the coarse flash of the almighty dollar. There is no ballroom in the world prettier than a New York ballroom. The apartment is a piece of decorative architecture in the best taste. The men look well, have a courtesy that has in it something of a genial chivalry, have as little awkwardness as self-sufficiency, and can talk as well as dance, and dance as well as talk. And the women—well, they dress and carry their dress as no other women out of Paris do. They have the gift of being natural in their best frocks, they have the air of fascination, and it is "the thing" with them to be gracious. A large proportion have a bright piquant beauty of a type that is all but peculiar to the American lady. There is with them a gay independence that has in it no flavour of forwardness. There are no dowds; and, the Frenchwoman not excepted, I regard the New York belle as the "brightest" talker in the world. It may be and mostly is the merest frivolity, but she imparts to the persiflage an unique spirit, a scintillation of unexpected repartee, a quaint turn of originality. She is never dull. She could not be heavy if she were to try; and she is not the woman to try—not much. Beauty alone will not make the "belle;" the beauty must be lit up by *esprit*.

The New York season is a delirious whirl. In regard to its time it is a sensible season, contrasting in this respect with the London season, which begins when the buds are forming, and lasts, in a stupendous insult to nature, until the heat of the dog-days are turning brown the leaves. When the short American spring begins to have its pale face flushed by the foreglow of the dawning summer, New York society sets to getting itself ready for emigrating from the city. Whither it hies itself, and how it deports and disports itself, I will take leave presently to outline. The season ends in a gush of weddings, and the marriage bells ring out its passing hours. Murray Hill is dead then until after the "Indian Summer," and the gray paper is up in the windows of the brown stone houses all the way from Madison Square to Morrisonia. The good time is over for a period; and it was a good time—a specially good time for the "old country" visitor, because of the zest he has found in its differences from the accustomed routine at home. The Englishman who is familiar with our own "morning park," that period between twelve and two when all the world of London society is in the Row—the throng of men as great as the crowd of women, who has memories of countless bisexual luncheons, if the term be permissible; of afternoon at homes where there were as many frockcoats as bonnets—such an one is struck on his first introduction to social New York by the absence of men from "up town" during the day.

The truth is, that all the men of New York, from the Vanderbilts to little Jerry Kane, are more or less—chiefly more—strenuous workers, who have business avocations which engage them "down town"—the New York correlative for our "in the City"—during the day. "Have you not a leisure class here?" asked the simple stranger of a live New Yorker. "What sort of a class is that, anyway?" queried the latter. "A class that do nothing, that are idle men," was the explanation. "Why, certainly," alertly responded the New Yorker, "we call 'em tramps." Now the tramp is no doubt an institution in America; but it may be said of him in a general way that he has not free access to the best society. In the comparatively Adamless Eden of New York "up town" in the daytime the ladies make up gay gossiping luncheon parties among themselves, and later—the men begin to trickle up town as the afternoon draws on—there are "coffee parties," with music or readings, and recitations. This latter form of entertainment is greatly come into vogue of late years, and certain ladies and gentlemen have earned high repute as practitioners. If they can give original pieces of their own, and these are interesting or graceful enough to be acceptable, their prestige runs high, and they become personages in great request.

The single man in London society who has made good his *entrée* I have often thought to have a specially good time of it. His circumstances may make him a "detrimental" in a matrimonial sense, but this apart, he does as well in a general way as can the best match of the season. It is astonishing how cheaply he can get along, assuming him a man on whom economy is encumbent. He has his club address on his card ; he lives there, and his adjacent bedroom costs him a few shillings a week. As a bachelor, there is no obligation on him to any reciprocity of entertainment. His sole society expenditure is made up of clothes, gloves, and hansom cabs. I have a young friend who seems to me to go to most places, who certainly neither plays nor bets, and whose income consists of a patrimony of £300 a year, and perhaps another £100 made by a little dilettante painting. But New York is no such thrifty paradise for the bachelor of modest means, however *bienvenu* he may be. There social etiquette virtually enforces an expenditure which "closes out" the man with the scanty dollars.

Let us imagine our ingenuous young Briton arriving in that city with good introductions, and a high-souled resolution to "make the campaign" in a fashion that shall not discredit his nationality in the eyes of keen although kindly transatlantic critics. With his letter to a society leader he of course leaves his card, but if he desires to begin well, he will accept the hint he may have received from one having the map of the country, that he should leave with his card a basket or a bouquet of rosebuds. Now, in a winter season the nocturnal temperature of which thinks nothing of dropping a few miles below zero, rosebuds are not to be culled from the hedges on the roadside. In point of fact there are no hedges; the rosebuds have been brought express from Florida or the Bermudas, and a creditable posy is cheap at twenty-five dollars. As he gets into the swim he will find the otherwise delightful fairway studded with frequent rocks that take the form of conventionally obligatory bouquets. The lady to whom he has brought an introduction gives a dance for him, perhaps; and the call after that spells "bouquet" imperatively, even if he should not have been moved to send flowers to the ladies of the family with the request that they wear them on the occasion created to do him honour. A young lady is gracious unto him, and gives him within reason all the dances he asks. If he has been well advised he will not neglect on the morrow of the dance to send her a floral souvenir. If he is fortunate enough to attain the relation with her of an intimate, all the more if he nourishes a hope to be something closer still, it behoves him to endeavour assiduously that whereever she goes, she carry flowers of his presentation. A New York bachelor friend—and he is a level-headed man who has never been accused of forcing the running, showed me his florist's bill for the New York season. It footed up over three thousand dollars, and his view was that he had "got out" rather leniently.

Then our properly self-respecting Briton who

has had a good time, when the period of his stay is drawing to its close, will be fain to do something toward the erection of a white stone to his social memory; and that it may be said of him that he has carried out his bat with credit, his mentor will probably suggest to him a "theatre party." There are theatre parties in other lands than that watered by the Hudson, but they are comparatively small potatoes. A little dinner at the Café Anglais or at the Bristol Restaurant, with a box to follow at the Français or the Criterion, doubtless is a good kind of a thing enough in its way, but is a mere colourless adumbration of a New York "theatre party." The planner of that function will do well on the threshold to investigate the state of his balance, and to proceed in his design only should that be satisfactory. That little detail being auspicious, he proceeds to secure a couple of undeniable chaperones, for whom he will look among the most brilliant and popular young married ladies of his more intimate acquaintance. Then he issues invitations to a well-assorted selection of bright and pretty girls, and to an equal number of congruous gentlemen. He bespeaks one of Delmonico's private dining-rooms, and gives the chef his head loose. Then he chooses his theatre and secures as many front seats on the balcony, all in a row, as he expects ladies, and the corresponding seats behind in the second tier. Finally, he visits his florist, and has with him a long and serious consultation.

That dinner-party should have all the elements of gaiety, and if there should be a shadow of black care on the shoulders of the host because of the cost he is incurring, he will do well do get rid of the incubus for the time with the greatcoat he left outside. Nowhere in America at mixed parties is there any long after-dinner sitting ; and pretty lips are pressing the velvety brunette cheek of the mid-winter peach as the hour approaches for adjournment to the theatre. Meanwhile the florist's men have been quietly bustling about the adjacent toilet room. As the ladies go in to cloak, they find a long table on which are displayed a series of hand and bosom bouquets, each set labelled with a lady's name. Sometimes the bouquets are all alike, so that the party has what may be called a floral uniformity. But it is regarded as more "high-toned" if the entertainer shall have been at the pains to remember or discover the favourite flower of each of his lady-guests, and to make her the compliment of having her bouquet consist of that for its staple. It was the fashion three years ago—there may have been a change since, for the breast flowers to commence at the girdle on the left side, and expand on the ascent till the spray of topmost rosebuds and of fern fronds interspersed among them broke and spread itself up against the white throat. The ladies have their breast flowers fastened on, take up their hand bouquets, and descend to the carriages. Imagine what a parterre of beauty and roses, what a bank of bright faces, sparkling eyes, delicate green fern-tracery, flaunting *Gloire de Dijon*, delicate *Maréchal Niel* hovering between the choice to be yellow or pink, lavish swarthy *Queen of Sheba*, and white moss rosebuds with a fickle faint blush on them, the horseshoe bend of a theatre balcony presents when its whole front tier is occupied by theatre parties such as I have tried to outline. Often the giver of the entertainment has had the broad-topped ledge in front inlaid with roses, and on the upturned blossoms lie satin and scented bills of the play which are works of art. When the performance is over, "Good-night," is still a long way off down the vista. The cortege returns to Delmonico's. The dining-room has been cleared, and is now a ballroom. Music is waiting to begin, and does begin, and with it the dance. Somewhere about two A.M. there is a hint of plovers' eggs in the next room, and it becomes apparent how elastic is the force of the English language as used in America, so that plovers' eggs may come to mean a somewhat elaborate supper. Then the prizes for the "German," which is American for what is known with us as the cotillon, are brought in; and in New York the "German" has been known under favourable auspices to last as long as a parliamentary debate in the House of Commons when the Irish brigade have got their war-paint on.

This is magnificent, but it can scarcely be called war suited to the resources of a modest gentleman who may not have achieved a sweeping financial triumph in a skirmishing campaign carried on in the precincts of Wall Street as an interlude to his social pleasures. If on the improbable hypothesis that he has come out "right side up" from that speculative combat with the particularly knowing wild beasts of the Wall Street Ephesus, he may "spread himself" in a variety of social directions and achieve the proud reputation of being a "white man." But the "theatre party," as I have cursorily described it, is an entertainment of which there are no unfrequent instances in evidences on most nights toward the end of the New York season. Such an entertainment, at the lowest computation, will certainly cost the giver of it full £500, something beyond the annual income on which the friend whose case I have cited manages to get creditably through the whole of his London season and the rest of the year to boot. But in very truth money is as dirt among those phenomenally pecunious New Yorkers. A building site in a coveted neighbourhood, and a cramped narrow quarter acre slip it was, was bought not long ago for £65,000. Mr. Vanderbilt's new house on Fifth Avenue cost £3,000,000 sterling to build, decorate, and furnish, the pictures not included. For the wooden carving and panelling of a single hall Mr. D. O. Mills, a Californian capitalist who has recently come east, and who in a financial sense is his own ancestor, disbursed £100,000. Till the other day Mr. Vanderbilt chose to drive in his buggy team the celebrated trotting mare Maude S., whose record is the fastest the world has known up till now, and for which he might by holding up his hand, at any moment have had a score of offers of a larger price than that which Mr. Peck paid Mr. Merry for Doncaster.

Boston society has an atmosphere of much greater repose than that of New York. The gay New Yorkers genially jibe at it as musty, dreary, pragmatic, and desiccated. I think there may be a flavour in those taunts of that assumed contempt which is a second cousin to envy. Boston sets its handsome composed face resolutely against ostentation. Life there has a savour, a brightness, and a purposefulness of its own. Æstheticism—not the Oscar Wildish travesty, but the cultured quest after true art brought into the home life—is much cared for and thought of in Boston. The painter is a power in Boston society. One quaint, genial little New Englander, Frank Millet, who earned for himself a brilliant name in our own profession when serving as a colleague of my own during the Russo-Turkish war, but who ever was an artist first and a journalist afterwards (unless, indeed, it may humbly be advanced that the true journalist must always be an artist, and make his artistic gift an handmaiden to the loftier cult), may be said to be a Boston Art Autocrat. Millet dictates dress from Greek and Egyptian models; he settles the *mise en scène* for the classical dramas of which Boston is or feigns to be so fond. I am not sure that he has yet interfered with the glorious sunsets over the picturesque contour of the Brookline heights.

Boston amuses itself, it is true—drives, dances, flirts, and dines; but it lives for higher things. It is the city of the wits. The humourists—the quaint men who have invented and elaborated that development of painfully grotesque incongruity which, now in its decadence, has been wont to be known as American humour,—can live around in less superfine places, such as Hartford, Cleveland, Detroit, and Danbury. Their slangy crudities are not to Boston's taste; she prefers the apt crisp *bon-mots* that turn on an allusion, to make and to follow which requires that the wit and the listeners should have culture. The Bostonians set on a pedestal their tried and approved sayers of good things. A *bon-mot* from the lips of Oliver Wendel Holmes—and he makes *bon-mots* with a clean-cut, facile grace that is peculiar to himself—is received with a hushed intensity of respectful interest. For myself I am like my memorable countryman, "I jock with deffeeculty," but when, with pain and writhing, I am haply delivered of an unaccustomed jest, I own I like to realise in the laughter of the listeners that it has told. Now the venerable Autocrat of the Breakfast-table is like that other rarely-gifted countryman of mine—" He jocks juist spontawneous;" and I have often thought it must somewhat dismay him to have his *jeux d'esprit* received with so portentous a solemnity. I know why this is so, and that it is a compliment to him of a kind that it should be so ; it is because of the proud reverence in which the Bostonians hold their great wit. Mr. Howells, the novelist, is another fine luminary among them ; and the professors of the adjacent University of Harvard find their self-love flattered when they cross the long bridge and travel into the city. Henry James junior, a Boston boy himself, was a great pride to the people of the " Hub ;" but they shake their heads rather mournfully now, and sorrow that he has fallen away from being an American to become a cosmopolitan novelist.

Till comparatively recent years nobody lived in Washington who could help it. Among those who could not help themselves were the people of the Foreign Ministries, the permanent heads of departments of administration, civil, military, and naval ; the man in all America who has the worst life of it —I need not say that I mean the President of the Republic, and the members of his Cabinet. Even under those comparatively narrow conditions the Washington coterie had an individuality of character such as no other society in the Union could then show. To begin with, it had comparative permanency. The general in supreme command of the army was a fixed entity. The same officer served as quartermaster-general from the beginning of the Civil War until three years ago. The Foreign Ministers were wont to have a long term of Washington ; when a man once gets to understand the

American character and brings himself into accord with it, he is so useful a man that his home powers do not care lightly to tear him up by the roots. And if attachés come and attachés go, as is the nature of the genial butterfly creature, the attaché has a generic character ; and, besides that he by nature spontaneously dances into lighthearted talk about all things and certain other things, the Washington variety of him has ever evinced an alert eagerness to fall in love with at least one American girl at a time, with the ultimate result of giving himself in marriage to the most lucrative damsel in other respects at least passably eligible.

This circle gradually widened its borders without in essentials changing its character. People from elsewhere who found themselves during visits in affinity with its spirit, and whom fortune had favoured with means adequate for a life of comparative relief from their local business cares, have taken to erect for themselves permanent and beautiful residences in the Federal capital, and to occupy these during the winter months. Washington is fast becoming a capital in reality as well as in name. It has no commerce to speak of, and is purely a legislative, executive, and residential city ; its streets are spacious, beautifully asphalted, and scrupulously clean ; its landscape-gardening, in regard to the laying out of its squares and its numerous open spaces, as well as the assiduous plantation of shade trees along its boulevards, is attended to with taste and zealous care. Most of its mansions stand detached and have front as well as side gardens ; and among its newer ones I cannot call to mind a commonplace structure. The subdued tint of the bricks—though new they are not garish—contrasts effectively with the greens of the creepers that trail up the house-fronts, and with the environment of ornamental shade-trees.

Around this calm, somewhat supercilious, and not a little exclusive inner circle of Washington society, there surges and rages a turbulent, discoloured, and often unsavoury sea of political or rather politician quasi-social life ; a sea in whose vexed, dingy waters splash, swim, drift, or drown senators, congressmen, logrollers, pension agents, lobbymen, so-called agents, office-seekers, appropriation-cormorants, intriguers, panderers, news-purveyors and news-inventors, sharks, gamblers, and indiscriminate scum. To the calm inner circle this pool of Acheron is as if it were not. The President of the Republic may have the countersign of admission into it, or he may not ; if he has, it is nowise in virtue of his position as the president. But if by a surprise of fortune he may happen to be a gentleman in spite of being president, he is free of it in virtue of the personal attribute. When I say a gentleman, I don't mean to use the expression in the narrow insular sense of a gentleman born, but that he is a gentleman by the grace of God and the personal virtue of having, in the face of the strong temptation of a political career, refrained from having damaged God's handiwork. Garfield was "raised" in a log shanty, and began his working life as a teamster on the canal; but what of that, when his clean hands, pure heart, and noble self-culture made him, apart altogether from official position, an ornament to any society? President Hayes never attained to the consigne, nor did Andrew Johnson.

The characteristics of the Washington inner circle, which it must be understood is in a certain sense the sublimation of all society throughout the Union, are clean cut. Its fashion is to be well informed as well as well educated. It is the only circle in the United States, save an Anglo-American coterie in San Francisco, that has any pretence to even superficial conversance with European international politics. There are drawing-tables outside the dwellings of the diplomatic corps on which may be found the *Kölnische Zeitung*, *Le Temps*, the *Neue Frei Presse*, and the *Times*. To Washington go monthly more *Nineteenth Centuries* than to any other city in the Union. In a Washington salon you may hear half the languages of modern Europe being talked at once; one group speaking German, another French, another Italian, between each there fluctuating a dropping interchange of polyglot stragglers. Boston concerns herself with science and the severer literature; Washington plays on the lighter literature of Europe with epigram-flashes, and hovers with equal ease of poise over Castelar and Tourganieff.

Ostentation is out of the question in such a circle as this ; one would as soon adventure horseflesh as an appropriate novelty in the menu of a ball supper. Lavishness however tasteful, with the exception perhaps of a vent in flowers and in artistic furniture, is not good form, and is put down with a certain quiet sternness that is singularly efficacious ; graceful simplicity ; a tone of refinement incompatible with the echo of the chink of the dollars ; a cultured brightness in everything ; such are the attributes of this best Washington society. Among its most delightful entertainments are the breakfasts, which in reality are early luncheons, and which have an airy freshness that they seem to catch from the yet young unfatigued day.

An interesting phase of American society is its keen sympathy with things artistic. Mr. Oscar Wilde went to America with a sham and self-constituted mission, to infuse into its benighted people the principles of what he and the paltry filigree-work school of which he is an accident, prate about as "true art." He found to his discomfiture that cultured Americans knew a great deal more about the principles of art than he could tell them ; and that they had learned in a school the canons of which inculcated a higher ideal than could be attained by what lavishness soever in sunflower and lily decorations, spite of what he called the "gaudy leonine beauty" of the former vegetable, and the "tender grace" of the latter. It must be said that the career of art in America has been somewhat arduous and chequered. People in a new country have to commence at the beginning of things. If you go out into a bush shanty in the "back country" of New South Wales, or into a shepherd's "humpy" in Queensland, you will find the logs or the bark pasted over with illustrations cut from the *Graphic* and the *Illustrated London News*. This is simply the evidence of the artistic instinct struggling to make the little artistic best of very adverse conditions. The Americans began in bad copies of good pictures, and in spurious rubbish with which their ignorance was defrauded. It has been by dint of hard-bought experience that some of them have ripened into discriminating connoisseurs. Let me give an instance. I know an old gentleman who lives in a beautiful house in the picturesque uplands which overhang the Rhine-land-like city of Cincinnati. Many years ago he made his fortune in hardware, sold out, and determined that for the rest of his life he would devote himself to art. Well, he didn't know anything about art, but he could learn, couldn't he? So he went to Europe, and opened his purse. Of course he got "stuck" with awful rubbish. But he went to school on the rubbish, so to speak. Next campaign it needed a higher style of rubbish to take him in; and in the course of a long sedulous career of art investment he has now ripened into a connoisseur of admirable taste and faultless acuteness. The wiliest vamper-up of bogus art treasures will not now adventure the hopeless enterprise of throwing dust into the eyes of the ex-hardware man. His beautiful house, itself an art treasure because of the varied beauty with which its interior is inlaid in native American woods, is an art treasury of admirable taste and high intrinsic value. But, if he takes a liking to you, the old gentleman will disclose to you the steps of the ladder by which he has ascended to connoisseurship—the milestones on the arduous, costly journey. Here is a room in the basement crammed with the utterest impositions—sham Etruscan vases, sham china, sham old masters, sham tapestry, sham everything. Then, here is another room wherein most things are frauds indeed, but less glaringly obvious frauds. Yet another room of comparative genuineness, but of comparative humility also, representing a real advance into the realm of artistic truth, but penetration only inside the outlying confines of that realm. Since this new birth the ascent to skill was severe indeed, yet the upland path was now well defined. That path is illustrated in old Probasco's mansion by not a few chambers that are the cupboards in which are hidden the skeletons of his long and finally successful struggle with art mysteries.

The millionaire Americans are profuse picture-buyers in Europe as well as in America. To any stranger visiting San Francisco the picture-galleries of Mr. Charles Crocker and ex-Governor Leland Stanford are readily accessible. Mr. Vanderbilt long shared with a countryman of our own now dead, the distinction of being the horror of the agents charged with the purchase of important pictures for the National Galleries of Europe. Neither Vanderbilt nor Crocker is a connoisseur of painting; but both know of what schools they like the exemplars, and they aim at securing the pick of the work of those schools. They employ skilled experts to ensure genuineness and to make their purchases, and when the pictures come along, they employ other experts to hang them to advantage. "Brutal capital!" exclaims the ardent but thrifty connoisseur, with a fierce sneer. "Capital," if you choose, sir—the dollars are not to be gainsaid; but wherein the brutality?

Some zealous members of New York society have recently established a sort of guild, under the title of "The Associated Artists," of which organisation the high functionaries are Mrs. Wheeler and Mr. Tiffany. The "Associated Artists" are designers of ornamental textile fabrics, and they have affiliated to them an establishment of accomplished and dexterous artisans, by whom their designs are embodied, by the processes of colouring and weaving. Mrs. Wheeler was lately engaged on a cartoon, to be reproduced in tapestry, representing Aphrodite rising from the waves with her attendant loves. My artistic friend writes to me in a rapture, "Aphrodite is a charmingly lithe buoyant figure." When I visited the unpretending establishment I was dazzled and amazed by the wealth of the embroideries, tapestries, portieres, curtains, and hangings that were shown me in such lavish profusion. I can make no pretensions to speak with any authority on art matters, but Herkomer raved over those fabrics, enthusiastically declaring that the work was far in advance of anything achieved in any of the art schools of England or the Continent. He was urgent that there should be an exhibition of it in London, convinced that it would raise the standard of art wherever shown.

Of Cincinnati society—New York would probably stick its nose in the air and superciliously ask how it is possible that there can be society in Cincinnati—the two favourite avocations are music and pottery. Probably the biggest thing of the kind in the world is Cincinnati's "Musical Festival." A vast building, specially constructed, is devoted exclusively to the celebration of the sacred fortnight of song. There are concerts in the afternoons; the evenings belong to opera. Patti has sung once and again, at the fabulous tariff of about ten guineas a note. The Cincinnatians lave themselves in the musical stream. It is no casual dip—one concert, say, or one opera; it is proper to hold and to occupy seats for the whole festival. These seats are sold by auction, and there is a keen competition for the more eligible ones, especially when the pork trade is in a flourishing condition. The ceramic art-study is less ardent but probably more thorough. The Cincinnati ladies copy vases from the most graceful classic models, or they give the rein to their fancy in making others with no other model than their own ideal. These vases, as well as plaques, cups, and saucers, they paint with patient and loyal aspiration after the beautiful, the quaint, and the fanciful. I call to mind some porcelain painting which three girls showed me in their workroom, in a pretty mansion in the Clifton suburb. On a set of vases of identical shape, severe yet graceful, were depicted brilliant-plumaged birds flitting through a tracery of wild-flowers, or perched on a spray in the heart of a mass of feathery foliage. Each bird was of a different species, each floral or leafy setting was distinct. The colouring was exquisite, as was the picturesque delicacy of flower and leaf. So far as my humble judgment goes, the palm for true artistic genius, as well as for intuitive taste in composition, and for vivid accuracy in the charming accomplishment of flower-painting, belongs against the world to a lady of Australia; but the work of those Cincinnati girls could at least have borne to be showed alongside of hers. The potter ladies of Cincinnati maintain among them a joint-stock oven, wherein their handiwork is baked with due pains and skill. Perhaps enough has been said to prove that if Cincinnati lives *by* pork alone, it cannot be said to live *for* pork alone.

At the risk of wearying the reader I would fain give a little sketch of yet another society, which has little in common with the bright dainty life of the fine city whose fringes are laved by the waters of the Ohio river. Before the war there were stately days and merry days in those fine roomy old mansions whose ornate fronts, showing over the low trees that shade the esplanade pleasure-ground, still confront the cool Atlantic breezes which blow across the fair expanse of Charleston Harbour. Those were the days of belles and balls in the beautiful capital of South Carolina ; of incomparable madeira served at the tables of planters whose ancestry went back to our own cavaliers. The earliest and the bitterest of all the seceding States was South Carolina. The iron of retribution was driven into her very heart. Her capital was blockaded for years, bombarded once and again, ruined up to the very hilt. The old families with the fine old names, whose wealth lay in cotton and slaves, were broken utterly in a financial sense, but not many of the men lived to know the pinch and sting of poverty. No, they were true to the gallant blood that flowed in their veins ; from the old men of sixty to the lads of fifteen they died for the Cause. It was all they could do ; nor can any man aver that they grudged their lives. But, ah ! for the women, the ladies whose laugh had been gayest, whose sparkle had been most winsome. Misery ground itself into their souls. They learned to be familiar with hunger, squalor, and wretchedness unspeakable. They lived in the garrets of the great shell-battered mansions, because these were unsaleable; even to-day you may buy one of them for the price of a London suburban corner shop. And now, when all things else have been changing and are changed in and around Charleston, when cotton mills whirr among the plantations that feed them, and the great steamers come and go in busy sequence, and cargoes of wealth-bringing pyrites are carried away to sea past the grim shattered carcase of the historic Fort Sumter, the old aristocracy of South Carolina stand aloof and apart from the new order of things. I know of grand old families whose women earn a pittance by seamstress work, so that the man of the family, who cannot or will not dig and who is ashamed to beg, although he permits himself to do a thing infinitely more shameful, may walk down to the club in fair raiment, and have the wherewithal to ask the room to join him in a drink, in accordance with an old bad custom which is not confined to the Southern States of America. Charleston lives in the dead past; it ever chews the melancholy cud of the great Rebellion. Let a club conversation begin where it may, it inevitably drifts into recollections of that fierce time. The stranger finds himself here standing, as it were, in a graveyard of men who indeed physically are not dead, but who have ceased really to live since Lee's surrender at Appomatox Court House. The realities of the civil war get crushed into his consciousness with a strange dramatic fierceness. I remember once adventuring an opinion in regard to the vexed question of the burning of Columbia. "On the balance of circumstantial evidence," said I, " it seems improbable that Sherman burnt Columbia intentionally. He is so bold and outspoken that I cannot see why, if he had done so, he should not have owned to it, and justified it as a military necessity ? "

" Circumstantial evidence be——!" exclaimed a dark man, whose face flushed as he spoke. " What does that count against personal proof? I was the last man of Wade Hampton's rearguard that evacuated Columbia as Sherman entered ; and I swear before God there was no spark of fire in any bale of cotton as I rode out between the tiers stacked in the street ! "

" And I, sir," said another man, whose eyes were glowing like live coals—" I, then a boy of twelve, was standing behind Sherman when he bade his bugler give the signal for the fire-raisers to get to work. ' Now let us have a bonfire !' were the words he used. I defy him to look me in the face and say he didn't burn Columbia !"

And so on, and so on. They do not plot, those people ; they simply smoulder moodily. It is the saddest ghost of a "lost cause." There are Poles who still hope against hope ; the Charleston ex-Confederate not only has no hope, but no wish. He has accepted the situation—only he cannot live up to it. The present generation must pass away before the people of Charleston take unreservedly to the still new order of things. Meanwhile they visit among each other economically, those ghostly folk ;

they are beautifully hospitable to the British stranger, with a proud apology for the *res angusta domi*. There is still a driblet of the famous old Madeira left, and I know no place in the world richer in old china, old silver, and rare bric-à-brac. But you cannot buy those heirlooms, although you may find people all but actually starving among them.

The superficial, not to say the supercilious observer, may be apt to say in his haste that the regulations of social etiquette are merely a bundle of arbitrary and petty enactments, whose chief object it is to impart to life an irritating artificiality. But if one looks deeper one will recognise something of a distinct principle underlying the apparent quiddities, and may interpret a specific meaning in the merest seeming triviality. Take our own code, that which obtains with insignificant local variations, in the mother-country and in her colonies. Examine its canons in regard to women. What are these enactments other than simply a refinement on the method of treatment of women that has inured in Eastern countries from the days of Rachel and Rebecca until now, glazed but a trifle by a lacquer made out of the débris of the days of chivalry? Yes, woman is to be a queen, a goddess; you are to defer to her in all sorts of pretty little ways; you are to approach her with entreaties if you are to win her; you are, if haply you have the knack, to write verses on her beauty, or, if you have the voice, to sing the lays of other men in praise of her charms. You doff your hat to her;

you accord to her the initiative of recognition ; you solicit the "honour" whether for a waltz or for a promenade into the Elysian fields of matrimony. You put the social crown on her brows—you concede to her the social sceptre ; only the crown is of tinsel, and the sceptre is hollow.

In effect we treat our women just as the Mahommedans do, making allowances for the differences between our civilisation and theirs. They immure their women in the harem ; they compel them to veil themselves when they go abroad ; they padlock them when the male owner goes away on a journey or a campaign. Their *a priori* attitude in regard to their women is the abiding conviction that the latter long for mischief, and that coercion, sequestration, and vigilant watchfulness are necessary to avert this chronic anxiety. The Easterns "shepherd" their women, and this because they consider shepherding eminently necessary.

And is not the keynote to our own code of etiquette a similar belief that the woman needs to be "shepherded," not among us indeed by bolts and bars, by harem guards, by the fear of poison or of the sack, but by a network of draconian conventionalities? But for those conventionalities which bear her up, such is her weakness, we say in effect, that she would be striking her little foot against a stone at every step. Hence, for example, chaperonage ; with the frequent reduction to absurdity of this conventionality in the solemnly ludicrous spectacle of a younger sister who happens to be married furnishing an elder sister who is still single with the seal of social propriety. Of what text is the chaperone the standing expounder, if only you will penetrate behind the flimsy screen of conventionalities that have become second nature with you, and look straight and frank into the heart of things? Does she not preach—" The heart of this single woman, and of every single woman, is by nature deceitful and desperately wicked ; she cannot be trusted alone lest she should gratify her natural instinct of coming to grief; it may be the blind leading the blind, but my function here is to save this poor creature from herself?" When you come to dissect things—to look into the principle of the mechanism of the social clock, it is just possible for an unprejudiced person, if he be very bold, to find himself tremblingly asking himself the question whether all this shepherding machinery of etiquette, so far from being a compliment, may not be an actual insult to the woman who is its flower-decorated victim.

America has dared to emancipate herself from what she regards as the disparaging bondage of this phase of conventionality. She has taken up a novel and startling attitude in relation to the young woman. She has developed the consummate and inconceivable audacity of regarding that ingenuous person as a sensible, reasonable, and responsible creature. She has been guilty of the sacrilege to believe that the tottering innocent can walk alone, and is all the better for doing so; that when the bodily swaddling clothes have been laid aside and dress-improvers adopted in their stead, the mental swaddling clothes may be dispensed with in favour of a neat purposeful attire of common sense. America takes the young woman into a corner very early in life, and says to her in effect: "'Seems to me the protection and conservation of your own honour and purity is a matter that affects you, as a rational being, more than it can anybody else. I propose, therefore, to vest in you the guardianship of your own honour Accustom yourself to rely on yourself. The atmosphere about you, taken by and large, is pretty sweet; don't chase the fair bloom off the flower of your youth by suspecting a snake in every tuft of grass; remember within limits the motto of *honi soit*, and understand how the ill-thinking spoken of in that motto, done into plain English, simply spells pruriency. Be fearless, be wise; your early training has had it among its aims to bring it about that you keep your head cool; on every hand you will find kindly and sympathetic women glad to advise and support you if need be. And so, my dear, go forward and prosper, in the name of God."

This is what America virtually said to her young women ever so long ago; so that generation after generation of young women have been born into and raised under the social creed. I have studied with much interest the working and issues of the revolution, and I make bold to put forward the averment that it answers. It is with fear and trembling that I do, because of a sinking consciousness of the chaperone's frown. I stand to my guns in the face of the cheap argument that one who is a partisan because of personal experience may be the slave of a glamour. And I am content to appeal to any one who has had the good fortune to have had some social familiarity with American ladies.

The frankness of the American young woman has in it, on the threshold, a certain bewilderment and even embarrassment for the British male person, especially if his collars be stiffly starched. She has so utter an apparent absence of self-consciousness; her mental equipoise is so serenely stable; her good-fellowship, if one may use the term, is so natural, that he cannot see his way easily to the solution of the problem. I assume him to be a gentleman, so that his intuition deters him from a misconception of the phenomena that confront him. She flirts, he finds; she is an adept in flirtation, but it is a flirtation "from the teeth outwards," to use Carlyle's phrase; and he is fain to own to himself, like the fox-hunting farmer who tried unsuccessfully to get drunk on the claret, that he seems to "Get no forrarder." But although the citadel of the fortress seems to him strangely impregnable because of the cool alert self-possession of the garrison, I have been told by heroic persons who have ventured on the escalade, that if the beleaguerer be he whom fortune favours, it will terminate an honourable siege by a graceful capitulation. Human nature is human nature all the world over. And there is no greater error than the prevalent one among us, that domesticity is not a leading virtue of American married couples. That there is too much of hotel life for American families I concede, and I am fully conscious of the faults and evils of the system; but that it entails any impairment of the higher domestic virtues I have failed to discover. It is not easy to see how a woman is deteriorated as the companion and friend of a man —as the participator in his aspirations, his troubles, his studies, his higher life—because her conditions release her from the duty of devising the details of a dinner, from the irritation of demoniacal domestics, from the drudgery of checking the grocer's pass-book, and the sad realisation that all bakers are liars, and mostly robbers as well.

The American girl, in her independence, has "a lovely time," as she herself would style it. I will pass over the precocious festivities of her childhood. But when she is due to "come out," her début is a notable circumstance. To give festive emphasis to that auspicious occurrence her parents must rise to the height of the occasion. That height may be a reception, or it may be a ball; but whatever it may be the function is a special one, and the speciality of it is duly notified on the cards of invitation. Floral offerings pour in from relatives, and from family friends who have already an acquaintance with the débutante. That radiant creature, with cool self-possession, stands by her mother as the guests are announced, and in a sort of halo of floral offerings, serenely receives the tribute of congratulations. And so she is launched, and her career commences. She has a latitude at which an English girl, nurtured on conventionality till it has entered into the essence of her being, would thrill with a shudder. If her "folks" are wealthy she has her own "parlour," and receives there the visits of her own friends. The friends may be her friends exclusively—that is to say, they may not know her parents, her sisters, or anybody that is hers. If one of us insulars chance to meet in London, let us say, a lady of his acquaintance from the country who is on a visit to the capital, and is fortunate enough to receive permission to call on her, he leaves a card as well for the lady of the house at which his fair friend may be visiting. A proper etiquette, surely, founded on the true principle that you are doubly grateful to the hostess, whose hospitality it is that has brought your friend within social ken of you, and whose threshold you have crossed to pay your respects to her guest. But in America this amenity is not necessarily regarded. It is possible for a gentleman to be a frequent caller on a lady without knowing any other member of her family. If she have sisters, and no separate "parlour" of her own, the sisters probably have each her distinctive day, and they make their arrangements in an accommodating and sisterly spirit. A girl in America can travel from New York to San Francisco without any thought of violated etiquette. She can cross the Atlantic alone, and not have the consciousness of a solecism until a fresh light comes to her with surprise when she would put up at a British hotel. She walks out with a gentleman friend who need not at all be the lover; she can go to the theatre with him, and ask him into her house to have a cup of coffee when he shall have escorted her to her doorstep. Or if she chooses she may go to the theatre, or anywhere else, alone; although her practice makes it sufficiently obvious that she prefers the companionship which she designates as an "escort."

Is all this very shocking? It rather startles one at first, but it is wonderful how soon one gets used to things, especially if they do not happen to be disagreeable. I do not ask any one to take my word for it, but I must record my profound conviction that the evil coming out of a liberty that at first sight seems to us marvellously close to licence is singularly small. There are occasional lapses, of course; but the lapses will bear comparison in unfrequency, of that I am assured, with those which occur under the conventional order, under the system of sedulous "shepherding." There is a significant old Scottish proverb—"He who will to Cupar, maun to Cupar." There are shes, unfortunately, as well as hes who "maun to Cupar," but just as they will hurry thither when left free agents, you will not hinder them from getting there by the most assiduous guardianship, short of the Eastern method of absolute incarceration.

And I think there are as few in America as in any other country, who set their pretty wicked faces resolutely in the sad direction of the Scottish borough town.

Before quitting a subject which I have very far from exhausted, I should like to say something about American summer resorts. Some years ago, Saratoga was the leading haunt of American summer fashion. It was an enlarged Homburg, with the Kursaal left out, and an infusion thrown in of the Grand Hotel at Brighton exaggerated twentyfold. Women dressed five times a day and danced half the night. The men whiled away a good deal of time in the unsatisfactory pursuit of "fighting the tiger." The visitors lived in huge hotels at one or other of which there was a ball every night—a "hop" was the charming Saratoga expression. There was little exercise save a dressed-to-death dawdle on the promenade. Saratoga is still to the fore; it is crowded, and the "hops" are as lively and the dresses as gay and as frequently changed as ever, but it is the resort now of only second-rate people, and of foreigners who think that they are studying there the eccentricities of American good society.

The latter has of late years undergone a wholesome change of sentiment as regards the pleasures of summer life. There has been a great awakening to the beauties of nature and to the sweet charm of simplicity. People crave to smell the fresh briny breezes, or to get away into sequestered upland regions, and live among leaves and rocks and waterfalls. Hotel life has "given out" in favour of the quieter and more domestic cottage life. Of course, there is luxury, but the luxury is accompanied by at least comparative simplicity. A lovely resort, much favoured by New Englanders, to whom it is what Oban or Penzance is to the Briton, is the cool picturesque island of Mount Desert, on the coast of Maine. There is scarcely any town—only a few fisher huts, two or three hotels, and a broad mountain slope studded from the waterside to the summit with picturesque cottages. But that no sea laves the feet of the hill capital of India, there is a striking resemblance between Mount Desert and Simla. Here the visitors have their own canoes, with a real Indian at the paddles, and they make horseback excursions to the glens and waterfalls inland. Even near New York, within an hour's ride or sail, are still to be found sequestered places whither the "hoodlum" excursionist—"hoodlum" is the American for 'Arry—does not find his way. Thus retired and quiet are villages in Staten Island, up Long Island Sound and here and there on the Hudson; and pleasantest of all, perhaps, Far Rockaway, looking straight into the face of the broad Atlantic. Farther off there is Long Branch, also facing the Atlantic, where an ocean esplanade seven miles long is lined with beautiful cottages, in one of which (Elberon) poor President Garfield died at last after his long struggle to survive Guiteau's bullet.

And then there is Newport. But to do justice to Newport one ought not to bring it in at the end of a cursory sketch. It demands not a paper but a volume to itself, and has indeed given the name to a what in England would have been a three-volume novel. It is a summer resort of a large proportion of the élite of American society, which here alone, save at Washington, assumes something of a cosmopolitan character, because visitors come to it as well from abroad as from all parts of the Union, although the New Yorkers arrogate to themselves the supremacy. At Newport people play with the fancy of being in Arcady, but it is an Arcady peopled by Watteau shepherdesses. It is a fabulously expensive place; the price of a site for a cottage would make a modest man like myself quite independent of the necessity for spoiling any more paper and slinging any more ink. Yes, they live in cottages; but they are cottage ornées of a very elaborate and sumptuous kind, whose interiors are museums of costly taste, while their exteriors are beautified by a wealth of rare flowers and exquisite foliage. In the mornings the quaint old town, in which yet dwell descendants of the Pilgrim Fathers, has its streets made lively by pretty little basket-phaetons, driven by ladies dressed with an elaboration of simplicity, who amuse themselves by spending money in buying utterly useless but expensive trifles. The afternoons are devoted to picnics, driving excursions, lawn-tennis gatherings, polomeets, short yacht voyages, boating, and hunting

—for there is a pack of English foxhounds which run a drag until it reaches a point where a wretched bag-fox has been turned down, and in its scared bewilderment seldom fails to furnish the hunt with the approved climax of a "kill." There is the casino, which in the mornings is a sort of "conversation house," and in certain evenings of the week is a ballroom; and there is the Redwood reading-room, where flirtations somewhat complicate the desultory pursuit of literature. Altogether, Newport is rather too lively for quiet people, and a good deal too artificial for those who desire to enjoy the charms of nature unsophisticated by the more or less eccentric conditions of exacting fashion.

DOUGHTOWN SCRIP.

PERHAPS I ought to begin by mentioning that this is not a "City Article." Nor am I either a broker or a jobber, although I do propound the question—Does any reader ardently burn to possess himself of some Doughtown scrip? If so, I am prepared to supply a considerable parcel of the same.

It behoves me to explain, first, what "Doughtown scrip" is, and secondly, how I came to be a holder of it. It is necessary to begin by being geographical.

Nearly the whole of the west coast of the Middle Island of New Zealand is auriferous. Fifteen years ago the diggings there were perhaps the richest in the world. It seemed as if you could hardly go wrong. A ship's boat disembarked you on the black sand of the sea-shore. You need have gone no farther, but simply have shovelled the black sand into your dish, washed it in the sea-water, and lo! there was a rich golden residuum. Ten thousand diggers—you could not call them miners—were delving in the black sand of a long strip of beach sixty miles south of Hokitika. On the low ridge behind the sand was a long row of canvas drinking-shops and canvas dance-houses. It was the same on the beach between Hokitika and Greymouth. Inland for miles the valley of every creek swarmed with toiling diggers. Hokitika to-day moulders along with a population of some 2000 souls, and a digger on the "bend" in its quiet decorous public-houses would be regarded as a strange curiosity. Fifteen or sixteen years ago there was gathered in and about it a population of some 30,000 able-bodied adults, with no thought in any mind but of gold. Teeming steamers arrived twice a week from Melbourne, and discharged their living cargoes to increase the busy, lighthearted throng. These were the halcyon days of the "Speckled Hen," the "Murrumbidgee Barge," "Topping Annie," and other gay allegorical persons of light heart and lighter manners, who looked scornfully at little nuggets, and thought poorly of the economist who called for a single bottle of champagne, after a couple of circuits in the waltz's giddy maze. The region had something amazingly like a civil war all to itself, when a small army of gentlemen of the Irish persuasion broke open the gates of the cemetery, and when a serried battalion of 600 Scotch Highland miners marched into the town with pick handle on each brawny shoulder, and in a quiet business-like fashion tendered their services to the warden "to drive the Fenians into the sea." A strong, wise, masterfully discreet man, Mr. Bonner ruled the storm and assuaged it, but not until he had locked up a revolutionary priest, and exercised martial law carried out at the pistol muzzle by volunteers who had rallied to his support. It was a great triumph for him to be able to decline the offer the colonial government made him of a battalion of regulars to help him keep the peace. He knew the men he had to deal with, and to have had the soldiers would have been to draw the sword and throw away the scabbard.

Gold-mining is still an industry of this remote, isolated coast-line. But there is hardly any "surface" work now. A "rush" occurs occasionally, but it is a very mild "rush," with no feature of the old buoyant, reckless, wicked rushes. "Kentuck," after a brief acquaintance with the "Luck" for whom and with whom he died with so tender a manhood, knew more about babyways than the mass of the New Zealand miners of the old days. A decent woman in a mining camp was a phenomenon in petticoats. Now gold-mining is a settled industry. The miner is married, has a wonderful genius for a large small family, and as like as not, owns his cottage. When he migrates to a new rush, he takes his live belongings with him. The track through the tree-stumps among which are dotted about the tents and the shingle huts, swarms with children. There is a school in gear before the temporary settlement is a fortnight old. Mrs. Miner brings her man his dinner in a basin out to the hole in which he is at work, or sends it by one of the bairns; when he drops work for the day he comes home to the domestic tea, and to his own fireside if it be winter-time—to the family mosquitoes in the summer. There is no dance-house now on all the west coast. "The Speckled Hen" as the wife of a mining manager, is the "leader of society" in an outlying mining township. "Topping Annie" is the sedate widow of a local government functionary, and has the reputation of devoutness and considerable wealth. Altogether the region has long since ranged itself, abjured sack —I won't say whisky—and taken to live in a cleanly decorous fashion.

I suppose that this "Westland," as the province is called, is the most universally gold-impregnated region in the world. You may "wash" anywhere you please within ten or twelve miles of the sea, and you will not fail to get "colour," only the proportion of gold to soil is not everywhere sufficient to make gold getting profitable : nor is an adequate supply of water uniformly procurable. But there is gold everywhere. The region is overlooked by Mount Cook, a huge snow-capped mountain some 17,000 feet high. A soaring genius proposed to assail Mount Cook bodily on the hydraulic principle, by directing on it vast compressed jets of water raised from out old ocean's bed. He has not yet carried out his neat little project ; but if he ever does he will have locally stolen a march on the day specified by prophecy as that on which the mountain-tops shall be overwhelmed in the great deep. But although Mount Cook stands yet scatheless, the jet of water from the nozzle of the gold-miner's simple hydraulic apparatus is eating shrewdly into banks and ridges of a more humble altitude. The process is simple enough. The water must be plenteously forthcoming. The stream from the nozzle of a huge hose is directed dead on the auriferous "face." Everything comes away under the remorseless play of this fierce douche —soil, boulders, the spreading root-stools of felled trees. The chaotic torrent rushes downward, along a compressed channel, in the bottom of which are the long narrow boxes wherein the particles of gold fall and lie, partly because of their weight, partly because intercepted by roughnesses and holes that act as traps. Some of these hydraulic enterprises are on a large scale, and pay steady and increasing dividends.

It was not as a gold-miner that I visited Westland in a recent March—that is the autumn season in New Zealand—but as a lecturer. With all its roughness there is hardly any more intelligent chance aggregation of humanity in the world than a gold-mining community. It is sure to possess in its curious mixture, that would perhaps be more accurately defined as a jumble, an exceptional number of educated men who retain their taste for reading. Out of the world by force of their conditions, gold-miners retain a keen interest in the world, especially the world of action. They follow the story of a campaign with engrossed interest. They take sides while Britain is not in the arena; in that case they are all on one side with a grand fervour. They stand with Chard and Bromhead inside the frail stronghold of Rorke's Drift, and in fancy, with flushed faces and sparkling eyes, they charge home with the big troopers at Kassassin. It was, as I suppose, because the plain blunt stories I tried to tell on the lecturing platform were tales of campaign and battle-field, that they sent to tell me they wanted me to go among them.

The message came to me at Christchurch just as I was making ready to make a reluctant departure from beautiful, hospitable New Zealand. I took it as among the best compliments that ever had been paid me, and postponing my departure, proceeded to obey the summons. Then came the question how to get from Christchurch to Westland. Christchurch is close to the east coast of the Middle Island, the capital of the province of Canterbury, the most fertile and the most socially charming region of all New Zealand. Westland lies on the opposite coast of the same island. But between the inhabited portions of the two provinces there stretches a lofty range of rugged precipitous mountains, with snow-covered summits and glacier-clad sides. Through the ravines of these there has been made a road, compared with which, in dizzy boldness of engineering, any road-making of which I have had experience, whether in the Alps, the Carpathians, the Balkans, or the Himalayas, is tame and prosaic. A coach traverses this road three times a week. On this coach I booked myself for a box-seat. My Christchurch friends cheerfully asked me where my will was, in case of accidents, warned me to sit tight, and if I got nervous to shut my eyes; and away I went by train across the fertile Canterbury plains to Springfield, the village at the foot of the mountains where the railway ends and the coach begins.

It was a staring red vehicle—was the coach—hung in the American plan on long leather bands from front to rear. The team consisted of a pair of wheelers, and three leaders harnessed abreast. The coachman was a quiet self-contained man, a friendly companion, and apparently not bothered with any nerves. It was a pleasant ride until the evening. There had been awkward descents done at a hand-gallop, that suggested unpleasant speculations as to the vehicle's, not to say the passengers' ultimate destination if a wheel should come off. But there had been nothing very trying, and much that had been very beautiful. The gaunt mountain-tops all around, the lovely lakes down in the basins, whose deep blue waters we had skirted; the long pale green stretches of upland; the romantic wooded valleys into which we had plunged so abruptly and emerged with equal abruptness; the cheery wayside taverns, lonely in the midst of the solitude, whose succulent mountain mutton we had eaten with appetite whetted by the pure keen mountain air—all went to make up an exceptionally pleasant and indeed memorable experience. We had lost time somewhere, and the short southern gloaming was about us, when the driver quietly muttered, as we turned sharp round a corner, "I don't like the Waimakariri gorge after sundown." It is with every emphasis that I record my assent to this expression; and yet when it was all over I was not sorry that the experience had befallen us. We went at a hand-gallop on a track just wide enough and no more, for our three leaders abreast. About 500 feet sheer below—sheer except in places where the cruel jagged crags reared their horrid heads—roared and boiled the furious torrent of the Waimakariri river. One could just discern through the gathering gloom the deep blackness of sullen gloomy pool alternating with the dingy white of the tortured rapids writhing their vexed course through the rocks that impeded the river-bed. Above us towered a beetling crag-wall as high, where the eye could catch its sky line, as the drop on the side next the river was deep. But this was only in places; for the most part it actually overhung us, and the narrow road was notched out of its looming face. It overhung worst at the sharp bends of the road, as it followed the curves, the projections, and the indentations of that serrated precipice. Not once, but often, the leaders as they galloped round a turn were clean out of our sight, and there was but the point of the pole projecting over the profound, ere as yet the wheelers, urged close to the verge that the wheels might clear the projecting buttress, complied with the sharp bend, borne round on their haunches by the driver's strong left arm. His attention was con centrated on his work, but once he spoke, and I would rather he had held his tongue. "Do you see these dim white specks on the flat top of that crag below us? They are the bleached bones of some horses. The beasts were pasturing on the upland above us, when a sudden scare sent them over the precipice. They fell clear outside the road without touching it, and brought up where you see their bones down there."

It was full dark ere we got through the gorge. Then the moon rose as we galloped across the upland flat, and drew up in front of "The Bealey" Hotel, the half-way house. "The Bealey" is a sort of hospice several thousand feet above the sea-level. All around it hang the everlasting glaciers. From their smooth, cruel, cold blue faces, we saw the moonbeams refracted inhospitably. But there was no inhospitality inside "The Bealey." A great log fire blazed in the ample chimney of the old-fashioned panelled parlour, and how good was that juicy slice of mountain mutton eaten with the great floury potatoes! The landlord gave me a posy of edelweiss that he had culled the same day on the glacier edge behind the house; he had tried the plant in his garden, but it would not thrive. The thin ice was on the bath-tub next morning, and it was cruel cold when, long before sun-up, the coach renewed its journey. A long heavy stage in the shingle bed of the Bealey river, where we saw the wreck of a coach that had been caught in a freshet and whirled down a few miles ere it had brought up, led to a steep climb on to a bare saddle whose summit was the highest point of the journey. Then followed the abrupt tortuous descent into the dismal Gehenna of the Otara gorge.

I remember nothing so weird. Whatever lay before us beyond the summit of the saddle lay unrevealed and mysterious in a veil of dense white mist. Into this vagueness we plunged at a gallop, whirling with startlingly sharp twists down a steep zigzag. From out the hidden mist-wrapped depths rose an ominous roaring turmoil. There were fleeting glimpses of sheer precipice, its lip just grazed by the coach-wheels. Down and yet down, till in a sudden wheel, one looked dizzily over the edge to see white water tearing and struggling far below. Then cataracts dashed from the rocks above us sheer down into the water below us, leaving road and the wayfarers on it dry behind their feathery spray that sparkled in the early sun which was fighting with the fog. Stretches of road down in the gorge here were laid on tree trunks that bridged the spaces from projection to projection. Places were worn to a slant by the torrents that battled and foamed their way across the track, and here and there the outer edge of the road crumbled and gave under the coach-wheels. One final sharp wriggle, we had darted across a wooden bridge hanging above the foaming torrent; and then the Otara gorge was behind us, and we were pulling up outside the lonely breakfast-house. We were in Westland.

A few miles farther, and we were in the "twelve mile avenue." Surely there is no avenue under the sun to compare with this wondrous natural arcade! High overhead the tall pines interlace their dark green branches, their sombre stiffness diversified by the tenderer tint of beech leaves and by the long graceful pendulous sprays of the weeping birches. That is the roof of this glorious aisle of nature's cathedral; but of it, and of the sunlight struggling down through it, you catch mere glimpses. For the aisle has a lower roofing of green lace. The avenue is lined by the boles of tree-ferns, up whose brown bark the delicate ivy and the flowering creepers twine; and the arching fern fronds, springing gracefully in wide curves from each stem-top, meet and interweave droopingly overhead. In this fairy avenue it is always cool and shady. There is ever the sound of lazily dripping water from some hidden rill percolating through the lavish tangled undergrowth. The greenery oppresses you with no sense of monotony. For clambering out on every branch, and clinging to every frond stem, the creeping rata expands its wild wealth of crimson blossoms. If there be a break in the avenue for an instant, there is a glimpse of the mountain face opposite, its lower slopes hazily purple with the flush of rhododendron blossom; higher up the cold blue glacier, and above everything, towering into the azure sky, the fantastic snowy peaks. This avenue is simply a dream of beauty twelve miles long. Were there no pink terraces in New Zealand, were there no Sydney Harbour with its lovely picturesque indentations, were there no Mount Macedon in Victoria, no Blue Mountains in New South Wales, no Mount Lofty in South Australia, no Hawkesbury, no Fitzroy, no water-sheen from Rangitoto, no Sounds between Nelson and Picton more picturesque than any Norwegian fjord, were there no more scrap of scenery in all the Australasias, the soft mystic beauty of this avenue would repay the pains of a journey across the world.

But it is not yet—at the end of the " twelve miles avenue" where Doughtown is to be found. Emerging from the avenue the coach has to ford the Takamakow river. Even in the quietest time this is no easy feat, for the boulders in the river-bed are big and shifting, and the deep current flows swift. This river comes down in the most strangely sudden freshets. It is told of a flock of sheep that it was driven from Canterbury to Westland without crossing the Takamakow. That happened thus. At night the shepherd drove his flock across an old dry bed of the stream on to a grassy patch that had once been an island. There was rain during the night up in the mountains. In the morning when the shepherd went on with intent to ford the river, he found no river to ford, only a bed in which some pools still lingered. While he slept the river had come down in flood, and carved its way back into the old bed! From the Takamakow the coach whirls on through the Kumara mining township, and beyond through others till it reaches its destination, in moist, quiet, sleepy Hokitika.

The day after a lecture night in Hokitika, on which occasion necessity compelled the use of a "property" monument as a reading desk, the cover of which of course fell off at the most enthralling passage, and disclosed, amid the cheers of the audience, an inscription which described the monument as "sacred to the memory of the sainted Maria," some friends were kind enough to drive me out to look at the "Humphrey's Gully" gold-mining claim. It was a pleasant drive, through picturesque country, in which nestled quaint mining hamlets that already had taken on a strangely old-world aspect. Everywhere were ferns such as would have given ecstasies to a British fancier; and over the fern-verdure waved the tall sombre pines. A broad placid river flowed gently down to the sea, margined by paddocks whose grass had the greenness of the old country. And above the flowing water, clinging on the slopes between the river-meadows and the ferns, there were pretty picturesque cottages over whose porches and gables trailed the roses and honeysuckles. About ten miles from Hokitika we pulled up at a lone public-house, where we were to leave the vehicle; for the rest of the way to where Humphrey's nozzle played on the "face" of his Gully was to be done only on foot, and not very easily thus, as I had occasion to discover.

As we halted, there emerged from the bar of the

public-house, a man. He wore the long boots and the woollen jumper of a miner, but he had accentuated his mission by accoutring himself with a tall hat considerably the worse for wear. This article of attire he took off, and deliberately set down on the stoop under the public-house verandah. From its depths he produced a voluminous blue pocket handkerchief which he used with effusion and replaced. Then he accosted the inmates of the vehicle.

He set forth, using grotesquely the longest words he could unearth, that he was a delegate from Doughtown, which he explained was across the swamp and beyond the ridge. Doughtown had heard that I was being brought out to visit Humphrey's Gully, and had sent its representative to beg with all respect, but with vehement urgency, that I should pay a visit to Doughtown, and favour the inhabitants of that camp with a lecture. It was a young and sequestered place, was Doughtown, he explained; still chiefly in the canvas stage of development. He had been appointed town clerk in advance of the town; and he spoke therefore with some official position. If I consented, he would immediately return to Doughtown with the news, whereupon a deputation should betake itself to where we now were, to await our return from Humphrey's Gully, and escort me across to Doughtown in worthy and seemly fashion.

There was only one reply possible to so flattering a request. The delegate reinstated his hat, and diffidently offered to "shout" for drinks round; he was told, he explained, to spare no expense, only he wished to avoid seeming presumptuous. We walked on into the Gully; he started across the swamp for Doughtown. Of the Gully I will only say that it was very rugged, very slippery, and not a little damp. But even in the remote recesses of Humphrey's Gully, civilisation was justified of her children. We had "afternoon tea" with a miner's wife in a shanty whose canvas walls were lined with pictures from the *Illustrated News* and *Graphic*. The good lady had some children, but professed concern about her eldest son, a live youth of twelve. She could not get him to mind his books, for there was no minute of any day that he did not spend in assiduous prospecting. The young gentleman took me aside later on, and tried to open a negotiation in relation to a claim which he averred would beat the Humphrey's Gully into fits.

As we approached "Webster's Corner," on the return journey, the Doughtown deputation were visible, lounging under the verandah. We were greeted with a cheer as we drove up, and every member of it, duly introduced by the "town clerk," who by this time was himself rather limp although his tall hat retained its aggressive stiffness, solemnly shook hands. They were a fine manly-like set of fellows, those Doughtown men; strapping, upright, bearded, with heads well up, and frank honest eyes. The speech bewrayed that most of them were Scots.

They had a final drink round, and then we set out for the two miles' trudge to Doughtown. There was no cart road to that place, and no wheeled vehicle had ever been nearer it than "Webster's." The "town clerk" hilariously led the way; we followed in a posse; and a lone man in the rear trudged with a big stone jar slung by a strap over his shoulder. When we got into the swamp the miners insisted on carrying me on a "king's cushion." With interclasped hands two abreast made a sort of seat on which I sat with an arm round the neck of each of my bearers. I was not in robust health, and they had somehow come to know this: they all but resorted to physical force to ensconce me in the living chair in which I sat. Then we climbed a low green ridge, and lo, Doughtown lay at our feet.

As regards looks, Doughtown had no great pretensions. There was a higgledy-piggledy of tents and shanties among the stumps, and all around was the oozy stunted sour-looking forest. Some holes there were, and hillocks of sweaty soil, and here and there a "whim," and yonder a windlass with a bucket close up to the cross-bar. The population, numbering about two hundred able-bodied men, a good many women, and a large assortment of children, had clustered in the foreground, and welcomed our appearance in the distance with vehement cheering and a desultory gun-fire. A few flags waved in the damp languid wind. As we drew near, Doughtown came out to meet us. A grey-bearded man was in advance; him the "town clerk" introduced under the high-sounding title of "the reeve of Doughtown." Then with indiscriminate hand-shaking we passed on, until the reeve halted in front of a central shanty which I assumed was the Guildhall and Mansion House of Doughtown all in one. We —my Hokitika friends had accompanied me—were invited inside, where the brown jar made good its appearance, and where, after formal introduction to the conscript fathers, the health was enthusiastically drunk of the person whom the worthy reeve was so good as to call "our distinguished visitor." After those preliminaries the formal business commenced on the stoop outside.

Modesty needs that I bury in oblivion the flattering expressions which his worship permitted himself in introducing me to the Doughtown audience. It was necessary for me to explain that having been taken by surprise, I could only speak from memory. But the excellent folks of Doughtown were not exacting. Any pause that occurred from a lapse in ready words they filled up with applause. One longer interval than usual they melodiously utilised by singing "For he's a jolly good fellow," right through to the bitter end. When I had made an end of speaking, "God save the Queen" was sung, partly as a finale, partly as introduction to the speeches in which a vote of thanks was proposed. Then it became time for us to go. But I must not go empty-handed, as it seemed.

I had noticed the "town clerk" with his hat in his hand, dodging about among the audience standing there out in the open. Presently he came up on to the stoop and whispered to the reeve. That civic chief spread his red cotton handkerchief on the table which had been brought outside, and the town clerk emptied into the handkerchief the contents of his hat. It was a curious collection. There was a sovereign, several half-sovereigns, at least one threepenny piece, and quite a number of little nuggets. And this miscellaneous assortment of metal the reeve announced was Doughtown's contribution in requital of my lecture. He wished, said he, he was sure all wished, that the collection had been four times as liberal, but "things," he explained, "are just now rather quiet with us." Of course I could not take the offering—that was out of the question. I declined with some expression of full satisfaction in the compliment that had been paid to me, the pleasant memory of which any recompense would utterly mar. I picked out a small nugget which I would have set in a shirt pin as a souvenir, and concluded by wishing success to Doughtown.

But the authorities were obviously not quite satisfied with this arrangement. There was a consultation between the reeve and the town clerk. The latter went inside, and came back with a small packet which he handed to his worship. Then his worship commanded silence, and spoke thus:—

"Sir, to-day will be memorable in Doughtown

annals. It marks the first step in Doughtown's intellectual career. You, sir, have come among us. We are a remote community, but we have energy, perseverance, and industry. You can tell the old country when you go back to it, that in becoming New Zealand colonists, we have not ceased to be Britons. You have heard us, sir, sing 'God Save the Queen,' and that with us, sir, was no unmeaning chant; it came from out our very hearts. We are a peaceful folk. You have described battles to us, and I am sure you had no listener who was not glad that his lot has not been cast in such scenes. But there is no man of us who would not brave all the dangers and horrors you told us of, on behalf of queen and country. You will do us a good turn if you will let that be known at home. And, sir, you decline to take any recompense for the trouble you have given yourself this day on our account. But we may beg of you to take away with you such a souvenir as may give you an interest in the fortunes of Doughtown. Some of our citizens have just united their mining interests into a company, the prospects of which, it is true, are still in embryo, but in which we allow ourselves firmly to believe. I hold in my hand, sir, the scrip of two hundred shares in the 'Doughtown United Gold Mining Company, Limited,' and of that scrip, sir, in the name of the community of Doughtown, I respectfully request your acceptance. For the present you will find it unsaleable at any price; but the time may come, sir, when, in the words of Dr. Johnson, it may 'enrich you beyond the dreams of avarice.' Your acceptance, sir, will give Doughtown a fresh incentive to make the enterprise a success!"

I took the scrip. One share I have pasted into my album as a souvenir. The rest I do not care particularly about holding. The rumour of an imminent call has reached me. Perhaps I should mention that there is a liability of fifteen shillings on each share. The worthy reeve did not mention this petty circumstance, and of course I could not look the gift-horse in the mouth. Are there any applicants then for 199 shares of the "Doughtown United"?

A POET WAIF.

IN the spring of 1883, in the course of a long visit to Australia, I happened to visit the Queensland town of Rockhampton. During my stay in that pleasant place, where by the flowing Fitzroy prosperous squatters and stalwart bushmen rub shoulders with sturdy miners, I casually came across a little volume of poems, published obscurely enough in Rockhampton in 1869, and bearing on the rag of green paper which formed its cover the title of *Voices from the Bush*. The verses, apart from the question of their merits, had for me a singular and a painful interest, the nature of which I shall presently explain. But first let me make a few observations on the intrinsic character of them.

It takes time for a new country to mature into literary expression in the poetic form. If there are writers of verse among its early people, these for the most part go for inspiration to the abstract rather than the concrete. They soar aloft in generalisations, and fail to note how pregnant with poetic suggestiveness are the new, fresh, unconventional conditions in the heart of which their lives are cast. So far as

I remember, the blue lakes, the full-flowing streams, the lone pine-forests of Canada have inspired no local poet to sing their beauties, their glories, their grand solemnity. It was an Irish poet, writing in a London Street, who indited the "Canadian Boat Song." It was a modern American poet whose mellifluous strains told of the "forest primeval" and of the life and love under its shadow in that Acady, where now the Novia Scotian farmer tills his fields and hauls their produce to the nearest railway station. Where is the early local poesy of America? When at length its crop of poets grew, their verse for long took little heed of the common life around them. Longfellow was in type rather an Anglo-Saxon than an American poet; Hiawatha and Evangeline, it is true, are localised, but they are no more imbued with, what for want of a better expression I may call contemporary local colour, than is Gertrude of Wyoming. Poe, with all his genius, has written no line racy of his own soil or his own countrymen. Emerson has sung of abstractions; Walt Whitman's beauties, like his pruriency, range free of any specific localisation. The great war, indeed, stirred souls to martial poetry, and the fighting lyrics of Buchanan Reid stir the blood like the sound of a trumpet. The Argonauts of the Pacific Slope found, too, their commemorators in the verses of Bret Harte and Joaquin Miller, gifted men who, products in the first instance of Eastern culture, carried their impressionability with them when they went out West, and stirred by the provocation of their wild picturesque surroundings, flung a halo of poetry round the rocking of the miner's cradle and the camp-fire under the quivering pine-trees that clothe the shoulders of the snow-crested Shasta.

There is strangely little Australian poetry that has for its subject the unchallengeable picturesqueness of that free unconventional life which is now already so nearly extinct, that the traveller may "do" Australia from Port Lincoln to Cook Town, from Cooper's Creek to Wilson's Promontory, and scarcely find a trace of it. Save in the outlying regions, the boundary-rider has taken the place of the stockman; paddocking has all but abolished the lonely shepherd. Gold mining is now an industry of capital and elaborate machinery, and the rare casual "hatter" poking among the débris of twice turned dirt, is a curiously inadequate and colourless substitute for the busy thousands who thirty years ago were burrowing in the golden dross of Forest Creek and Eureka Flat. And one searches strangely in vain for the story of this old new life told in verse, for expression of the poetic side of that life, a side of which it was surely rich to exuberant affluence. If there be any lays of the gold-fields within the yet narrow precincts of Australian literature, it was my misfortune to have failed to discover them. Poor Gordon, with a pathos that swells the heart, has let "the Dying Stockman" sing his own requiem in verse that will not die, and who but must sorrow that the hapless author of

"Galloping Rhymes" did not let himself live to enrich the garden of poetry with more flowers of quaint pathetic *insouciance ?* The rich field of Australian scenic description, so far as I know, is all but virgin soil, save where Kendall here and there has turned a furrow which makes us mourn that it was not longer and broader. But Kendall, with all his sensitiveness to beauty, all his sweet gracefulness of expression, does not strike his ploughshare into the everyday life of young Australia. Gordon, indeed, stirs us with a genuine crack of the stock-whip, and makes our nerves tingle to the long strong gallop of the stock-horse. But who has given us a glimpse of the poetic side of the strange lone life of the solitary shepherd ? Who has made our ears ring to the stroke of the pickaxe as it struck the boulder nugget, or essayed to picture the emotions of its wielder as the thrill of gold ran up his arms to his heart ? Where are the verse tales of bush life and bush death ? Of the " shout " of the not yet " lambed down " bushman, flush with the unmelted cheque— of the reefer watching with eager hungry eyes the " washing up " after the crushing—of the feverish life-spasm of the gold-fields—of the tragedies which beset the miner's toil ? Surely there is indicated here a wide and fertile field that must have lain ripe unto rich harvest to the hand of the husbandman wielding the sickle of a poetic spirit, where that spirit gay or serious, buoyant or sombre.

But I had searched with little fortune for sheaves

of such a harvest, until I chanced upon those all but still-born *Voices from the Bush*. They are rugged, doubtless, careless, and here and there turgid when meant to be impressive; but it seems to me that they go right home. They speak in no dilettante tone. The writer of those verses proves in every line, in every phrase, that he tells of that which he does know, testifies of that which he understands. He has lived every phase of the life he sings. Yes; this man, manifestly, has spent his New Year's Eve in the shepherd's lonely hut; he has "smashed his cheque" with his eyes wide open to his own folly; he has stood by the miner's grave, and seen the dead shepherd buried "between two sheets of bark"; he has held a share in a reefing claim, throbbed with eagerness that it should yield "23 dwt. to the ton," and made genial game of his own disappointment when the crushing proved a blank failure. He has lived and moved and had his being in the atmosphere whose lights and shadows he sets himself to depict with a brush that is faithful, if careless and sometimes rough. He opens for the outsider the arcana of this quaint, picturesque, half-merry, half-melancholy, all-reckless life that is now all but obsolete in that Australia which is now so fast undergoing the process of reduction to conventionality.

Up among the heather hills of Northern Scotland two brothers were reared together in a Presbyterian manse. They went to the parish school together, and thence to the university. Both, it seemed, had rebellious, froward blood in their veins. The elder, his college career over, went out into the world. It was for him a somewhat turbulent world, or rather, it might be the truer to say that he made it so. From the boat of a timber-drogher water-logged in its voyage home from Quebec, he slid into the saddle of a heavy dragoon, and out of that into the career of a war correspondent. Of him more need not be said. The younger, and by far the more brilliant brother remained at the university until "sent down" for a madcap piece of youthful folly; either snowballing or lampooning a professor—the tradition is not exact. In shame for this mishap he must needs run off to sea, and sailored all over the world till at length, some twenty-two years ago, still scarce more than a lad, he stranded somehow on the shore of Queensland. For years but vague and piecemeal tidings of him reached his relatives. There had been none at all for ten years, when it happened to the elder brother—the war correspondent lecturing brother—to pay a visit to Queensland; and he naturally gave his attention to search out the career of the vagrom son of their father. The story of that career came to him in scraps. One and another casual informant told how the scapegrace had been now on a cattle station "up north"; now shepherding on the Burnett; now reefing on the Morinish goldfield, itself all but a memory for years; again in sugar culture in the Mackay district; later, roadmaking about Roma, and then another spell of roadmaking at Mount Abundance; still later in the washpool at shearing time about Toowoomba; and last of all in the graveyard of that place, after a long illness in its hospital. The old familiar sad story of a wrecked life and a premature death! Yet no voice anywhere to utter aught save kind and loving words of the brilliant reckless waif, always cheery, always a true friend—to all save himself, alas!; strewing his desultory path with blithe humour, with yet-remembered scraps of verse, here jovial and boisterous, there tenderly pathetic. To the searching brother came men from afar, earnest to testify to the love they bore in their memory to "poor old Alick"; rugged miners from Charters Towers, grizzled and bronzed bush hands from the Downs, managers of sheep and cattle "stations" who had "bossed" him, and had been chaffed or eulogised in his ever ready verses. And the hospital warder, too, of Toowoomba, who had at last closed his eyes, his own somewhat dim, honest fellow, as he told the sad simple story; and the good old Presbyterian minister, also, to whom, as the sands were running out, the son of the manse turned with the rekindled instinct of his boyhood. There were vague stories of a little book of poems that had been published somewhere, but that trail was faint, until at length a Rockhampton man who had known and loved him whose name among his fellows was "Alick the poet," brought to the brother the little green volume on whose title-page was the legend "Voices from the Bush, by Alexander Forbes."

The "Voices" are very unequal, but they are very genuine. Many of them are so local and so full of topical allusion as to have little further interest than in so far as they lift the curtain from that curious phase of life—the life of a gold-field—with which they deal. But others, I make bold to think, may well bear extrication from the obscurity of the green paper covers. These stanzas, for example, if they disclose none of the abrupt force and now cynical, now tender, contrasts of Gordon's " Dying Stockman," seem to me to have a wistful haunting plaintiveness that finds a ready access to the heart, and may, perchance, even rise to the eyes :—

THE SHEPHERD'S GRAVE.

On a grassy bank doth the shepherd lie
   Which the creek's dull waters lave,
Where the gum-trees nod to the azure sky,
And naught one hears but the curlew's cry,
   You may see his lonely grave.

In a distant land, long years ago,
   A tender mother smiled
O'er the cradle of him who sleeps below ;
And she often, I ween, would a kiss bestow
   On the lips of her slumbering child.

*   *   *   *   *

When his father died, in that trouble great,
   She turned to her sturdy boy,—
Ah, little she dreamed of his dismal fate !—
And she prayed that he, in her widowed state,
   Might grow up her hope and joy.

*   *   *   *   *

> Even yet she may think that her boy doth roam,
>   And her aching heart may burn
> With hope that again he will seek his home,
> As she wistfully gazes across the foam
>   For him who will ne'er return.
>
> For low and deep doth the shepherd sleep,
>   By the Queensland waters lying,
> He hath laid him down in a nameless grave,
> Where the curlews shriek and the gum trees wave,
>   And the southern winds are sighing.

But this miscellaneous " Laureate of Queensland," as he jocosely claims to be, will not have it that the followers of his capricious muse shall stand overlong sadly by the shepherd's lonely resting-place. He whisks them with a turn of the leaf from the nameless grave to the mining claim, and rattles off a comic ditty of a warmly speculative complexion.

His castle in Spain rises story after story; and, when the whole imaginary structure topples to the ground, the laughing philosopher makes a quaint jingle of the misfortune, and distils the catastrophe and its consequences into a dozen lines of spasmodic " patter ":—

NO. 2 REEF, BEFORE CRUSHING.

> Now, if this claim turns out an ounce,
>   Right joyful I shall be;
> I'll walk into the Morinish
>   And have a jolly spree.
>
> And if two ounces it should run,
>   By Jove that would be glorious;

Rockhampton I'd turn upside down,
    And spend a month uproarious.

And if three ounces we should get,
    That just would suit my kidney;
I'd take my passage in the boat,
    And have a trip to Sydney.

If we four ounces should obtain,
    No longer here I'd tarry;
The steamer which takes home the mails,
    This male should also carry.

And if a duffer it should prove—
    But, Lord! I'll say no more now;
I have a guardian angel,
    And he's stuck to me before now.

AFTER CRUSHING.

D—NATION, vexation, tribulation, starvation, consternation.

Too bad, poor lad, very sad, close up mad, grog not to be had.

Sanguinary rot, queer lot, soon must trot, gone to pot, quite forgot.

Limited tick, publicans sick, blocked quick, dirty trick, no longer a brick.

No cash, frightful smash, too rash, can't be flash, final crash.

Up a tree, here with me, plain can see, soon must flee, little glee.

Seven weights, cruel fates, all the slates, made up to dates, horrid straits.

Hard luck, everywhere stuck, no more truck, below zero pluck.

    Credit stopped, curtain dropped, heavy debts, no assets.
    Number Two, adieu!

I do not pretend to be an impartial reader of the touching verses which follow; but I am not ambitious to share the indifference of him who can read them without being moved, not less by their spirit than by their tender lingering cadence. If this be not something better than mere verse-making—if it be not true poetry, and all the truer because of its limpid simplicity, its unstrained felicity of word-painting, its completeness of the realisation of lonely bush solitude in a few casual yet how effective strokes —then I must submit to know that my test of poetry, whether it moves me or no, is a snare and a delusion. But the reader will let his own feelings be the test for him of the merits of

THE SHEPHERD'S NEW YEAR'S DAY

The shepherd was out in his hut alone
   On his pallet hard reclining,
Not a sound was heard but the night wind's moan,
Or the mope-hawk hooting with solemn tone
   To the stars which were brightly shining.

The fire had gone down to a single spark
   Which glowed in a smouldering ember,
But little he cared that the place was dark,
For he had no timepiece by which to mark
   The last fleeting hours of December.

And his thoughts went back to his native land
   Where the sweet church bells were ringing;
Where his kindred have met in a happy band,
And at twelve o'clock, joined hand in hand,
   Dear "Auld Langsyne" are singing.

    *   *   *   *   *

Ah! woe is me for those glorious days,
　　Alas for the youth-time squandered,
When I roved upon Scotia's snow-clad braes,
Or when the lark's sweet song of praise
　　O'er the verdant meadows wandered.

　　　*　　　*　　　*　　　*　　　*

And the shepherd knelt down by his lowly bed,
　　In the heart of the Queensland wild-wood;
And a fervent prayer to his Maker said,
His blessings to share on each dear one's head
　　Whom he loved in his happy childhood.

And hope came down from his Father's throne;
No longer his thoughts had a mournful tone,
　　As in solitude he was lying.
He was hushed to sleep by the night wind's moan,
And the creaking gum-tree's hollow groan
　　For the old year that was dying.

It has been well said of a parody that to be perfect it must be "pat," and I think the annexed fairly fulfils this requirement. Another method it possesses is its naked truthfulness. If the writer of the lines haply testifieth of his own experience, his testimony, I fear, could not be more ruthlessly at once and ruefully accurate.

FOR ALCOHOL.

THE shades of night were falling fast,
As through a Queensland township passed
A youth, who seemed to little reck,
So long as he could smash his cheque
　　　　For alcohol.

His cheeks were tanned, his brow was dun,
Through long exposure to the sun,
And like a brazen trumpet strong
He shouted as he went along
    For alcohol.

In well-lit bars he saw the rum
For which so many miles he'd come;
Far out the night was dark and drear;
Besides he had not for a year
    Seen alcohol.

"Try not the road," the landlord cried,
"You will be better far inside,
My house with comforts doth abound;"
In went the youth and "shouted" round
    For alcohol.

"Stay," said the barmaid with a wink,
"We'll serve you with the best of drink;"
A leer shone in his bloodshot eye,
And loudly he again did cry
    For alcohol.

And there he stayed until with rum
He got most blindly overcome;
So thoroughly they skinned him out,
No coin was left wherewith to shout
    For alcohol.

"Beware the gutter's miry swamp,
Clear out from here and find some camp!"
This was the waiter's last farewell,
And from the puddle came a yell
    For alcohol.

Next morning, by the watchful trap,
Half hid in mud, without a rap,

Was found that youth who did not reck
So long as he could smash his check
    For alcohol.

There, in a kennel smeared with clay,
Alive, but mortal drunk he lay ;
While from his lips so parched and dry
Escaped at intervals a cry
    For alcohol.

He who sings the requiem of the dead shepherd has seen in how awfuller, swifter fashion, death comes to another mate in the person of the working miner, and essays the task of chanting the dirge of the entombed digger :—

THE DIGGER'S BURIAL.

On the gory field of battle,
    'Neath the dun and sulphurous sky,
'Mid the cannons' thundering rattle,
    Bravely doth the soldier die ;
'Tis the death for him most glorious,
    When a bullet lays him low,
And the battle cry victorious
    Tells of many a vanquished foe.

Far upon the heaving ocean,
    When the storm king in his wrath,
'Mid the elements' commotion,
    Threatens all who cross his path ;
Mark yon hapless vessel founder,
    Gulphed beneath the greedy wave,
While the sea-birds shriek around her—
    'Tis the sailor's fitting grave.

In the freshness of his vigour,
   See, in yonder narrow hold,
Eagerly the hardy digger
   Sinks in search of hidden gold;
Fathoms down his way achieving,
   Deep into the earth's dark womb,
Foot by foot still stoutly cleaving—
   Digging for himself a tomb.

Hark! the earth gives way above him
   And falls in with deafening roar;
Woe is me for those who love him,
   For they ne'er shall see him more.
Down the shaft his messmates calling
   Listen with abated breath,
But the silence is appalling—
   Naught below but ghastly death.

*   *   *   *   *

Ah! the funeral of the digger
   Was a solemn thing, I ween;
Round the grave each mourner's figure
   Dim and indistinct was seen,
As the firelight o'er them streaming
   But a fitful radiance gave,
While the stars, serenely beaming,
   Shine upon the miner's grave.

Round the spot where he is lying
   Soft's the murmur of the breeze,
And like dirges o'er him sighing
   Is the rustling of the trees;
And the digger calm is sleeping
   'Neath Australia's dust-flecked sod,
There we left him to the keeping
   Of his Saviour and his God.

I humbly hope the reader will bear with me for having ventured to throw this stone on the cairn of a poor gifted shipwrecked brother, who with happier fortune might have taken some rank among the sweet singers of our language, and have been not without honour among us.

X

A CHRISTMASTIDE IN THE KHYBER PASS.

KINLOCH and myself had to ride long and hard to fulfil the tryst we had made to spend our Christmas day with the cheery comrades of Sir Sam Browne's headquarter staff. It had seemed a light thing, that promise, as we had ridden out of Shere Ali's dilapidated military cantonment on the bare plain of Dakka, three weeks previously. Kinloch's work with Maude's division, lying about the foot of the fortress-crowned crag of Ali Musjid, offered no prospect of being anything more than routine duty; and I had merely to make a hurried journey down to Lahore to gather up the skeins of the rather complicated political tangle. Be Sir Sam's headquarters where they might, we should be with them without fail for that Christmas dinner, on the preparations for which Hill of the Goorkhas, the headquarter caterer since poor old "Jock" Mure had gone back sick to Peshawur, had already begun to bring his ingenuity to bear. It is all "Khyber Pass" in the broad sense from where, at the mouth of the gap between the two grim precipices, the fort of Jumrood frowns out on the plain of Peshawur; and those crumbling ramparts of Jellalabad, erstwhile so staunchly held against Afghan force and guile by the "illustrious garrison" which the gallant Sale commanded, and in which Broadfoot and Havelock served as staff officers. For the Briton who traverses that rugged road between Jumrood and Cabul there are many memories—many sombre, others inspiriting. It is the road by which, during our occupation of Cabul which ended in '42, precarious communications were maintained with the plains of India. It is the road along which Elphinstone's hapless column, in its fatal effort at retirement from the Afghan capital, struggled through blood and snow and misery and humiliation incalculable, till utter annihilation befell it, where yet the bones of British soldiers bleach in the dark crannies of the Jugdulluck Pass. It is the road by which Pollock marched his "army of retribution" through the gloomy gorges of the Lower Khyber up to where the "illustrious garrison" were holding Akbar Khan at bay outside the earthquake-rent ramparts of Jellalabad; and onward through victorious fighting at Jugdulluck and Tezeen, till the British standard waved again from the turrets of the Bala Hissar of Cabul. The Khyber route has fewer associations with our more recent experiences beyond the Sulieman range, for it was from the more southerly Kuram valley that Roberts darted over the craggy Shuturgurdan to exact retribution for the massacre of the gallant Cavagnari; and, although the troops who were more or less within sight of Ali Musjid when the Afghans evacuated that place of strength in November '79, wear a clasp on which is graven its name, it cannot be said that the distinction was earned by any memorable display of prowess.

We "took our risks," as the American phrase goes, when we rode out of the Dakka camp and set our faces toward the plains. The Dakka force was in truth all but in a state of siege. No man was safe a thousand yards beyond the British lines. Communications between the posts established at various points on the line were maintained only by armed parties in some strength. The hill-men ruthlessly cut up baggage parties, and native stragglers died the death at their hands without mercy. The day before our start the post escort had been driven back, the mail-bearer killed, and the bag containing Cavagnari's despatches to the viceroy and the correspondents' letters to their journals in England, carried off into the craggy fastnesses wherein dwelt the Upper Shinwarries. The army chaplain had made good his passage, if not by the sword of the Lord and of Gideon, by dint of the free use of his Smith and Wesson; but the camel that bore his canonical vestments as well as the holy man's clean shirts, had fallen a prey to the fell Upper Shinwarries, who had "cut up"—that was the grim phrase current—his servant and the camel-man, and carried off the clerical plunder into their precipices.

We had been offered an escort, but had declined the offer. There were three of us white men—for Lord William Beresford, who afterwards won the V.C. so worthily in Zululand, was accompanying Kinloch and myself; and a posse of four or five native servants leading spare horses followed us. We were all well armed, and it was scarcely likely that the hill-men would tackle so large a party. As for their dropping fire at long range, which was sure to be an incidental accompaniment of our journey down the Khyber, no escort could fend that off.

Our sole casualty from the straggling jezail bullets was a hole through a brass vessel strapped to a cantle of a servant's saddle. But we had not gone three miles from the camp when we had to put up with contumely at once irritating and amusing. The Upper Shinwarries, with all their faults, have a fine sense of humour. On that rocky peak 300 feet above the hollow through which we were riding, stood a strange tall figure. White robes depended from his broad shoulders, and waved from his limbs out on the breeze. In one hand he brandished a fluttering scroll as of white paper. As we drew nearer he faced us, and made as if reading to us in a loud voice from the scroll in his hand, while with the other he performed gestures of an uncomplimentary nature. Kinloch adjusted his binocular, and intently regarded him. "The scoundrel!" he presently exclaimed, "he has arrayed himself in the parson's canonicals, and I verily believe that is

Cavagnari's looted despatch he is pretending to read. He is cursing us by his gods, and using the most unparliamentary language in his infernal Pushtoo!" whereupon Kinloch took a shot with his revolver at the extremely impertinent Upper Shinwarry. That humorous person answered to the fire by bursting incontinently into a war-dance of a violently gymnastic character. Cassock and surplice were whisked about in wild gyrations, and as for the despatch, it was applied to pantomimic uses of the most contumelious kind. When the hill-man had had his fill of dancing, he picked up his gun and sent a bullet or two after us by way of parting salutation.

From the clump of trees by Lundi Khana where Magenis' battery lay camped by the little stream, we climbed to the bleak Lundi Kotul by the zigzags of the old road that Mackeson had made forty years before, now fallen into bad dilapidation. Past Afghan tower-villages, whence the hill-men are wont to watch, jezail in hand, for a shot at the neighbour (and probably brother) with whom endures the ruthless blood feud; past Khoti Khestia and its tanks, down the precipitous hill face opposite to which Macpherson and his men had slidden to intercept the retreating garrison of Ali Musjid; across the Khyber stream, in whose clear sparkling water lurks a subtle poison, and through the gruesome gorge which the horrid rocks overhang on either side, and where the only pathway is the rugged bed of the stream; then out on the graveyard-meadow at the base of the fortress rock of Ali Musjid, with its memories for us of two days' starvation while as yet supplies had not come up; and up on to the Shaghai Ridge, whence the huge missiles from the 40-pounders had gone whistling to explode against the ramparts of Ali Musjid, and over which I had ridden at a headlong gallop carrying to the telegraph wire down at Jumrood the tidings of the abandonment of the fortress by its Afghan defenders. Over against us was the slope where poor Birch and Swetenham, with their valiant Sikhs about them, had fallen in the vain effort to gain the Afghan line of outlying *sungahs*. And, grateful sight for weary travellers, the garden ground in the hollow, and the bare brow of the ridge, were studded with the tents of friends.

Up in the Khyber, among one's minor inconveniences, was the utter impossibility of reckoning on a night of unbroken quiet. On this particular night, as well on to midnight the gunners' mess broke up and under the glorious moonlight we sought our sleeping-places, one might well have been excused for the conviction that there was not a hostile hill-man within the amphitheatre bounded by the cincture of jagged peaks. As I finished my cheroot outside the long empty sepoys' tent in a hospital dhooly inside which my man had made my bed, no sound broke the stillness save the occasional neigh of a cavalry horse down among the gardens, and the contented grunt emitted by one of the artillery elephants chained in a row right in my front. Two hours later there raged a din as if the fiends were having a "night out." A bicker of musketry fire rattled down in the valley, intermingled with the wild yells and defiances of the hill-men, who were making a *chapao* or night attack on the camp. Mules were braying, horses squealing, bullocks lowing; and the elephants in front of me were rattling their chains as they trumpeted uneasily. For my own part, I had grown callous to these pestilent *chapaos*. They were never pushed home, nor meant to be; their sole aims were to harass our people and stampede some of our animals, which then became the prey of the hill-men. Besides, in the confusion bullets were apt to fly about promiscuously; and if it is unpleasant to get shot at all, I have always thought it additionally unsatisfactory to be hit in a stupid casual fashion by a bullet that when it set out on its career had not known its own mind. So I lay still in the dhooly, and, indeed, being weary, had begun to dose off again. Suddenly there was a crash, the tent caved in, and the canvas came huddling down on my dhooly. There was a rushing sound, and then the dhooly splintered into fragments about me as I lay. I was quite unhurt, but the occurrence seemed peculiar and deserved investigation, so I extricated myself from the wreckage and began to take observations. These gave me the impression that I had had rather a narrow escape. A chance bullet had gone through the ear of one of the artillery elephants chained just in front of the tent. In a paroxysm of pain and scare she had broken loose, wheeled about, and in her frantic stampede had blundered right over the tent, and either trodden on or fallen over the dhooly in which I had been lying.

At Jumrood we lost Kinloch, who remaining with Maude's division shouted after me as I rode away, " Remember our Christmas compact!" From Peshawur Beresford, I think, made a dash into the Kuram, in the forlorn hope that with Roberts he might find a spell of that fighting for which his soul longed as the hart panteth after the water-brooks; and I took dâk down to Lahore, which for the time was the virtual capital of India, since the Viceroy had come down from Simla to get his finger closer on the pulse of events, and was devoting himself to the duties of his high office with that engrossed sedulousness which the situation no doubt demanded, but against which frivolous Anglo-Indians murmured vehemently, and longed for the gay days of the Northbrook *régime* back again, as an alterative to what they denounced as the dreary workfulness of his successor's vice-reign. A few days in Lahore gave me freedom to set my face again toward the Khyber and its Christmas obligations. A generation is passed since the home-folk of this island of ours were taking thought of Christmas comforts for their loved ones confronting the enemy on foreign soil. But in hall and cottage among us, there are yet alive women with whom the memory to this day is fresh, how thirty years ago they were filling boxes with the love-gifts designed to gladden the hearts and help to the comfort of sons, brothers, and husbands in those bleak encampments from out which daily the trench-parties tramped down through mud and snow to maintain the staunch weary struggle that resulted in the fall of Sevastopol. Too few of those souvenirs attained their destination in the confusion; of those that through multifarious vicissitudes at length reached the camp, some were over late to speak to the soldier of the tender home-thought that had prompted their despatch, since in battle, trench, or hospital, death, swift or lingering, had come to him. But our sisters in India, somewhere or other around whose borders campaigning, if not actual fighting, is almost constantly going on, are practised experts in the minor science of forwarding to their men-folk in the field the opportune and welcome *Liebesgaben*. I am not prepared to be definite, after seven years, as to the number of plum puddings forming that little hillock on the top of my dâk-gharry between Jhelum and Peshawur, on the apex of which sat the faithful John amidst a whirl of dust. At Peshawur the heap of Christmas gifts were loaded into the panniers of a camel, and the ship of the desert started on its measured solemn tramp up through the defiles of the Kyber.

I remained behind for a day that I might be the spectator of a strange spectacle—a camel chase, gentleman riders up. The competitors had been named after a somewhat startling fashion. I remember that at first "Viceroy's Ultimatum" cut out the pace, but died away, when "Chamberlain's Mission" took the running for a bit. "Russian Chicanery" was well up as far as the distance, but compounded when collared, and was not persevered with. "Frontier Policy" was never in it, and "Retreat" bolted off the course. Finally "Peace with Honour" staying well, made up his lost ground, and his rider coming with quite a Chifney rush at the end, landed him an easy winner. Camels when they canter are indescribably ludicrous animals; their best pace is the trot, in which they give one a vivid idea of a four-legged ostrich. At a trot a good camel can travel a short distance at the rate of eight miles an hour, but it may be said as a general thing that he infinitely prefers a walk at the rate of two miles an hour, and is much more partial to squatting down than to travelling at all. Up in the Khyber the camels used to squat down never to rise again, in most embarrassing frequency. They were supposed to find sustenance in grazing; but is the digestion even of an ostrich equal to boulders seasoned with gravel and sand? On this fare the camel trudged on, carrying his load to the bitter end, and with now and then a groan that had a curious plaintive eloquence in its rumble; till the day came it could go no farther, and then it let itself down with all its wonted gingerliness, and the poor, ugly, patient head dropped helplessly sideways on the sand.

Reaching General Maude's headquarters at Jumrood on the outside of a commissariat mule, for I had been forced to leave both my own horses sick at Peshawur, my earliest inquiries were for Kinloch. Kinloch was in camp right enough, and had not forgotten his tryst, but meanwhile there were military duties to be done. The nuisance of fighting with the Afghans and the hill-men their congeners is this, that you never can tell when your work is over. You may have bribed them into apparent peacefulness, and as like as not you will be attacked when returning from handing over the money. Then you will take out a detachment against that particular tribe, exchange a few long shots with fellows who somehow have attained inaccessable pinnacles, burn their wretched outhouses and the paltry stores of straw and brushwood gathered in and around them, blow up their rubbishing tower, and scour the whole vicinity with horse and foot, the net result being the capture of an old woman in a condition of abject dotage. All this achieved, you will be marching home in triumph, your "political" full of self-complacency because of the "example" and the "lesson" which he is never tired talking of, when, just as your little force is in that awkward defile, a brisk fire opens upon you on flanks and rear Then you of course unlimber that solitary field-piece again, blaze away into space, follow up your shell fire by a large expenditure of the Empress of India's rifle ammunition, lose a man or two, and have no alternative but to bustle out of the tight place with what speed you may regard compatible with a show of decency, chased by the hill-men till you get out into the open, when they cease to molest you, after having in a loud voice hurled aspersions on your nearest female relatives, and bestowed on yourself a varied assortment of disparaging epithets. My views in regard to Afridi hill-men, derived from some little experience, are much those I entertain in relation to hornets' nests—that both are wisest left alone.

But the Anglo-Indian "political" on the warpath is a strange and unfathomable creature. For a long time he forbids the troops to fire a return shot at a tribe who keeps them in a chronic fidget by cutting up stragglers, blazing at sentries, and stealing stray live stock. The nuisance has quieted down and the irritation is being forgotten, when some fine day the "political," with a *Delenda est Cartago* air, proclaims the tribe's cup of provocation to be full and running over, and enjoins the commander of the troops to move out and chastise it. Such was the crisis when I reached Jumrood on my return journey up the Khyber. A highland clan called by the barbarous name of the Zukkur-Kehls, were to be proceeded against; Kinloch in his capacity of staff officer had to accompany the expedition, while I had to go too, because there might be some fighting for me to write about. The programme was a night march to be followed by a surprise, but both details miscarried, since we lost our way, and were ourselves surprised by daylight before we had nearly reached the remote valley of the Zukkur-Kehls. Well, we duly burnt their wretched huts, caught and confiscated a few wretched cattle and scraggy sheep, and brought their towers down by a few charges of powder. The force from Jumrood started back whence it had come; but General Tytler had brought through the hills from Dakka a co-operating column, and since at Dakka we should be the nearer to our friends of Sir Sam Browne's headquarters, Kinloch and I transferred ourselves to it when it turned to march back. Tytler determined to make his exit from the Zukkur-Kehl valley by a previously unexplored pass, toward which the force moved for its night's bivouac. About the entrance to the glen there was a fine forest of ilex and holly; large, sturdy, spreading trees, whence dangled long sprays of mistletoe; the mistletoe-bough was here indeed, and Christmas was close, but where the fair ones whom, under other circumstances, the amorous youth of our column would have so enthusiastically led under that spray which accords so sweet a licence? The young ones prattled of those impossible joys; but the seniors, less frivolous, were concerned by the increasing narrowness of the gorge, and by the dropping fire that hung on our skirts as we entered it. However, there was but one casualty—a poor fellow of the 17th Regt. had his thigh smashed by a bullet—and we spent the night under the ilex trees without farther molestation.

But next morning brought us into mischief. Surmounting a rocky ridge, the head of the column plunged into a ravine stupendous in its stern grandeur. The sun in places never reached the bottom of this gorge, and the little streams as they trickled over the rocks were frozen into miniature glaciers. Our way was toilsome, nor was it any the pleasanter because of the straggling fusilade that came down on us from the overhanging crags. There was no surgeon with the advance, and I had to put into practice what rough knowledge of surgery campaign experience in other lands had brought me. None of the wounds had been dangerous until we reached a bend where the crags somewhat receded, leaving an open space of the torrent-bed's shingle, athwart which wayfarers had to pass. From a knot of hillmen on a ledge above the open space the bullets came slapping on to the stones rather thickly. We hurried under cover of the bank, but as I turned round I noticed that the soldier next to whom I had been walking had gone down and was lying on his back on the exposed spot. The men of the 17th gave me plucky assistance in bringing in their comrade from his exposed situation, but we could find no satisfactory shelter, and I had to see to him with the bullets splashing on the stones all about us. It was a bad case, a bullet right through the thigh, and the only expedient practicable was to plug the wound and bandage it tightly, after which we got him into a dhooly and went on. As we were working at him

—poor fellow, there was no more Christmas for him, for he died next morning under the knife—a curious thing happened. None of us were touched, but a bullet found its billet in the chest of the poor fellow whose thigh had been smashed the previous evening, and on whom, carried on a dhooly, I had been attending in the intervals between other calls. He was already all but moribund from the first wound; the second wound but quickened up inevitable death. The world is a very small place. Having done the best for my patient, I had jotted on a scrap of paper a word or two about the nature of the wound and what I had done in the nature of what is technically called "first dressing," and as the custom is among German military surgeons in similar circumstances, I had pinned the paper to the collar of the soldier's tunic for the information of the surgeon into whose hands he might come at the Verband-platz. The other day I was presented to a lady at a garden-party, who told me she had this scrap of paper in her album, given to her as a little souvenir by her husband, the army surgeon who dealt with the wounded soldier at the dressing-place.

Our start from Dakka next morning was delayed because of the funeral of the two British soldiers in whom I had a natural interest, and it was past noon ere Kinloch and myself rode through the Khoord Khyber Pass and struck across the bleak stony expanse of the Basawal plain to Chardai, our halting-place for the night. It was Christmas Eve when we sat chatting with young Beatson in his lonely post by the Chardai streamlet; but a few hours of morning riding would carry us to Jellalabad whither Sir Sam Browne's camp had been advanced, and we were easy on the score of being true to tryst. As in the cold gray dawn we resumed our journey, leaving the young officer who had been our host to concern himself with the watchfulness of his pickets and the vigilance of his patrols, there was a sound of unintentional mockery in the conventional wish of a "Merry Christmas" to the gallant lad, and there was a wistfulness in his answering smile. From off the stony plain flecked with dead camels, we cantered through the tombs of Ali Boghan, and before us lay the fair expanse of the Jellalabad plain—the garden of the Khyber; which to us, after the monotonous stony mass of the region we had been traversing, seemed a veritable garden of Eden. The sombre-silvery foliage of the wild olive groves glistened dully in the sunlight, the reaches of the Cabul river gleamed like burnished silver, the villages girt about with trees had a distant beauty that closer inspection might have dispelled. Flocks and herds straggled over the meadow-land by the river side, and the snowy ridge of the Sufed Koh, on which the sunbeams shed a glory of tender brightness, added to the scene a fresh and rare beauty. The road to the encampment, the white canvas of whose tents showed through the intervening hills, was traversed at a hand gallop; and presently Kinloch and myself found ourselves in the street of the headquarter camp, shaking hands with friends and comrades, and trying to reply to a medley of disjointed questions.

The bugles were sounding for the Christmas Day church parade as we finished a hurried breakfast. Out there on the plain the British troops of the division were standing in hollow square, the officers grouped in the centre. The chaplain was arrayed in his clerical uniform; perhaps the Upper Shinwarry man had yielded up his loot. There were some notable fighting-men in the group in whose forefront stood the parson. He was winning the Victoria Cross in the heart of a *mêlée* of Sepoy mutineers, when a trenchant tulwar stroke severed at the shoulder the left arm of the tall grizzled old chief, but since that day the Queen's enemies once and again have known to their cost that it was not his sword arm which Sir Sam Browne lost at Seerpoorah. The compact, ruddy man whose every lineament showed his Highland extraction, was that Herbert Macpherson who won the Cross by the dashing capture of the Sepoy battery at the Charbagh Bridge, when Havelock was cutting his path to the succour of the beleaguered garrison in the Lucknow Residency; and whose higher fame as fine commander, not less than gallant soldier, was waiting for him further into the heart of Afghanistan and on the Egyptian desert among the sand-parapets of Tel-el-Kebir. The name of "Jenkins of the Guides" is a terror in every glen of that turbulent frontier-land in which he has been fighting off and on for the past twenty years. By Jenkins, his second-in-command, the chivalrous Battye, the finest soldier of all his gallant race, stood, alas, on his last Christmas parade. A little apart Cavagnari, his usual environment of fierce-eyed hill chieftians left squatting among their quaint weapons in front of his durbar tent, was absently drawing lines on the sand with his sword scabbard, his fine Italian face grave with thought. For that bold, subtle brain there was little rest in those troublous times; the shadow of the lurid future, if it haply lay across the complications of the present, brought no concern to a man who for years had been confronting a violent death every hour of his strange, audacious life. Of such men as Cavagnari is our empire of India—a thinker, a doer, a darer. The skein had not been woven that knit with his fate, the fate of the blithe-faced stalwart young Guide officer whose fine-poised head rose above the group of comrades among whom he stood. Young Hamilton was by Battye's side when the latter fell; a few months later, among the bloody embers of the Residency at Cabul, he was himself to die, confronting to the last, with the calm, cool smile on his young English face, the fierce surge of the maddened fanatic horde.

"How you English leave your dead about the world!" There was something of cold cynicism in the comment, uttered as it was by a casual French visitor to Sir Sam Browne's headquarters, one of a little party that after church parade had strolled into the old city of Jellalabad, and to whom a survivor of the memorable defence, by rare chance still soldiering in the division now lying before the place, was describing incidents and localities still fresh in his memory after nearly forty years. The Frenchman's tone rather jarred on us Britons; but we were looking down on an illustration of the truth of the remark. Below the rampart in which we stood there was a bit of waste ground, covered with the rubbish of an Oriental city. "Down there was our burial ground," said Major Bayley, who as a sergeant in the 13th Light Infantry—Havelock's old regiment—had been of the "illustrious garrison." Yes, under that area of dirt, old pack-saddles and broken crockery poor General Elphinstone, whose body, after his death in captivity up among the mountains, was brought down to Jellalabad by his faithful soldier-servant, sleeps that long sleep which ended all his troubles and misery; there, too, lies valiant Colonel Dennie of the 13th, slain in a successful sortie against Akbar Khan; and there also are the graves of the nameless dead of the long, stubborn, heroic defence. The squalor of this British dead-place Major Bayley explained:— "After the abandonment of the city, had the place been marked, the Afghans would have disinterred our dead; so we carefully obliterated every token of interment, and left it intentionally much as you see it." As we sauntered round the ramparts we came to the "Cabul Gate" of Jellalabad, the watchers on which, as they looked anxiously up the wide valley down which should lie the path of the Cabul force which they knew to have commenced its retreat, saw that January afternoon a sight which chilled their blood. That lone survivor of all the slaughtered thousands, tattered, bloody, sore wounded, huddled in a heap on his saddle as he urged his fagged pony on with what strength was left him, riding from out that fearsome valley of death to the city of refuge that he had not dared to hope he might reach—is not the scene depicted in all its awful significance, in Miss Elizabeth Thompson's wonderful picture? Until not many years ago, a quiet elderly Scottish gentleman fed his sheep and raised his oats on his Ross-shire farm, prescribing now and then for an ailing shepherd, or the sick bairn of a neighbouring crofter. I have often thought what memories must have haunted this man as he strolled about the north-country braes and straths. For he was none other than the Surgeon Brydon whom the officers on the Jellalabad gate-work saw riding down the gray slope to them, saved, he alone, from the pilgrimage of slaughter that began outside the Cabul cantonments and ended at Gandamuk. And a later only less fell experience was among the surgeon-farmer's memories. It befell this man whom fortune buffeted yet spared alive through so much, to bear his part in all the terrible vicissitudes of the long memorable defence of the Lucknow Residency.

The sun was in the west when we left Jellalabad with its strange medley of associations, and strolled back through the gardens to the camp. The headquarter street we found swept and garnished, the flagstaff bedecked with holly, and a regimental band playing "Home, sweet home." Dear old Sir Sam Browne did not believe in luxury when on campaign, but now for the first time I saw him at least comfortable. This snug tent with the spreading awning in front, and its cane chairs and carpets, was rather an improvement on that chill bivouac among the rocks on the Shagai Ridge, that refuge in a tomb on the Ali Musjid graveyard-meadow, and that cave above the Lundi Khana stream in whose damp recesses a rheumatic night had been spent after a meal composed of a mystic stew to which everybody had contributed some detail of provender. But over against the general's residence was a grander tent than that inhabited by the old chief. A large double-poled marquee had been set up for the use of the headquarter mess, and under its shade a table groaned with cold joints, while beer flowed like water from a great barrel in the corner. An informal luncheon was just flickering out. Men had eaten beef and had drunk beer; but they lounged about the place, casting lingering contemplative glances at a huge wickerwork crate, on the lid of which sat Captain Knox, the confidential ally of Hill, the mess caterer. Knox was on duty over that crate, with the firmest orders to keep its lid down against all odds, no matter how overwhelming. The contents of it were magnums of champagne. Not without arduous planning and loyal co-operation had this triumph been achieved at so great a distance from what, in military phrase, might be termed the champagne base of operations. It had been Hill's daring idea. It need not now be described by what genius of plan and what energetic persistence in execution, his conception had grown into triumphant realisation. Suffice it to say that within that outwork of wickerwork there reposed eight magnums of Christopher's Perrier-Jouet. Including the recent arrivals, Kinloch and myself, the Christmas Day diners at the headquarter mess would number sixteen. A trifling arithmetical calculation gave the result that to the lot of each diner, supposing the drinking were fair, would fall a bottle of champagne. Was it then to be wondered at that an ardour of expectation should burn in the bosoms of the prospective participants, when it is told that the camp had known no champagne for many weeks, and that there had been periods when the mess had been forced to go without even the ration of commissariat rum?

Hill and I were old cronies; but on this afternoon I instinctively felt he was in no frame for light gossip. A sense of responsibility possessed his mind; on his manly brow the frown of strong thinking made wrinkles as he sat apart and absorbed in his tent, with chance interludes in the shape of raids into the open air kitchen in the rear, whence his voice would sound in strident objurgation of his native subordinates. Nor were there wanting occasional howls, indicating to the intelligent listener that discipline sterner than mere scolding was being administered. In the short eastern gloaming the committee of arrangement gathered in the mess-tent under a solemn sense of responsibility; on its members devolved the duty of setting out the tables. Not that, in strict truth, there were any tables; that luxury was as yet unknown in the headquarter camp. But substitutes were available in planks raised on boxes, in the lids of those boxes, and in a couple of half doors that had been picked up somehow. These appurtenances so disposed as to bear securely the viands that presently were to be spread, the question of seats gave some trouble. The regular company had stools or chairs of their own, but there were the two French noblemen who had straggled up the Khyber with letters of introduction to Sir Sam, and my baggage with my camp-stool was not up. To the Frenchmen was alloted the empty champagne crate; to me was assigned the beer barrel set up on its end.

The mess ante-room was the camp street outside the dining tent; and at the fashionably late hour of eight we "went in" to dinner, to the strains of the "Roast Beef of Old England." It was a right jovial feast, and the most cordial good-fellowship prevailed. He would have been a cynical epicurean who would have criticised the appointments; the banquet itself was above all cavil. Rummaging among some old papers the other day, I found the *menu*, which deserves to be quoted:—" Soup—Julienne. Fish---Whitebait (from the Cabul river). Entrées—Cotelettes aux Champignons, Poulets à la Mayonnaise. Joints —Ham and fowl, roast beef, roast saddle of mutton, boiled brisket of beef, boiled leg of mutton and caper sauce. Curry—Chicken. Sweets—Lemon jelly, blancmange, apricot tart, plum-pudding. Grilled sardines, cheese fritters, cheese, dessert."

Truth compels the avowal that there was no table-linen, nor was the board resplendent with plate or gay with flowers. Table crockery was deficient, or, to be more accurate, there was none. All the dishes were of metal, and the soup was eaten, or rather drunk, out of mugs and iron tea-cups. But it tasted none the worse on this account, and let it be recorded that there *were* champagne glasses, while between every two guests a portly magnum reared its golden head. Except " The Queen " of course, there were but two toasts after the feast—one was " Absent Friends," drunk in a wistful silence, and the other, the caterer's health, greeted with vociferous enthusiasm. The gallant officer who gave the latter toast proved himself as eloquent at the board as he was known to be vigorous and forward in the field ; and only Anglo-Indians can appreciate the full significance of the title " Bobajee Bahadur," which amid general acclamation he conferred on the comrade who had contrived so purposefully for our Khyber Christmas feast. The Bobajee Bahadur was not an orator, but as one watched him resting from his labours, now that his *bundobust* had ripened into triumphant fulfilment, one noted how the glow of modest complacency irradiated his manly countenance. Our Bobajee Bahadur is a brevet-major now, and a staff officer, and may scorn the gifts that in other days made him popular among us. Yet if he live to be a field-marshal, that will be no loftier title than Bobajee Bahadur.

A few fields off the fuel had been collecting all day for the Christmas camp-fire of the 10th Hussars, and by ten o'clock the blaze of it was mounting high into the murky gloom. A right merry and social gathering it was round the bright glow of this Yule-log in a far-off land. The flames danced on the wide circle of bearded faces, on the tangled fleeces of the postheens, on the gold braid of forage caps, on the sombre hoods of beshliks. The bright streaks of the firelight alternating with the dark shadows would have rejoiced the soul of an artist. In the half gloom behind the seated or reclining inner circle stood groups of stalwart troopers, ready with cheery chorus or deep-voiced solo; for the recognition of good comradeship between all ranks on service never in a well-ordered regiment tends to the relaxation of discipline. In the foreground native servants regarding the heat with salamander-like indifference, attended to the supply of refreshments, or rather of refreshment; for it was campaigning time, and there was no variety. A kettle of neat rum was kept on the boil, and from this reserve store the cups were kept supplied with a fluid whose warmth was on a par with its strength; and the dandies of a corps that "don't dance" but knows how to fight, lay or sat on the dusty ground and sipped with hearty relish the red-hot rum. It was a pleasant rendezvous of friends, but there were those round the camp-fire who missed one soldier-figure from the circle, and recalled with sad hearts other days with the 10th, when the leading spirit alike in the field and in the messroom, was one who was ever staunch comrade as good soldier, and who has been sore punished for an offence for which he himself never pleaded excuse. The songs ranged from gay to grave; the former mood in the ascendency. But occasionally there was sung a ditty the associations with which brought it about that there came something strangely like a tear into the voice of the singer, and that a yearning wistfulness fell upon the faces of the listeners. The bronzed troopers in the background shaded with their hands the fire-flash from their eyes; and as the familiar homely strain ceased that recalled home and love and trailed at the heart-strings till the breast felt to heave and the tears to rise, there would be a little pause of eloquent silence which told how thoughts had gone astraying half across the globe to the loved ones in dear old England, and were loath to come back again to the rum and the camp-fire in Jellalabad plain. Ah, how many stood or sat around that camp-fire that were never to see old England more! The snow had not melted on the Sufed Koh when half a squadron of the troopers were drowned in the treacherous Cabul river. No brighter soul or sweeter singer round that fire than Monty Slade; but the life went out of Monty Slade with his face to the foe and his wet sword grasped in a soldier-grip; and he lies under the palm-trees by the wells of El Teb.

THE END.

Printed by R. & R. CLARK, *Edinburgh.*

www.ingramcontent.com/pod-product-compliance
Lightning Source LLC
Chambersburg PA
CBHW050124170426
43197CB00011B/1705